WITHIN THESE WALLS

WITHIN THESE WALLS

Memoirs of a Death House Chaplain

REV. CARROLL PICKETT
WITH CARLTON STOWERS

First published in Great Britain in 2003 by Fusion Press,
a division of Satin Publications Ltd.
101 Southwark Street
London SE1 0JH
UK
info@visionpaperbacks.co.uk
www.visionpaperbacks.co.uk
Publisher: Sheena Dewan

Originally published in the USA in 2002 by St Martin's Press.

A catalogue record for this book is available from the British Library.

ISBN: 1-904132-23-5

Printed and bound in the UK by Mackays of Chatham Ltd, Chatham, Kent

To those who have done acts of goodness
without knowing it, been there when needed without being
asked, and said the words that needed saying without
being coached or coerced.

To my children –
Karel, Anne, Steve and Charlotte – who have chosen
special times to do special things. Each is remarkable in ways
I cherish and deeply appreciate.

To my wife, Jane,
who came into my stressful life and proved to me that it is
not good for man to live alone. And to her children – Kelley, Stacy
and Jody – who have blessed my life.

And to one very special brother,
for advice and presence, for service and sincerity, for being
involved in prison ministry, and for learning a great lesson: that all
men are not all bad. And for finally realizing that I am not the
bad brother he thought me to be when we were kids.

Must we kill to prevent there being any wicked?
This is to make both parties wicked instead of one.

from *Pensées*, by Pascal (1660)

After review of your taped senior sermon, I am convinced that your ministry
is destined to focus on the dying; lending comfort to those faced with death
and those who are losing loved ones …

a written evaluation of seminary student Carroll Pickett in 1957

FOREWORD TO THE UK EDITION

As prison chaplain at the Huntsville unit of the Texas prison system – 'The Walls' – Reverend Carroll Pickett ministered to nearly one hundred men in the final hours of their lives, seeing their despair, remorse, shamelessness, anger and fear. He gave comfort to these condemned prisoners, who were moved to the Death House to eat their final meal, receive final visitors and write farewell letters. He then offered spiritual solace, should they want it, while they were strapped to the gurney and executed by lethal injection. It is from this unenviable vantage point that he is able to give such a moving and powerful insight into the cruelty of the death penalty.

Reverend Pickett's experiences at The Walls led him to ask himself throughout his ministry, and more vocally after his retirement: What good is being achieved by the death penalty? How can the state kill a person to show other people that killing is wrong?

What purpose, then, does the death penalty serve? There are many arguments given to justify its use. Deterrence. Protection for society. Retribution. But after these arguments have been factually undermined or argued to be morally indefensible, one has to conclude that there is no justification for the death penalty.

Take deterrence, for example. Criminologist and social theorists worldwide have found no consistent, credible evidence to suggest that the death penalty is more of a deterrent than any other punishment. The United Nations itself has concluded, '… research has failed to provide scientific proof that executions have a greater deterrent effect than life imprisonment. Such proof is unlikely to be forthcoming. The evidence as a whole still gives no positive support to the deterrent hypothesis.' Texas has the highest number of executions and also the highest rate of violent crime in the US whereas since the abolition of the death penalty in 1975 Canada has seen a significant drop in violent crime.

When arguing that executions protect society, people often state that imprisonment has not prevented individuals from offending again once set free. It is impossible, however, to determine whether those executed would actually have re-offended. Also, many violent crimes are committed without premeditation, under the influence of drugs or alcohol or with emotion overcoming reason. The answer has to be to review the parole procedures with a view to preventing relapses into crime. The answer is certainly not to increase the number of executions.

If you are left with retribution as justification, you are also left with the uncomfortable reality that the state is no better than a murderer. If killing is wrong, it is always wrong. Morality cannot be upheld by legalised murder.

Thankfully the world is becoming increasingly aware that there are alternative punishments to the death penalty, punishments that are effective and which do not involve the premeditated killing of a human being by the state in the name of justice. Over half the countries in the world are now abolitionist in law or practice, and the trend continues with three countries abolishing the practice each year. In 2001 only four countries accounted for over 90 per cent of the world's known executions – China, Saudi Arabia, Iran and the USA.

The death penalty in the USA was reintroduced in 1976 with the execution of Gary Gilmour. Since then, and up to the time of this book going to print, over 800 people have been executed in the USA. Of the 805 executed, some were mentally ill or impaired, some were children when they committed their crime and some were almost certainly innocent.

In 1997 Kerry Max Cook was released after spending 19 years on Death Row in Texas. He was freed on bond but faced a fourth trial that could well have sent him back to the Row. After waiting for two years he was offered a plea bargain – which was no admission of guilt – in which he would give up any claim for compensation for being fully released. He was given 15 minutes to decide his fate, and he chose freedom. After his decision, DNA evidence was released by the state that proved his innocence. He spent all those years in a five by nine foot cell and once came within 11 days of execution.

Reverend Pickett himself ministered to people where serious doubts over their guilt were never resolved. The peculiarities of the Texas legal system mean that new evidence is only admissible if brought before the court no more than 30 days after sentencing has occurred. In the light of this legal intransigence, Leonel Herrera's final statement is particularly chilling. 'I am innocent, innocent, innocent. Make no mistake about this … Continue the struggle for human rights, helping those who are innocent … I am an innocent man, and something very wrong is taking place tonight.'

The irreversibility of the death penalty also makes a mockery of the notion of rehabilitation. Reverend Pickett remembers many men who showed genuine remorse for their crimes. Some of those who did not receive the death penalty went on to further education, successful business ventures and family life. Poignantly, the Reverend remarks that often the man he met in the Death House was in no way the same person who had committed a terrible murder in an impulsive and mindless moment in his teens.

Here in the UK, the Guilford Four, the Birmingham Six and many other individuals would have been executed had the death penalty remained on the statute books. Politicians in the UK have recognised the fallibility of the system, and after a long struggle it is finally abolished for good. This realisation is slowly dawning in the USA as well. In response to thirteen innocent people being released from Death Row, Governor George Ryan of Illinois imposed a moratorium on executions, and is now considering how to go about granting clemency for the rest of the Death Row population there. The Supreme Court recently ruled that executing the mentally impaired is unconstitutional and appears to be moving in favour of ending the practice of executing child offenders as well.

Within These Walls provides a courageous and clear testimony to the futility and waste of the death penalty and argues powerfully for a radical rethink to its use. In the end, Reverend Pickett concludes there can be no justification for the state to kill in the name of justice. This is absolutely right. The struggle towards abolition is a slow but essential one.

Janet Hague,
Death Penalty Campaigns Manager,
Amnesty International UK

INTRODUCTION

During the fifteen years I served as chaplain for the Texas prison system, I ministered to ninety-five men who were put to death by lethal
injection. I stood by them as they were strapped to a gurney and as
the needles that would pump lethal chemicals into their veins were
inserted. I heard their final words and watched as they took their last
breaths. I was the last friendly face they saw. I spent the final hours
of their lives with them, hearing stories of troubled childhoods and
crimes committed, seeing the anger and arrogance, the sorrow and
remorse, and, finally, the resolution and fear on their faces. Often, I
would conduct their graveside ceremonies in the prison cemetery the
following day, generally accompanied only by the warden and inmates
assigned to dig the grave.

It never got easier.

Since 1952 I have been a Presbyterian minister and should admit
that there was a time in my life when I embraced the idea of putting
murderers to death. Like so many Texans, I was raised in an atmosphere that insisted the only real justice was that which claimed an
eye for an eye.

I was wrong. As I participated in the endless process that would
earn my state infamous recognition for its death-penalty stance, I
found myself wondering just what we were accomplishing.

That is what this book is about. It is not so much a story about me
as it is a rememberance of a dark and troubling corner of the world I

once occupied, a journey that I'd never planned to take. It is a story that examines that frightening twilight time between life and death, issues spiritual and moral, and the most basic concepts of right and wrong. It is my honest-as-possible observations of what prison life is all about, a portrait, as well as I can draw it, of an ever-growing segment of our nation's society that all too many wish only to forget.

And it is about the death-penalty issue, which screams to us almost daily from headlines and the six o'clock news. On the following pages I will introduce you to men who faced that penalty, those charged with carrying it out, and loved ones affected by the process. And I will share the questions that have never been far from my mind since that December day in 1982 when I accompanied a condemned murderer named Charlie Brooks into the death chamber, where he became the first prisoner in the world ever to die by lethal injection.

Does the death penalty serve as a deterrent to crime? When I started as a prison chaplain two decades ago, there were 100 men on Texas's Death Row. Since that time the state has executed over 250, yet the number of those sentenced to die has climbed to almost 500. I submit that there is absolutely no proof that execution in any way deters murder.

And there is the matter of "closure," which we hear so much about. In those dark early mornings following an execution, I spoke with the loved ones of crime victims—husbands and wives; mothers, fathers, and children—and almost without exception found that the feeling of relief so long anticipated was not realized. A death, however horrible and senseless, cannot be erased by another death, however quick and humane.

As a young woman once said to me following the execution of the man who murdered her mother, "It really doesn't change anything, does it? It doesn't bring her back. Her grandchildren still won't ever be able to see her."

All the death penalty does, I strongly believe, is create another set of victims. By killing a person, we inflict great damage on yet another family. While I do not wish to be viewed as some naive apologist for the evils of those deserving punishment, I know that they, too, have loved ones, who grieve just as desperately as do the families of their victims. I've watched them make tearful visits to the Death House, knowing it would be the last time they would see their husband, father, brother, or son alive.

I've seen prison guards turn in their badges, wardens walk away from their jobs, and fellow chaplains sink to such depressed states that they were forced to turn away from their calling. They, too, have been victims of a legal system that insists not only on the right but the duty to take the life of another human being.

And so, yes, I am among those growing voices who believe it is time that lawmakers and peacekeepers, members of the greatest society in the world, come to the civilized realization that the cruel act of revenge—however cloaked in legal terms—nets us nothing and diminishes us all.

On the pages that follow, however, I promise no sermon, no indignant rant that insists I have found all the answers and should, above all others, be heard. I would simply ask that you travel along with me, hearing the voices, seeing the faces. Over the years, I ministered to men so far removed from the social mainstream, so callous and mean-spirited, that any attempt to describe their evil mind-set requires a talent greater than mine. I've been cursed, spat upon, and threatened. On the other hand, I've met men whose guilt sprang only from tragic youthful mistakes for which they spent lifetimes begging forgiveness from God and their fellowman. Many were illiterate, some too mentally challenged to fully understand what they had done and why they were to die. And, despite the insistence of our former governor turned president, there were those put to death in whose guilt I did not believe. I met men who had, indeed, committed the crimes for which they were sentenced to die and who displayed genuine remorse. In those years between their crime and their punishment, some changed dramatically. Even on Death Row I saw men whose lives had regained some degree of promise, purpose, and even dignity. Yet they died the same death as the unrepentant.

It was upon such matters that I'd considered writing long before I was invited to speak to a recent Texas House of Representitives committee hearing on a proposed bill that would bring a halt to executions while a two-year study of the process was conducted. It was early evening before the hearing ended, and as I walked into the Capitol Building hallway, a familiar-looking man with a graying ponytail stood waiting. He smiled and extended his hand. No sooner had I taken it than he pulled me to him in a powerful embrace. "I'm so glad to meet you," he said. "There was a time when it could well have been under very different circumstances."

His name was Randall Dale Adams, and he had spent twelve years on Death Row, wrongfully convicted of the 1980 murder of a Dallas police officer. I remembered seeing his face in newspaper photographs and in the award-winning documentary *The Thin Blue Line*. Even today his case is recognized as one of the prime examples of a badly flawed judicial system sometimes too quick to condemn and convict.

Before his innocence was finally recognized, he told me, his mother had already purchased a new suit in which she planned to have him buried. He had been only seventy-two hours away from a trip to the Death House, where I would have awaited his arrival, when the insane process was halted and he was set free.

I drove home that evening silently studying the highway that stretched before me, my thoughts on all those I had met, men whose fate was far harsher than that of Randall Adams. The time, I decided, had come to put them in writing.

—Rev. Carroll Pickett
Huntsville, Texas

ONE

It began as one of those glorious Texas days when the summer sun's warmth feels like a soothing balm and the blooming lantana and honeysuckle give a rich and intoxicating fragrance to the air. Having just begun a vacation from my position as pastor of the Huntsville First Presbyterian Church, I was eagerly looking forward to a lengthy list of carefree activities. There was the long-planned reunion of my wife's family that we would host, our twins' fourteenth birthday to celebrate, then, perhaps, a leisurely weekend on a Gulf Coast beach. I'd also planned a few days in Victoria, visiting my father, who was ill with cancer. On that July Wednesday afternoon in 1974, however, I had planned nothing more demanding than joining some friends to determine just how badly my tennis skills had deteriorated.

Then, shortly after 1:00 P.M., a dark and ominous cloud fell over the quiet, friendly city I had called home for seven years. In time, I would look back on that moment, pinpointing it as the time when the direction of my life and career spiraled off in a direction my wildest dreams could never have conjured.

I was forty, happy and comfortable in my calling. And when my oldest daughter, Karel, arrived at the tennis courts to say that Jim Estelle, director of the Texas Department of Corrections and a member of my congregation, wanted to see me in his office, I had no way of knowing that from that day forward nothing would ever again be the same.

"He says it's urgent," she told me.

Despite the years we had been friends, I had never visited Estelle's office; didn't, in fact, have any real grasp of the difficult job he had as the director of the ever-expanding Texas prison system. Like everyone else in town, I was aware of the towering redbrick structure that loomed on the edge of the downtown area and also aware that it served as the well-guarded home of two thousand men whose social debts were being paid in months and years, even lifetimes. Nor did the Chamber of Commerce have to remind us that the prison was a primary source of our city's income, employing more residents than even the local college or public school system. Still, for many, The Walls, as the local unit was called, was the proverbial elephant-in-the-living room—there but not really seen, a ranking topic of conversation only among those who worked there.

Live in Huntsville long enough, I'd been told when we first arrived, and you will forget the prison. You'll never give a second thought to the fact that only its thick walls and guards separate murderers and thieves from the law-abiding man on the street. In truth, had it not been for the fact that director Estelle and a number of other prison employees regularly attended my Sunday services, I might well have gone for months without giving a moment's thought to the prison, its staff, or the men it confined.

It simply wasn't a part of my world—or, I thought, my responsibility.

On the second floor of the Texas Department of Corrections (TDC) administration building, I was greeted by Estelle's secretary, Dorothy Coleman, grim faced and businesslike, who explained that her boss was across the street in the warden's office. "He asked that I call him as soon as you arrived," she said.

The voice I soon heard on the phone was not that of the warm, outgoing man I'd so often talked with following Sunday morning services. Even more to the point than his secretary, he spoke in strained, measured sentences. "I need your help," he said. "We've got a hostage situation over here." There was a brief pause, as if he were coaxing into his lungs the air he needed to continue. "It's bad," he finally added.

Three inmates, he went on to explain, were holding fellow prisoners and a number of prison employees inside the unit's library. Armed with guns that had somehow been smuggled in to them, the convicts were demanding that arrangements be made for their escape and threatening to harm those held captive if their demands were not met.

He said that families of the hostages, already being alerted to the situation, would soon be arriving and that he wanted me to make myself available to them until the matter was resolved. "I need for you to be my representative to the families," he said. "Do whatever you can—anything you can—to make them comfortable and keep them calm. See that they have whatever they need and assure them that we'll pass along any information we have through you."

Though he mentioned no time frame, I had the strong feeling that the crisis he was dealing with—and asking me to become a part of—would not be short-lived. Suddenly glad I had stopped by the house to shower and put on a suit, I assured him I would help in any way I could.

"You can set up in the conference room," he said. "Whatever you need, just tell my secretary, and she'll see that you have it."

Again he paused briefly. "One more thing," he finally said. "Two of your people are in there."

A knot formed in the pit of my stomach as he spoke their names: Judy Standley and Yvonne Beseda.

For a moment I stood speechless. Why would people like them, loving mothers and faithful members of my congregation, be subjected to such an outrageous nightmare? For the past several weeks I had been meeting regularly with Judy, a librarian at the prison, to discuss plans for her oldest daughter's wedding. Only a month earlier Yvonne had come to me with the exciting news that she had been hired to teach math and reading to inmates. I had baptized her youngest child. Two wonderful women, filled with joy and anticipation when we had last spoken, were now faced with a terror beyond my imagination.

Dorothy's voice finally interrupted my thoughts. "Reverend Pickett, what can I do to help you?"

"Show me where the conference room is."

Thus began my involvement in the longest prison siege in U.S. history.

In the first few hours, details of the horror story playing out across the street were sketchy. An inmate named Fred Gomez Carrasco, a convicted drug lord who had come to The Walls only six months earlier to begin serving a life sentence, had solicited the aid of fellow inmates Rudolfo Dominguez and Ignacio Cuevas in an attempt to carry out an escape he'd been planning since his arrival. A prison trustee had smuggled three guns and ammunition to them, hiding the weapons among a grocery delivery he routinely made.

Fifty prisoners and ten employees had been inside the library, which was located on the third floor of the unit's education building, when the gunmen suddenly barred the door and ordered everyone to line up against the walls.

A few minutes later, when unsuspecting prison guards began walking up the concrete ramp leading to the library, a warning shot rang out. It was the clarion call that first signaled the seriousness of what was beginning to unfold.

Prison officials had hastily gathered to consider how they could diffuse the situation and return order to the unit. Yet no plan suggested was deemed workable. Carrasco and his lieutenants had, it seemed, selected the ideal place in which to barricade themselves. With its glass front door the only entrance to the library, any kind of direct assault was judged too dangerous. Nor did the facility have any windows through which snipers might attack the gunmen. Brief consideration was even given to using explosives to blow a hole in the back wall of the building to provide an entryway. Like most of the plans, however, it was dismissed when it was determined that the risk to innocent lives would be too great.

While all but four of the inmates would soon be released, five at a time, silently walking single file from the building, the ten prison workers—five teachers, four librarians, and a guard—were to remain as hostages. It was their lives that became the overriding concern, not only of the prison officials, but of those who had begun arriving at the conference room, frightened and angry, to await word about their loved ones.

From their homes and workplaces in the community and outlying towns, they came to the headquarters we'd quickly established, each asking the same questions. Are they okay? Can we talk with them? How long will this last?

I had no answers to give them. It was, in fact, not until late that night that I began to have some idea of what lay ahead. Jack Kyle, one of the prison officials, came over and led me into a nearby office. "We have a full-blown crisis situation," he began, "and it isn't likely to be resolved quickly. So prepare yourself for a long haul." He explained that Carrasco, a man said to be responsible—directly and indirectly—for as many as forty murders during his career as a drug dealer, was demanding additional weaponry and arrangements for transportation to freedom. Already he had begun making threats to shoot hostages if his requests were not met. He had begun to divulge part of his escape plan; it was to use some of the hostages as shields. "What he's telling us," Kyle said, "is that he'll die before he surrenders."

I asked if there was any chance that Carrasco and his men would, in fact, be allowed to leave. The silent stare from Kyle sufficed as his answer. "For now, all we can do is keep negotiating, going along as far as we can to buy time," he explained.

Back in the conference room, I surveyed the strained and weary faces. Yvonne's husband, Buster, had come alone, explaining that he'd not told the children what was happening, hopeful that it would end quickly and that he could take his wife safely home. He sat quietly, alone with his thoughts. Throughout the day, Herman Fleming, the husband of Ann, one of the librarians, had been on an emotional roller coaster—angry at one moment, wrapped in cold fear the next. Now he, too, sat quietly, staring at the floor. The family of teacher Jack Branch, a friend I'd known since moving to Huntsville, sat holding hands, praying. Others were gathered in small groups, speaking softly among themselves. Occasionally a husband or wife, son or daughter, would give in to their nausea and quietly ask directions to the restroom. Some paced, Styrofoam cups of coffee in hand, as midnight neared.

I knew that if I was to be of any help to those who had come to this insane vigil, it was important that I quickly gain their trust. Honesty, regardless of the pain that might accompany it, was essential. "I'm told that none of the hostages have been harmed and there are negotiations underway," I announced. "But it also appears that this could go on for some time."

Members of the media who had begun to gather across the street from The Walls were painting a darker picture. They were already referring to it as an "impending disaster." I prayed that they were wrong yet feared that they might be right.

Returning home in the early morning hours, I tried unsuccessfully to sleep, knowing that I had promised to be back at the administration building by six. In darkness, I entered the rooms where the twins still slept and woke them to wish them happy birthday. And then I tiptoed into the predawn to return to a place where there would be nothing to celebrate.

As the crowd continued to grow, I began to telephone other ministers in the community for assistance. Could they, I asked, contact members of their churches for help in providing meals for those who had arrived? Well before noon a steady parade of casseroles and covered dishes, cakes and pies, urns of coffee and gallon jars of ice tea, began to arrive.

New to the group was the brother of The Walls's Catholic chaplain. Fr. Joseph O'Brien, following a lengthy meeting with warden Hal Husbands, had voluntarily entered the library-turned-fortress in the hope that he might help to mediate a settlement. In a bit of dark irony, Carrasco had, shortly after coming to prison, been assigned to the work detail that occasionally assisted the priest in the chapel. Now the inmate agreed to allow the priest into his makeshift fortress, but only if he arrived in handcuffs.

Instead of an optimistic report, Father O"Brien returned with a handwritten list of demands from Carrasco that ranged from profane to trivial. He asked for immediate delivery of a television set, fifteen pairs of handcuffs, three M-16 rifles and one hundred rounds of ammunition for each, three bulletproof vests and helmets, and three walkie-talkies. Food, clothing, blankets, pillows, and cigarettes were also on his list.

A television set and handcuffs were delivered along with the requested food, blankets, and pillows. No rifles, director Estelle responded, would be delivered under any circumstances. The vests, walkie-talkies, and helmets were under consideration.

As negotiations continued through the day and into the night, it became clear that prison officials were stalling for time. In the meantime, they argued, why not allow the hostages to leave? As expected, the request fell on deaf ears. One minute, Carrasco was willing to talk, promising that no one would be hurt if his orders were carried out; the next, he was angrily slamming the library phone against a desk, threatening to soon begin killing hostages if his deadlines were ignored.

During one telephone conversation with the warden's office, Carrasco had gathered the hostages around him, demanding at gunpoint that they cry out for help. As a chorus of "Please help us" and "Get us out of here" resonated into the phone, a laughing, arrogant Carrasco turned into a cruel and psychotic cheerleader. "Louder," he repeatedly commanded.

To fortify the only entrance to the library, filing cabinets and bookcases had been pushed against the glass door. Then, teacher Glennon Johnson was handcuffed to a chair that was placed atop the cabinets. In full view of armed prison guards assigned to watch the library doorway, he became more than a hostage. He was a target. By late evening, the stress overwhelmed him to the point where he began developing symptoms of a heart attack. Begrudgingly, Carrasco placed a call to the warden's unit, advising, "Somebody should come get this guy to a hospital before he dies." Johnson was thus released from the ordeal. But soon replaced.

When Father O'Brien returned later that night to deliver sandwiches, a wary Carrasco had forced him to eat one first to make sure officials had not treated them with some drug that might cause loss of consciousness. Then, at meal's end, he had informed the priest that if he left the library, he would not be allowed to return. Father O'Brien chose to become a volunteer hostage, replacing the ill Johnson.

While the tension in the warden's office across the street was heightening, so was the tension in the conference room, where fear was giving way to raw anger. Family members began to lash out at perceived failures of the prison system, hurling blame in every direction as the frustration level rose. When, in fact, several chaplains from other prison units visited, offering support, they were summarily dismissed by those waiting. To my regret, they were perceived as a part of a system that had placed innocent people in harm's way and clearly were not welcomed.

I was, I knew, in uncharted territory. Throughout my career I'd dealt with individuals and families in various crises, but trying to simultaneously calm and minister to as many as fifty people at once was a daunting assignment. When a longtime friend named José Garcia contacted me, his voice was an answered prayer. A highly respected Houston psychiatrist who had worked as a consultant for the prison for some time, he immediately volunteered to help in any way he could. "How soon can you get here?" I asked.

As he sat in the small office that had been assigned to me, he read the prison files that described Carrasco's criminal history—the drug dealings, the ordered executions, a daring helicopter escape from a prison in Guadalajara, and finally a motel shootout in San Antonio in which he had been wounded and finally apprehended. Convicted of the attempted murder of the officer who arrested him, Carrasco had arrived in Huntsville with a bad limp and walking with the aid of a cane. It was his medical condition, the files indicated, that had determined he would be assigned to The Walls unit where the prison hospital facilities were located.

Setting the folder aside, Dr. Garcia looked across the desk at me and shook his head. "This man," he surmised, "doesn't give a damn about any of those people in there. His only interest is in himself— and he's loving the attention. He feeds on it, sitting up there watching news reports on television and having the paper delivered to him every day. His feeling of self-importance is growing by the minute." Rising from his chair, he moved to the window and looked out toward the prison. "My guess is that he won't try to do anything until a Saturday."

I wasn't following his reasoning.

"He wants his prison break to be the big story in all the Sunday papers," the doctor explained.

Volunteering to remain in Huntsville for a few days, he joined me in the conference room. "I'm going to stay in the background," he said, "but if you see any indication that someone is about to really lose it, let me know, and I'll see what I can do to help."

When the weekend passed without incident, an unsteady resolve seemed to settle over the conference room. Angry outbursts disappeared, and tears came less frequently. What I saw in their place were remarkable displays of faith and strength, people lending support to each other, positive thoughts replacing negative. In this darkest of times, I saw strangers begin to embrace each other like family. A miraculous bonding, unlike any I'd ever seen before, was taking place.

We talked and prayed, resigned to a long and uncertain wait.

When another minister in town sent word to me that he wished to join us, I attempted to explain the fragile routine that we had become comfortable with. His intent, I knew, was genuine, but I tried to tell him that it had been made clear to me that no additional outsiders would be welcomed. Several people, in fact, had even dismissed my suggestion that their own ministers be asked to stop in.

Inside the conference room, trust for outsiders was in short supply. He persisted, however, and finally made a rather grandiose entrance, announcing, "The Lord has sent me to minister to everyone in this room." He was met by silence and cold stares. After sitting alone at one end of the room for almost four hours, he left.

True to Dr. Garcia's evaluation, Carrasco made no secret of the fact that he was enjoying the attention of the press. He'd demanded to talk with several reporters by phone, and when he was allowed to do so, he lashed out against prison conditions in long, rambling interviews. If people died, he repeatedly insisted, it would be the fault of the Texas Department of Corrections, not his. To prove that the hostages had not been harmed, he occasionally let them speak to reporters.

Then there would be long and agonizing stretches when nothing seemed to be happening. In those hours of silence I could feel the expectant eyes of everyone in the room focused on me, following my every move, wondering if I might have some new bit of information, however small, to share. Often I would return from a phone conversation with the director's office with nothing more than a new word of warning. Yet another of Carrasco's deadlines was approaching, I would announce. It was a signal that everyone should stay away from the windows in the event gunfire broke out.

Then, in the middle of the week, Carrasco began to allow selected hostages brief telephone conversations with members of their families. The calls, routed through the warden's office, would come to the administration building, and Carrasco would inform me who to summon to the phone. The calls would begin each day at 6:00 P.M. One evening, he said he wanted to talk with me before putting Jack Branch on to speak with his wife. "Preacher," he said in a gravely voice, "I know that you've got people in here. They've been talking about you. And I've got a question for you."

"What's that?"

"I want to know what makes your women so strong?" he asked.

. . .

As a new week began, the small world in which we were living seemed frozen in time. Days began to blur. Concerns inside and outside the prison grew. For a time, word spread through the streets of Huntsville that the inmates were armed with homemade bombs and were preparing to blow a getaway hole into the prison wall. Several times a day there would be a false rumor that Carrasco had killed a hostage when one of his demands was refused or a deadline ignored. Raising the fear level even higher was a story that a group of Carrasco's drugworld associates had driven up from Mexico and were gathering at a highway rest stop just outside of town, planning an assault on the prison. Everyone was feeling the pressure. Like many in the community, my wife, Sonya, feared that gunfire might eventually spill into the city streets, and she announced that she was taking the children to Fort Worth, where they would stay until the insanity ended. Karel, my oldest daughter, refused to go. "Daddy might need me here," she had argued until allowed to remain at home.

The tensions inside The Walls was even greater. Carrasco continued making demands. He wanted an armored car, equipped with two-way radio and telephone, to be made available for his getaway, specially made bulletproof helmets and vests, even new suits that could be worn on his flight into the free world. At one point he'd even offered to exchange the hostages for Director Estelle, Warden Hal Husbands, and several other TDC officials. So desperate was the situation that the idea was briefly considered until members of the prison board unanimously voted against it.

A San Antonio attorney was summoned to participate in the negotiations but made no headway in his effort to persuade his client to surrender and end the standoff peacefully. On Wednesday, as a new deadline was given, lawyer Reuben Montemayor wrote a note to prison officials while he and his client talked on the phone. "Deadline 8:00 P.M.," he scribbled on a notepad, "or prepare for war!!!"

Fred Carrasco and his dictates were not the only problem. Since the seige began, the entire prison population had been in a state of lockdown. Inmates were confined to their cells, allowed out neither for recreational nor work activities. Even showers and hot meals had been suspended. Cold sandwiches, delivered to the cells, had become the daily menu. In the only bit of levity that managed to penetrate the somber atmosphere, a prisoner had written a note, folded it into a paper plane, and sailed it out his window. On it he had written, 'I'm holding my cell mate hostage. Unless I get a hot meal immediately, he dies.'

There was no such attempt at humor inside the administration building. As the week dragged on, the physical toll became as great as the angst. The month of July ended with nerves raw and tension reaching new levels. The break for freedom, we began to hear, would come soon.

It was on Saturday afternoon, August 3, when I picked up the phone to hear Carrasco's voice. "We're leaving," he announced, describing in detail how he and his associates would make their way from the library to the armored car that had been positioned in the center of the recreation yard. One of the inmates he'd kept inside the library had already been sent outside to make certain it was fully gassed and running well. For several minutes we talked of the fastest route through the city of Houston. They would, he added, be taking two of the female hostages with them. "After we get to where we're going," he said, "I'll call you sometime in the next twenty-four hours to tell you where they are so you can come get them." Judy Standley, Yvonne Beseda, and teacher Novella Pollard, he said, had already volunteered. "I'm going to let you talk to them."

The strength I heard in Judy's voice amazed me, and Carrasco's earlier question returned, echoing in my mind. *What makes your women so strong?* And suddenly I had the answer that I wish I'd given him. *Because they have great faith and love in their hearts. Because they are comfortable with themselves and have long known the im-*

portance of lending comfort to others. Because they care more about others' well-being than their own. Because they are ladies of remarkable conviction and courage. . . .

Judy went straight to the point, explaining that she had volunteered to be handcuffed to Carrasco as they moved from the library toward the waiting armored car. They would, she said, be hidden away inside a makeshift shield that had been built during their descent from the library to the prison yard. If they made it that far, she would be among those accompanying the prisoners on their getaway attempt. "I'm going to die tonight," she said. "I've known for several days this time would come, and I'm prepared. I'm not afraid; please tell my family that I know where I'm going and that God will be there to take care of me."

I made a futile attempt to encourage some optimism but was quickly interrupted. "I need to talk with you about my funeral," she said, a firmness masking the exhaustion I knew she must be feeling.

It was obvious that she had given a great deal of thought to her request. She listed favorite hymns she wanted sung and messages she wished me to deliver to her five children. Her mother, she noted, was a member of the Church of Christ, a denomination that does not embrace the idea of musical accompaniment in its church. "If there is something special you can do for her," Judy said, "I would appreciate it." I promised an a cappella choir.

Engraved on her tombstone, she wanted the words "She died so others might live."

"One other thing," she said. "Promise me that you won't let Dru call off her wedding. It's just two weeks away, you know."

"I'll see to it. It will be a fine wedding."

She began to cry softly. "Tell her," she said, "that I wish I could be there." And with that she handed the phone to Yvonne.

Again I was soon taking notes for funeral plans. Like Judy, she too had volunteered to remain a hostage during the escape attempt, knowing full well that survival was impossible. She passed along messages for her children.

"What," I asked, "do you want me to tell your husband?"

"Tell him that I love him very much," she replied, "and that I'm not sorry that I took this job. All I wanted to do was help people. . . ."

And then the phones went dead, cut off by prison officials. It was the signal that a final confrontation was about to begin.

For several minutes I sat alone in the office, a sadness that I'd never experienced sweeping over me. I wasn't sure that my legs would support me even if I attempted to get up.

Finally, though, I began making my way down the hall toward the conference room. Walking toward me was Buster Beseda. "You've been talking to Yvonne, haven't you?" he said.

I nodded and motioned for him to return to the office with me. There, I told him of the escape plan that had been described to me and of the things that his wife had said. Saying nothing, he began to cry. And for the first time since this ugly, painful experience had begun, so did I. "God, how will I tell the kids?" he finally asked. "I don't think I can do it." His pain filled the silent, tiny room as I reached out to embrace him.

"I'll do it for you," I whispered, wondering even as I spoke if I could muster the strength to do so.

Outside, a new kind of urgency filled the street in front of The Walls. The large tent, which had become the headquarters for the still-growing number of reporters, had been dismantled. The street running in front of the prison, barricaded for days, was suddenly filled with fire trucks, and their hoses were being unloaded and hooked to nearby hydrants. An army of law-enforcement officers—Texas Rangers, state troopers, sheriff's deputies, and prison guards—was moving into place. The plan that had finally been formulated in the warden's office called for powerful bursts of water to be leveled at the convicts' protective shield, knocking it over as it made its way down the ramp. Immediately thereafter there would be a quick attack by officers who were hidden nearby.

Inside the conference room, the silence became deadening as the wait began. Suddenly I felt the need to be in several places at once. I escorted Buster and his children into one room, then gathered Judy's children to wait in another. The Pollard family, aware that Novella had also volunteered to be handcuffed to one of the convicts, followed me down the hall to privacy. I assured each family that I would return as soon as I had any information. Then, after stopping to say a quick prayer, I returned to the others.

At 9:40 P.M., the gunfire began.

With the telephone no longer in operation, the only way I could determine what was happening was to race to Estelle's office, where his secretary was in contact with the command center across the street. She had a walkie-talkie to her ear as I entered. Pale and tired, she nodded in my direction, motioning me to a nearby chair. Then, cupping her hand to the receiver, she said, "They didn't make it." Her voice broke as tears began to fill her eyes. "Stay right here," she continued. "Mr. Estelle is sending someone over to brief you on what's happened." We looked silently at each other for several seconds before she again spoke. "I don't envy what you've got to do," she said.

Ron Taylor, the public information director of the prison, soon appeared and began to cry even before he spoke. "Judy and Yvonne," he finally managed, "are dead. Father O'Brien has been shot but is going to be okay. Everyone else is safe."

He had a quickly prepared statement to give to those waiting in the conference room. "How do you want to do this?" he asked me.

"Let me talk to the families of the victims first," I suggested. He nodded and slumped into a nearby chair to wait. I made my way into the hallway, every step an effort.

Buster was waiting in the doorway, ashen and shaking. "She's dead," I said. From somewhere deep inside him came a sound of agony unlike any I'd ever heard. His son, Robert, a promising stage actor who had returned home from New York, jumped atop the desk and drove his fist into the ceiling, oblivious to any kind of physical pain as several bones in his hand broke on impact. I stood silently as he vented his rage. Finally, his father managed to calm him, then looked in my direction. "What about Judy?" Buster asked. I could only shake my head before turning to go find her two daughters and three sons.

For all the unsufferable grief being felt in those two small rooms, a burst of joy had filtered down the hallway from the conference room, where other families, more fortunate, were told that the siege had ended and that their loved ones would soon be returned to them.

In the street below the atmosphere had turned carnivalesque as reporters mingled with curious and relieved citizens. Once more I reached out to Estelle's weary secretary for help. "These people can't face all the reporters milling around outside," I explained. "I need some help getting them out of the building and to their homes." Almost as if by magic, ten Texas Rangers appeared, ready to serve as escorts.

When the last person was safely out and en route to reunions that we had all been praying for, I collapsed into a chair and surveyed the empty room. In the silence I pondered the long days and nights during which it had become its own kind of hellish prison. And I attempted to visualize the dark, insane drama that had been played out inside The Walls.

In the early morning hours, Carrasco had freed hostage Linda Woodham, sending her out with a blueprint of a four-sided escape shield he and his associates had designed and constructed from large blackboards. His deranged mind's version of an armored tank. Taken to the warden's office, she detailed the escape plan and described the makeshift shield. Reinforced by thick law books taped to the sides, it was large enough to hide the convicts and the three hostages from view. Yvonne, she reported, would be handcuffed to Carrasco, Judy to Rudy Dominguez, and Novella Pollard to Ignacio Cuevas. Father O'Brien would be handcuffed to the rear opening of the shield. The three convicts, she continued, would be wearing the bulletproof helmets that had finally met Carrasco's approval. Alongside, the remaining five employees and three inmate hostages were to be handcuffed to ropes that encircled the structure. Their job was to help navigate the turns necessary for the portable shield to successfully descend the ramp.

The route they planned, then, was simple: out the library door, down the three-story ramp to the exercise yard, then, with Yvonne, Judy, and Novella, into the armored car and out the gate to freedom. "He's fully prepared to go out in a blaze of glory," she had added.

At a few minutes after 9:00 P.M. the escape attempt got underway.

What the prisoners had not planned for was the sharpness of the turns they were facing en route down the ramp. Almost twenty minutes were needed to make it from the top level as impatient officers and guards waited two stories below, hidden inside the darkened inmate dining room.

When the cumbersome shield had finally been guided to the second floor, law-enforcement officers appeared from the darkness and pointed the high pressure water hoses toward it. The powerful rush of water was supposed to topple the structure, providing precious seconds during which lawmen could rush it and bring things to a peaceful end.

However, when one of the hoses ruptured, the force necessary to overturn the shield was lost. What resulted was nothing more than a soaking of the inmates and their hostages. And the immediate sound of gunfire from inside.

Rushing toward the structure, several officers were knocked back as bullets pounded into the armored vests they wore. Others managed to reach the shield and turn it over. A prison guard cut the outside rope, to which several hostages were handcuffed, allowing them to flee to safety. There were two more quick shots from inside, then silence as a helicopter hovered overhead, bathing the gruesome scene in a wide circle of light.

As dozens of armed officers approached, Father O'Brien, wounded in the arm and chest, called out a warning that Dominguez was still alive and attempting to reach for a gun. Officers shot and killed him. Then all fell silent.

During the carnage, Carrasco had died of a self-inflicted wound to the head, keeping his vow to not be taken alive. Judy Standley, shot four times in the back, was dead. Yvonne Beseda had been killed by a single gunshot to the chest. In the days to come it was determined that Carrasco and Dominguez had executed the women. Cuevas had apparently fainted when the gunfire erupted and was alive and unharmed. Aside from Father O'Brien, the only other hostage wounded was an inmate named Martin Quiroz, who had suffered a flesh wound to the arm.

After eleven seemingly endless days, the nightmare's climax had lasted only a few tragic minutes.

It was midnight when Dorothy gently placed a hand on my shoulder and told me that Jim Estelle, still in the warden's office across the street, wanted to see me. "He'll send someone over to escort you through the crowd," she said.

He was seated at a desk, his face a mask of sadness and fatigue, as I entered. On the floor nearby were the handmade helmets worn by the convicts during their deadly escape attempt. Nearby lay the guns that had ended the lives of Judy and Yvonne. From the window I could see the blue-and-white armored car, still parked in the center of the exercise yard. Imagined or real, my nostrils quickly filled with the scent of gunpowder.

Gathering around him those who had been involved in the negotiation attempts, he thanked each for his efforts, then requested that I say a prayer.

It was only after everyone else had left that he asked if I would accompany him to visit the Standley and Beseda families the following afternoon. I assured him that I would, then turned to leave. "You understand," he said, his voice weak and plaintive, "that there was no way that we could have turned violent people like that loose on the free world. Any hostage taken through the gate would have had no chance to live."

It was an explanation that he need not have offered. The suffering that he was so obviously feeling would, I knew, haunt him for the remainder of his life. All because he had performed an impossible and unpopular job that, by its nature, offered so few alternatives.

Daylight was beginning to break as I made my way home. Not wishing to wake Karel, I quietly made my way into the living room before hearing my daughter's welcome voice: "Daddy, is that you?" Suddenly my body did not ache so badly, my spirit lifted. I went up the stairs to her bedroom, where she greeted me with a hug. "I've been so worried about you," she said.

For several hours we sat on the floor, holding hands, quietly talking. And for the first time in her life, she saw her father cry.

While the siege was over, its aftermath would dramatically overturn the routine of the community for days to come. Estelle and I spent Sunday afternoon with the Standleys and the Besedas. The following day, I conducted Judy's funeral in the morning, then Yvonne's in the afternoon. In what I can only look on as a fitting tribute, both services were televised worldwide. In time, however, the cameras and microphones disappeared as reporters left in search of a new story.

For days afterward I had a steady stream of calls from those who had become a part of the conference-room vigil—some offering thanks, others seeking assurance that the anger and frightening dreams that still troubled them would one day pass. I welcomed my own family home and finally got around to buying birthday gifts for the twins. I visited Father O'Brien in the hospital, pleased to find that he was recovering nicely, then made a trip to Victoria for the postponed visit to my father, with whom I'd not been able to speak during those days that had so consumed me. He had, he said, listened to my funeral sermons on television and was proud of me. That made me feel better than I had for longer than I was able to remember.

Four months later, I would deliver the eulogy at his funeral.

Ignacio Cuevas, the lone survivor of the trio who had terrorized the entire community, was quickly charged with capital murder. An investigation soon revealed that a prison trustee named Lawrence Hall had supplied the guns for the fatal escape attempt after receiving them from a San Antonio friend of Carrasco's named Benito Alonzo. In the months to come, they too would be tried and convicted.

And, finally, my thoughts returned to my church and the needs of its congregation. Dru Standley's wedding went off as scheduled, just as her mother had requested. Determined to practice what I had long preached, I knew that life, while not as simple as I had once thought it to be, goes on. It would take time, I knew, to come to a full understanding of the events that had transpired. It would be some time before the frightened and solemn faces that I'd looked into daily would take leave of my dreams. Forgetting what had taken place would be impossible.

There was, in fact, but one thing I knew for certain. I had shared it with Dan McKaskill, the prison official who had helped me avoid the media en route to Jim Estelle's office on the night the siege finally ended.

In what was more vow than simple statement, I had assured him that under no circumstances would I ever again set foot inside the prison.

Little did I know.

TWO

How people are drawn to lifetime careers has always been a fascinating mystery to me. I've often wondered what mixture of interest and aptitude, happenstance and encouragement, must merge to steer one person toward becoming a test pilot and another toward becoming a big-league ballplayer. Is there some magic gene that sets the course for doctors, lawyers, and political movers and shakers? At what stage in life does a divine finger point the way for men of the cloth?

As a youngster growing up in South Texas, I had briefly entertained the idea of following in my parents' footsteps and becoming a teacher. As I began to enjoy some success at tennis, it occurred to me that I might even combine the best of both my worlds and grow up to become a teacher-coach. Then, however, shortly after I'd enrolled in junior college, my minister, Rev. John Newton, asked my help in cleaning up an abandoned USO building that he hoped to convert into a youth center for his church. As we became closer friends, I found myself increasingly impressed by the passion and dedication he brought to his calling. I found his sermons moving and thought provoking. In time, he persuaded me to direct his youth choir. My course, then, was set.

Long before I finished college and enrolled in the seminary, I knew that what I wanted was to be a preacher.

My calling, I was convinced, was not to save the world but, rather, to minister to a small congregation of familiar faces. Believing that

my greatest strength as a pastor lay in the ability to deal with people
one-on-one, I was quite comfortable with the idea of pursuing a career
in relative obscurity. In another time, my career choice might have
been referred to as "country preacher." I simply liked the idea of being
able to call people by their first names, knowing what grade their
children were in, and who's birthday or anniversary was being celebrated.

Such was the case in the early days of my ministry in out-of-the-
way Texas whistle stops like Pottsboro and Sinton.

And it had begun that way in Victoria as I'd first stood before a
Sunday-morning gathering to preach on the importance of the church
being an extension of the family unit. With God's help, I assured those
who had come to welcome me to the pulpit, we would share in each
other's joys and strengths, collectively mourn one another's sorrows,
and learn that a loving, helping hand was human nature's most treasured gift. In that sermon I shared my philosophy and convictions, and
in the weeks and months to come, the members of my congregation
embraced them.

One could not have asked for a more rewarding experience.

In time, however, the church membership grew far beyond my expectations. After six years, my primary function had evolved to that
of chief fund-raiser for construction of a new building and unwilling
mediator to the unfortunate political infighting that had accompanied
the growth. After a great deal of prayer and soul-searching, I became
convinced that I was no longer the man for the job. I had become a
country preacher with a big-city flock, more businessman than minister. The time had come to move on.

Even as I was arriving at that realization, a call came from the First
Presbyterian Church in Huntsville. Once thriving and well-attended,
it had fallen on hard times. Philosophical warfare among members had
resulted in people staying away in droves. What it badly needed, I was
told, was a pastor who could restore calm and begin a reuniting process. Would I be interested?

What the chairman of the search committee did not bother to tell me was that no fewer than forty-six ministers had turned down his offer before he'd gotten around to contacting me.

"Just bring your family to Huntsville for a visit and let me show you around," he urged. "Believe me, once you get here, you're going to like it so much you'll never want to leave."

The tour of the town didn't take long. We drove through the meandering campus of Sam Houston State University, into several well-manicured residential neighborhoods, then to the small downtown area where mom-and-pop business establishments were dwarfed by the towering redbrick walls of the prison unit and its nearby administration offices.

It had not even registered with me as we'd driven northward for the visit that Huntsville was, in fact, the headquarters for the Texas prison system. Nor did it occur to me that the lost souls it hid from public view might have anything whatsoever to do with the position being offered me.

I would, I told my host and his committee members, need some time before I could give them an answer.

Two months later, in September of 1967, I became the troubled church's new minister. At the first service I conducted, there were six people in the congregation. My choir consisted of a man, his wife, and their two children.

It would be the first in a lengthy list of challenges I would face. Yet, as time passed and attendance and renewed enthusiasm began to grow, I had every confidence that we had found a place to call home.

And perhaps if I'd been more insightful, I'd have even seen the subtle signs that pointed toward a calling I'd never anticipated.

Among the numerous prison employees who occasionally attended my services was Dr. George Beto, then the Texas Department of Corrections director. A bear of a man, he had years earlier made a career change that I could only describe as remarkable. A Lutheran minister, he had opted to become involved in the criminal-justice system, eventually making the climb to one of the most important positions in the state. Viewed nationwide as a pioneer in the penal sciences, he had spent much of his adult life arguing that society, when viewing the criminal element and the purpose of modern-day prison systems, had never made up its mind whether it wanted revenge or rehabilitation. Dr. Beto was an outspoken advocate for the latter. During his lengthy tenure as prison director, he had instituted a number of revolutionary programs designed to prepare inmates for the eventual day when they would be returned to the free world. Within the walls of the network of units he oversaw, he had ignored the controversy they were certain to cause and established things like Explorer Scout troops for younger prisoners and a Jaycees chapter for older inmates, and encouraged a relationship between the prisons and the local university that allowed those under his watch to earn college credits. Under his guidance, the Texas prisons had become virtually self-reliant as inmates worked on farms where food was grown and in prison shops where commercial goods were produced and sold to free-world consumers. Those with mechanical skills kept the prison vehicles in running order, while men with medical backgrounds staffed the prison hospital and others learned the skills necessary to provide the clothing and linens for the entire population. In a manner of speaking, the Texas prison system under Dr. Beto operated as a self-sufficient city determined not to burden the taxpayer.

For those trustworthy inmates whose parole date was nearing, he initiated a work-release program in which they were allowed to leave the prison during the day, returning for the evening head count and lockdown only after putting in a full day's work for local employers willing to offer them jobs.

Among Dr. Beto's goals was to assure that those who had served their time and paid their debts to society did not return once set free. I marveled at the fact that someone in his position could carry out his responsibilities with such a mixture of hard-nosed rule keeping and compassion for his fellowman. As we became friends, I came to admire him greatly.

And in time I would learn his one great weakness.

One midweek morning I answered the phone and for the first time since I'd known him heard tension in his voice. Bob Arrington, a Texas Department of Corrections pilot who was also a member of my church, had flown to Colorado to pick up an inmate and had not returned. He had, Dr. Beto said, begun his flight home during a snowstorm. "His plane is missing."

The pilot's schoolteacher wife, Ann, had immediately turned her classes over to an assistant and was en route to the local airport to await word, he explained. "Somebody needs to be with her," he said, "and I've got to be honest with you—I can do just about anything but comfort a distraught woman. I'm not the person to help her out. I simply don't know how to do it."

I told him I was on my way.

No time passes more slowly than that spent waiting in doubt. Throughout the day and into the night, we paced the airport terminal and talked and prayed as the search for the missing plane continued. Ann had arranged for a friend to pick her daughter up after school, and as the six-year-old's bedtime neared, her mother began to cry. "I need to tell Melanie what's going on," she said, "but I can't let her see me like this."

Assured that she would be okay alone for a half hour or so, I drove to the Arrington house and did my best to explain to the child why her father and mother were not there to tuck her into bed. I listened to her innocent nighttime prayers, assured her that her mother would soon replace the baby-sitter, who was staying the night, then returned to the airport. I said a prayer of my own as I made the short drive.

It was almost noon the following day when word finally came that the wreckage of the plane had been located. There were no survivors.

Weakened from the sleepless wait and badly shaken by the news, Ann was in no condition to drive home. Nor, I feared, would she be able to muster the strength to tell her daughter of the tragedy that had just befallen them. "I sent her on to school today," her mother said, "and she'll be coming home soon. I don't know what I'm going to tell her."

That difficult responsibility fell to me. With three children only a few years older and another two years younger, I tried without success to imagine how they might react to similar news. I prayed for gentle words that might somehow soften the blow to a child who had idolized the man now lying dead in the snow-covered Colorado wilderness, but none that seemed satisfactory came. There is, I learned on that painfully sad afternoon, no good way to tell a child that her daddy is gone forever.

The following Monday I conducted my first funeral service at which the majority of those in attendance were employees of the prison. Among them was Dr. Beto, who, as he neared retirement, was mourning the first loss of a member of his staff. After the ceremony he stood near me at the doorway to the church as people filed out, a pained expression on his face as he nervously waited to have a word with Ann Arrington. As if she instinctively knew how difficult the moment was for him, she reached for his hand and smiled. "My husband," she said, "had such great respect for you."

That day, as I surveyed the color guard the prison had assigned and the crowd of somber faces that filed from the church, I came to a realization that had eluded me during the early days of my ministry in Huntsville. Those who worked at the prison, daily dealing with the anger and hatred of the men they were assigned to watch over, were no different from the rest of us. Their tears flowed just as freely, and their pain was felt just as deeply.

It was the death of Bob Arrington that moved me toward a better understanding of those who made their livings behind those rust red-brick walls—and while I didn't know it at the time, it helped to prepare me for that seemingly endless nightmare that would draw us even closer during those eleven torturous days in the summer of 1974.

In the years following the prison siege, I would often be reminded of the prophetic words of that pulpit committee chairman who had first invited me to Huntsville: "You're going to like it so much you'll never want to leave. . . ." I'd found the city's people warm and welcoming. Old-time, golden-rule values dominated the community, and the university lent a vibrant intellectual atmosphere that I found appealing. And the tennis courts weren't bad. It was, by every measure, a great place to raise children.

Soon I was venturing well beyond my duties at the church, agreeing to serve as the emergency-room chaplain at the hospital and helping to create a ministerial alliance designed to bring preachers of the various faiths and colors in Huntsville closer together. We formed groups called Christian Organization for Missionary Endeavors and Helping Out Widows, which would stand ready to lend spiritual aid in times of tragedy. I ran for the school board along with prison teacher Jack Branch, one of the surviving hostages of the Fred Carrasco siege, and we were both elected. I volunteered to serve as treasurer for the local chapter of the Salvation Army and watched our kids grow and develop friendships. I coached their Little League teams, taught them to play tennis, and, in my role as a school board member, had the honor of handing out diplomas to each when they graduated. I was busy, happy—and blind to the dark clouds forming over my own home.

In the years following the siege, my wife had developed a growing resentment toward my involvement in the community. My priorities, she insisted, had become badly misplaced. Admitting that I had spread myself too thin, I eventually began to reduce my volunteer activities in hopes of mending a marriage that was clearly beginning to unravel. Nothing I did, however, seemed to satisfy her, and, in time, she even began to view the church as an adversary.

As the seventies drew to a close, the situation had deteriorated to a point where she had told me that the only way she would consider any attempt to continue our marriage was if I resigned my ministry.

Then, on the last Sunday afternoon in December of 1979, she announced after another in a growing series of heated arguments that she was leaving to stay with her sister in Houston for a while. Her resentment had spread to everything in which I was involved. The latest focus of her ire was the fact that there had been a rash of holiday-season automobile accidents that required me to spend an extraordinary amount of time at the hospital emergency room. While packing to leave, she had telephoned two women in the church and confided her frustrations.

Word spread quickly. Almost immediately members of the church were dropping into my office, expressing concern that I might have "problems" that I needed to talk about. And while I chose not to discuss my martial difficulties, still hoping that things might somehow work out, I quickly realized that my position in the church was in jeopardy. One member went so far as to say, "You know, if you and Sonya get a divorce, you won't be able to continue as our pastor." Another was even more blunt: "I think your ministry here is over." I felt a sudden swell of resentment building toward those who had taken judgmental stances without any real knowledge of the problem.

The following Sunday, with my wife not among those in the congregation, I felt unworthy to take communion for the first time in my life. In my heart I knew that I was soon to lose a job that meant a great deal to me. Yet all options had been eliminated when my brother came to me, offering to help. Sonya had contacted him, suggesting he act in the role of mediator. In truth, there was little he could do. "She says," he explained with a helpless shrug, "that she will return home only if you resign from the church."

Thus on January 8, 1980—our daughter Charlotte's seventeenth birthday—I met with the officers of the church and tendered my resignation. I had served the First Presbyterian Church for thirteen years, and the decision was, at best, bittersweet. The church had grown and prospered. I had made friends in the congregation who would, I knew, remain with me for a lifetime. On the other hand, the profession has an unwritten rule that a minister's tenure of service to a particular church has limitations. There comes a time when new leadership is demanded if God's work is to continue to move forward. In truth, I had offered the membership all I had to give. It did not, however, lessen the painful knowledge that there were those who no longer wanted me as their pastor.

A few days earlier, Sonya had told our children that I would soon be leaving the pulpit. "He did it," she explained, "so we can have a happy home life again." Charlotte, who had come to view the church as her second home, burst into tears at the news.

Agreeing to stay until a new pastor was hired, I was soon barraged with questions about my plans for the future. The truth was I had not the slightest idea of what I would do. But for years I had preached the importance of faith. I could only hold firmly to mine and rest assured that God would point the way.

It took only ten days.

One morning, as I worked on a sermon, trying to avoid thoughts of what my future and that of my family held, I received a call from a member of my congregation. Jim Estelle, who had replaced Dr. Beto as director of the prison system, expressed his regret that I would soon be leaving. We talked of the close friendship our teenage daughters had developed. "You know," he finally said, "it would be a shame to pull Charlotte out of school before her senior year." I confided that it was a concern that had weighed heavily on me.

"I'd like for you to come to work for me," he said. "I need a chaplain."

I thought he was joking. Or perhaps extending an offer born more out of charity than genuine need. I expressed my reservations. "Give it a try for a year," he suggested. "That will provide you the opportunity to see if it is something you feel comfortable with and also give your daughter the chance to graduate from high school with her friends. Come in, and let's talk about it."

For some time I sat alone in my study, replaying the conversation. I had received a few calls about possible job opportunities—teaching, working for a firm that sold religious materials; a couple of churches had even contacted me—but I had not seriously considered any of them. Now, to my surprise, I was thinking of becoming a prison chaplain despite the fact that I had little idea what the responsibilities were. How did one go about trying to save souls that the laws, the courts, and most of society had already judged lost? While certain that God's loving hand reached well beyond brick walls and iron bars, I wondered if I could do the same in a world so foreign to me.

And I thought back to that dark night years earlier when the smell of gunpowder and death had been so suffocating, prompting my solemn vow to never again set foot inside the prison. For years I had routinely gone out of my way to avoid even driving past it, fearful of the dreaded memories that it was certain to summon.

Sonya, meanwhile, seemed excited by the idea. "It will be good for you to have a boss to answer to," she said. "And regular hours. You've tried too long to be all things to all people, and it very nearly destroyed us."

Proving that God does, indeed, work in mysterious ways, I took the job and was assigned to The Walls. My primary duties, I was told, would be to conduct regular worship services in the small Chapel of Hope that occupied one corner of the prison yard and to minister to patients in the unit's hospital. When I asked my predecessor for advice, his suggestion was short and to the point. What I was about to encounter, he said, was light-years removed from any kind of ministry the rest of the world had to offer. "If you're not very careful," he warned, "you can let the prisoners take so much out of you that you have nothing left for yourself." I wondered if it had been such a fate that had caused him to leave, but I stopped short of asking.

By the summer of 1980 we had moved from the church parsonage into one of the neatly kept duplexes reserved for prison employees. It was located just across the street from my new workplace, and I held high hope that my new adventure—what else do you call a journey into the unknown?—might provide a fresh start for my wife and me. With only my responsibilities as chaplain to attend to and my office within walking distance of our front door, I was sure that I would be able to spend far more time with my family. Meanwhile, the officials of the Presbyterian Church had lent their blessing to my job change, which they officially termed a "specialized ministry," and I had spent considerable time with Warden Jack Pursley, a fellow officer on the school board from which I'd resigned, learning the rules and regulations that would form the strict boundaries of my new challenge.

Had I known at the time what the future held, I might well have made a cowardly run for safety before ever preaching my first sermon.

Prison life is a world unto itself, a mind-numbing routine in which the punishment of those who call the prison home is to be held accountable for their every movement. Meals are served at the same time each day, head counts done morning and night, showers last exactly three minutes, time for "lights out" never varies, and small privileges are awarded for only the best behavior. There are so many rules that no man can be expected to remember them all. It is a world, I would soon learn, filled with paranoia and grinding loneliness, anger and dispirited resignation. The prejudices and cliques of the free world are only magnified behind prison walls. Racial tensions are a constant, the educated view the uneducated with disdain, the strong bully the weak, and those in authority are routinely viewed as the enemy. Many bring to the cell blocks the violence that they once acted out in a free society. Even those who wish only to pay for their crimes and be left alone must do so in an atmosphere of fear that never sleeps.

Like all units in the system, The Walls employed two chaplains—one Protestant and one Catholic. My ministerial partner would be Fr. Joseph O'Brien, who, after recovering from the gunshot wounds he suffered in the aborted escape attempt that ended the siege, had courageously returned to his duties. It soon became obvious that, after six years, he was still troubled by those terrifying days and nights he and his fellow hostages had endured. From my first day on the job until he finally retired, it was rare when we had a conversation that did not eventually wind its way to discussion of that fateful night when the trip down the ramp ended in a fusillade of gunfire. "You didn't know," he laughed one day after talking of the fears and doubts that remained with him, "that one of your jobs here would be to serve as priest to the priest."

Each of us was assigned an inmate who served as our clerk, handling paperwork, collecting the mail, and running errands. As proof of the extraordinary circumstances that make prison life unique, Father O'Brien's right-hand man was Jewish. My own man was a self-proclaimed agnostic with a sizable chip on his shoulder. Everyone called him Blue. A habitual criminal with a lengthy list of felonies to his credit—bank robberies had been his specialty—he had clerked for the chaplain I was replacing. "I know my way around," he advised me. "I'll do your paperwork and protect you, but I don't go to chapel."

Obviously there would be plenty of time in the days ahead to try and change his mind about the latter. But, for the moment, it was his promise to "protect" me that had my attention.

Blue grunted. "You're naive, man, just like the preacher was before you. Probably same as the guy before him. Until you learn the ropes, you don't go anyplace without me, okay?"

I could only shrug. "Hey, you're the boss," I replied. And, for the first time, Blue smiled. Clearly he liked that idea.

Some friends were aware of the career change that I'd made, and their response was often accompanied by a time-worn joke. At least, they noted, I would be delivering all future sermons to a captive audience. What they didn't know was that attendance at the regularly scheduled Sunday and Wednesday chapel services was not a mandatory requirement for the inmates.

As I preached my first sermon, an unsettling flashback to that initial Sunday at First Presbyterian occurred. Of the over two thousand inmates confined in The Walls, a grand total of six sat in the chapel pews. A lone prison guard stood near the door, his expression speaking loudly to the fact he would also rather be somewhere else. As I spoke of my reason for being there and outlined future plans for worship services, I realized that the challenge would be a greater one than I had anticipated.

My disappointment deepened when a prison major introduced himself and pointedly told me that he would respect me only when I'd earned it. It was two years later, following a stroke, when that same major called me to his bedside as he was near death and asked that I conduct his funeral.

While aware that the rules offered myriad restrictions I could do nothing about, I was determined to make the chapel a welcoming place, as close to a free-world church as possible. I hoped that one day music would come from the piano that sat silent in one corner, that a choir would soon lift its voice, that the empty pews would be occupied, and that guards would not feel the need to stand on alert. I outlined plans for Bible-study classes and regular visits from clergy of all denominations, and explained that I had not come to judge, simply to minister. The door to my office, I promised, would stand open to anyone who wished to visit.

As I spoke, I looked out on blank stares and skepticism.

"You can't expect people to come to you," Blue later told me. "They're waiting for you to come to them. That's how it works in here. Folks are suspicious of everybody until they get to know them." My first order of business, then, was to earn trust.

Among those he suggested I get to know was an inmate named "Redbird" McCarter. "You need this guy," Blue said. A convicted murderer, McCarter was the acknowledged leader of the unit, tough and feared by his fellow inmates. When I finally located him, he was in one of the isolation cells in solitary confinement for a laundry list of offenses: fighting, refusing to work, and showing disrespect to guards. When I arrived, Bible in hand, he was seated on a cot, eating his evening meal of beans and a single biscuit. Overhead a twenty-watt lightbulb barely illuminated his stark surroundings. Aside from the bed, there was nothing else but a commode and a bare concrete floor.

While I did not specifically ask that he put in a good word for me to fellow inmates, I did outline for him the plans I had. When I mentioned my hope of one day conducting services at which no guards stood watch, he only laughed. Out at the Darrington Unit, I knew, church services were conducted under the watchful eyes of as many as twenty guards, there to make certain no contraband was exchanged and no untoward physical contact went on during sermons.

During the course of our half-hour visit, I heard nothing but skepticism and allegations of bad treatment. Prison, he said in a voice filled with more anger than I'd ever heard, was an us-against-them world. Yet, as I turned to leave, he thanked me for coming. "We don't see many preachers down here in solitary," he said.

I left the Bible with him and told him I'd be back.

Several Sunday chapel services later, all of them dismally attended, I looked up to see Redbird among the scattering of early arrivals. Taking a seat, he looked at me and nodded ever so slightly. To my amazement, the pews began to fill. Freed from solitary confinement and back into the general prison population, he had obviously put out the word that attendance was no longer optional.

Things began to slowly fall into place. One of the first things I learned was that there was an incredible supply of musical talent in the prison population. Several pianists came forward, then an accordionist who had studied under a member of Lawrence Welk's orchestra. A gospel quartet was soon formed, composed of a murderer who had been a backup singer for Hawaiian pop singer Don Ho, an armed robber who had sung in a group that had toured the country performing in Holiday Inn lounges, and a father-son team serving time for bank robbery. The father and son had been, respectively, an evangelist and a Christian music director before their arrests and conviction. The piano player who accompanied them was serving time for the murder of his wife. Next we formed several choirs—including one composed of black gospel singers, another made up solely of Hispanic inmates—and began to have occasional competitions among the units after persuading a deejay from a Fort Worth religious music station to serve as judge.

So remarkable was the talent that his was not an easy job. In fact, when Public Broadcasting System newsman Bill Moyers decided to do a television special on the origin and history of the gospel favorite "Amazing Grace," he dispatched a film crew to Huntsville to record the Chapel of Hope Choir's version of the song and included it in his documentary.

One of the most difficult assignments I faced was to arrange for the weekly Bible-study classes. Because they were considered part of the prison's educational program, they were to be held in the building where, six years earlier, Carrasco and his men had barricaded themselves and their hostages. My first trip up that long ramp, past the spot where I knew Judy Standley and Yvonne Beseda had died, was not easy.

Taking Blue's advice, I made myself visible throughout the prison, visiting cell blocks and workplaces and walking among the inmates in the yard. When it came to my attention that some hospitalized prisoners were physically unable to attend services, I requested permission from Maj. A. J. Murdock to ask members of the inmate Jaycees to bring them. Soon, each Sunday morning a dozen or more wheelchairs were being pushed across the yard in the direction of the chapel.

Ultimately guards no longer appeared at services. I strongly felt that if it was to serve its purpose, the chapel would have to stand as a test of faith. And if I didn't show it toward the inmates, how was I to expect it from them?

A great deal of my time was spent in the prison hospital, particularly the third floor, where the terminally ill patients were being treated. Every Thursday, Blue and I would arrive to see the seventy beds lined in rows filled by men coming to grips with the fact they would soon die. That, I soon learned, frightened even the strongest and healthiest inmates. Regardless of the length of their sentence, no matter how far in some distant future a parole hearing might be, they were all afraid that death might occur before they were freed.

For those in the terminal unit, all hope of being freed had disappeared. My job was to provide whatever comfort I could. I took writing materials and envelopes and offered to help write letters, and I had my Bible with me in the event a patient wished to have a favorite Scripture read. Mostly, however, I was a listener.

I soon learned that it was not unusual to spend time with a patient one day, then soon afterward carry out another of my assigned responsibilities. Those without family or friends on the outside world were buried in the prison cemetery. I conducted their funerals. With rare exception, the only people in attendance were the warden and the inmates assigned to dig the grave and serve as pallbearers.

I had made a request of the medical staff that I be alerted whenever an inmate was brought into the emergency room or if it became obvious that one of the terminal patients was nearing death. I believe that no one should die alone, and I felt it was my responsibility to offer whatever final comfort I could. It was during one such vigil that I saw a dramatic example of the fact that compassion for one's fellowman did not exist only in the free world.

Late one evening a call came to the house, alerting me to the fact that an elderly inmate, riddled with cancer, was dying. Like the rest of the prison, even the hospital units had a regularly scheduled "lights out," and so, when I arrived, the third floor was dark. Making my way to the patient's bed, I quietly pulled a chair up beside him and sat holding his hand. I'd been there only a short time when I heard a whisper. "He don't like the dark," another patient explained. "It scares him. I don't think it's right he should die in the dark." I turned to see this aged black man, his body also cancer ravaged, with a tiny reading lamp in hand. Plugging it into a nearby socket, he stood at my side, ignoring his own pain as he held the light above his friend's bed for the last four hours of his life.

I have never witnessed a greater act of human kindness.

I had agreed to a one-year trial period at the job, and it seemed to fly past. And while I'd spent it in a social climate far different from the one I'd known outside The Walls, I quickly learned there were similarities. Inmates fell ill, just as other people do; there were those who wanted to run things, and others who struggled to fit in. They, too, had questions and fears that haunted them in the darkest hours of the night.

They were people, and I had made up my mind to treat them as people.

Even as I became increasingly comfortable in my role, I constantly faced questions of my own. Just as the prisoners followed rules, I had strict rules to follow, too. Choir practices and evening worship services had to be kept to a rigid schedule, ending well before the nightly head count. The paperwork required for an inmate to visit my office for a counseling session seemed endless. The slightest rule infraction was cause to deny prisoners the right of attendance at chapel. In my early days, I thought nothing of shaking the hand of an inmate who had come to my office or occasionally giving a pat to the back of some newcomer to my services or a Bible-study class. But I was soon written up by one of the assistant wardens. I was reminded that physical contact of any kind between members of the staff and the prison population was a violation.

It was just one of many things that made no sense to me. I realized that there were also larger questions, which no rules-and-regulations book could answer: What was our purpose as a prison staff? Were we to simply lock offenders away and toss the key? Were our motives punitive, or was rehabilitation a real goal? What, for that matter, was the definition of my role as spiritual leader of the unit?

I found no one who could give me specific answers. Warden Pursley, I suppose, came closest as we sat in his office one day. "I can't say I'm sure what your philosophy should be, any more than I can give you a short answer of what mine is," he admitted. "I'll leave it to you. There are few things in this business that I'm certain of, but I do know how to do my job. And I'm convinced that you know yours."

And to that he added the only words of encouragement I needed to hear: "You're here," he said, "for the right reasons."

Unfortunately, my wife did not share Pursley's opinion. Initially, she had seemed pleased with my new career. In time, however, the late-night calls alerting me to some emergency at the hospital began to anger her. If a meeting I was required to attend ran long, causing me to be late returning home, she made clear her impatience. Whatever rebuilding we had accomplished had begun to deteriorate. Clearly, Sonya was not happy. And neither was I.

Still, I prayed for the miracle that would mend our differences.

Two days before Charlotte was to graduate from high school, her mother and I went out to dinner in celebration of our twenty-sixth wedding anniversary. It was a pleasant evening, with gifts and laughter that gave me hope that things might be on the mend. Yet the following day, while I was away, Sonya moved out.

She had not mentioned—even as we celebrated our anniversary— that she'd filed for a divorce three weeks earlier. In fact, I did not find out until late June, when I attempted to purchase a new car for my daughter Anne. A student at the University of Texas at the time, she had wrecked the one that we'd given her before she'd left for college. It was only when the salesman pointed out that my bank account had been frozen that Anne took me by the arm and pulled me from the man's earshot. "Daddy," she said as tears formed in her eyes, "I thought you knew."

"Knew what?"

"Mother has filed for a divorce," she said. She went on to explain that Sonya had told her and the other children that she would soon be leaving, that with her mother's help she had already purchased a mobile home in which she planned to live.

For a time I fought the idea that a quarter-century-old relationship could so suddenly end, convinced that there were no problems too great to be worked out if enough energy and effort were applied. Among the strongest of my Christian beliefs was that God abhorred divorce, and I prayed that He would show me some way to resolve the problems that had been festering for so long. Somehow, some way, I was determined to repair the damage that had occurred.

Soon, it became obvious that I was trying to accomplish the impossible. During court proceedings, Sonya swore to a lengthy list of alleged cruelties that I had inflicted on her. She even told a judge that the dress she wore to court was the only one she owned, and that it had been purchased for her by her sister only when it was learned that I had refused to provide even the barest necessities for her.

I was forced to admit that it was over.

It was a time during which my faith was severely tested. I fought to control my anger as I questioned why God would allow such a tragedy to befall me. The overwhelming disappointment I had felt in those members of my congregation who had earlier chosen sides and determined I was no longer fit to minister returned. I was angry at a wife who I felt had demanded the impossible of me. And I cursed my own shortcomings.

Only gradually did the pain and doubt begin to fade as I came to a new realization. If I was to properly demonstrate the faith I had preached all my life, I had to move forward. Though I had made mistakes that cost me dearly, I felt that God was not yet through with me. That message, I came to understand, had been relayed by Jim Estelle when he expressed his need for a prison chaplain. It was his way of saying, "I still trust in you."

And, I would ultimately realize, it was God's way of telling me where He wanted me to be. By helping convicts to rebuild their lives, perhaps I could move ahead with my own.

Even in the darkest times, I would quickly learn, there is reason to smile. During chapel services on the Sunday after Sonya moved out, several of the inmates came forward to tell me that they had pitched in money from the commissary accounts to purchase flowers. "What for?" I asked.

"Well," one finally acknowledged, "you know, word gets around pretty fast in here. What we heard was that you just lost your wife. We thought maybe you would like some flowers for her grave."

I couldn't help but laugh. "She's gone," I admitted, "but she's not dead."

THREE

Hope does not flourish in prison. Everywhere I looked, from the hospital's terminal ward to the isolation cells, I encountered faces frozen in despair. For all the bad jokes about there being a Bible in every foxhole and prison cell, I found that many of the inmates had lost whatever faith might have once guided their lives. The men who lived behind The Walls daily woke to stare squarely into the mouth of a pitch-black tunnel that seemed to have no end.

In time they began coming to my office in a steady stream, bringing with them burdens so dark and weighty that I wondered if the small favors that the rules allowed me to offer would be of any help. Still, I had pledged to try.

It was rarely easy, as some days left me so drained and confused, so frustrated and depressed, that I would remain alone in my office long after the last inmate had visited, well after the final head count of the day had settled the prison into the quiet that visited only at night.

These, I kept reminding myself, are also God's people. Regardless of their flaws and the crimes that they had committed, and of the evil and anger that had brought them to this place, they were in many ways no different from anyone else. They cried out for an inner peace while enduring the pain of separation from loved ones. They worried about ill and dying mothers and fathers they could neither touch nor comfort. Most did not come to me to talk of spiritual matters but rather of troubles that invaded their daily lives: a son back home who was refusing to attend school and had been arrested for drug use, a daughter who had fought with her mother and run away from home, a girlfriend who no longer came to visit. And they lived in a constant state of fear and doubt, vainly searching for a strength that would allow them to endure another day.

The level of fear that pervaded prison society was made clear to me early on.

Blue, still concerned about my physical well-being, routinely remained at his desk in the office we shared as I counseled inmates. Despite the fact many of my visitors requested that we speak privately, only rarely did my clerk agree to step into the hallway. Generally, I deferred to him. In the system for the third time, he knew the present dangers and the men to watch.

One morning, after a call from the hospital had informed me that an inmate was refusing to submit to a physical examination before speaking with me, Blue instinctively recognized that my visitor's needs were of a private nature. As the prisoner—a newcomer to The Walls—entered, Blue said he'd be outside the door if I needed him.

Seated across from me was a man in his early twenties, pale, tired, and in tears before he even spoke. His face was badly bruised, and even though he folded his hands into his lap, I could see they were shaking. Not-yet-dried blood was visible on the leg of his white jumpsuit.

It was several minutes before he could control his sobbing enough to speak. "Is what we talk about confidential?" he asked.

I assured him that it would be.

"I've been raped," he blurted. "I'm afraid I'm hurt pretty bad. I'm bleeding. But I can't tell anybody over at the hospital."

I was still more naive than I wished to admit. "Why not?"

"Because they'll write up a report, and eventually somebody's going to come and ask me to say who did it. And I've already been warned that if I tell, it will happen again."

In another world, another time, I would have immediately taken him from my office and driven him to the nearest emergency room. Here, however, where logic often seemed a foreign concept and an incomprehensible kind of jungle law trumped all written rules, no such option existed. Somehow, I knew, I had to convince him to get medical attention in the prison hospital, while at the same time I had to determine some way to assure his safety. He explained that he'd only recently arrived to begin serving a six-year sentence.

"My situation," he said, "is hopeless. I can't go through this over and over again. They told me I was 'theirs' whenever they wanted me. I have no way to protect myself. I'd rather kill myself than go through it again."

I listened as he graphically described being beaten and sodomized by three older inmates, his despair echoing throughout the small room. And I felt absolutely helpless. Among the rules was one that required me to report all suicide threats to the warden. Doing so, however, would only bring pressure on the inmate to discuss his reason for wishing to take his own life. And, should he do so, an investigation into his rape charges would surely be initiated, further adding to the dilemma.

Finally, however, he agreed to return to the hospital and have his wounds tended. As soon as I reported his threat of suicide, I knew, he would be placed in isolation, where a guard would be assigned to keep watch over him around the clock. If nothing else, it would buy a small measure of time and safety.

A few days later he returned to my office, no longer crying but in a state of depression unlike any I'd ever seen. A prison psychiatrist had visited him and recommended that he be immediately transferred to the hospital's psychiatric unit. It was the safest haven the prison had to offer.

In time the young man became a regular at chapel services, but he would sit silently, a blank expression on his face, all joy of life gone. Diagnosed as manic-depressive, he showered only when forced to by the doctors or guards and feared even going into the dining room for meals. I watched him become an old man in a matter of months. The experience had destroyed him. And I agonized over the fact that I had been able to do so little to help him.

He never spoke the names of the men who had assaulted him.

In truth, prison lore is filled with disquieting tales of sexual brutality. Stories similar to that of the raped inmate came to me all too often, and I felt a new level of anger each time I heard them. I wondered what kind of person would do such a thing, and why prison guards, paid to watch over the activities of the inmates, could not prevent such horrors. Only when the math was explained to me—there were twenty-two hundred prisoners at The Walls and fewer than one hundred guards on the payroll—did I realize that watching everyone all the time was impossible.

The best safeguard of a young, vulnerable prisoner, I soon learned, existed within the inmate population itself. Despite the myths of bad Hollywood fiction, sexual predators do not run rampant behind prison walls. They are, in fact, a small segment of the population and generally viewed by the other inmates with the disdain otherwise reserved for child molesters. I soon learned of an inmate code that offered some measure of safety. There were those who took it upon themselves to play the role of protector to younger convicts. When possible, the newcomers were assigned as their cell mates. It was an imperfect answer but more effective than anything else prison officials had come up with.

My greatest challenge, then, was to fight against an enemy I could only see in the eyes and hear in the voices of those who came to me. And I had to come to grips with the realization that the performance of miracles was beyond me. I could only search for ways that gave brief respite to a prisoner's pain. In many cases, the best I could do was listen, be a friend for that day, and hope that the simple act of trying to understand lent some degree of comfort.

Among the concerns I heard regularly were those expressed about family members. Inmates constantly came to me, voicing concern that wives and girlfriends, children and parents, never visited or wrote. Some even refused the one collect call a prisoner was allowed to make every ninety days. Almost daily I made calls and wrote letters to strangers, attempting to gently remind them of the importance of making contact. Sometimes it worked; sometimes I was told in no uncertain terms that no interest existed.

An inmate named Cecil was, by all measure, one of the meanest, most feared men in the prison. When I first met him, I quickly judged him to be one of those who used visits to my office only to get an occasional hour's break from work detail. It was a transparent ruse I saw regularly, just as I saw those who could offer up chapter and verse of the Bible in a manner that would shame many ministers, or the inmate who once confided to me that he had, since his incarceration, been baptized no less than nine times by ministers of a like number of faiths. To cover all the bases, he'd explained. Yet I would quickly learn that such men felt no real conviction; that they were mocking Christianity and conning me or, more importantly, the parole board.

In time, however, Cecil's own frailties showed. His mother, he confided, was quite ill and no longer physically able to visit. He said that he worried about her constantly, to the point where he was unable to sleep. One afternoon as we talked, I asked for her phone number. While rules did not allow him to make a call, there was nothing that said I couldn't speak with her and ask how she was doing, then pass the information along.

By doing so I made a friend. And an ally. Though Cecil never once attended a service, he became one of the chapel's greatest supporters. He came to view me as his lone contact with the outside world. There were times, however, when the manner in which he displayed his loyalty was hardly what I would have asked for.

When, for instance, he learned that a fellow inmate had been bad-mouthing me and the chapel services, Cecil visited the exercise area in the yard and slipped a small weight into a sock. Then, waiting in a blind corner where the guards could not see him, he struck the man in the head with his makeshift weapon, knocking him unconscious.

A few days later he admitted to me what he had done, proudly proclaiming that the inmate, still recovering from a concussion, wasn't likely to speak ill of me or the chapel again. It did not seem to bother him that I was duty-bound to turn him in to the warden's office. He just shrugged and said he'd been in solitary before. No big deal. He'd gotten his message across.

When word came to me that his mother had been hospitalized, I lobbied for him to be allowed a rarely given furlough to visit her bedside. It was not an easy sell. His history of violence, both in the free world and in prison, made him a security risk. My argument was that if prison officials wished for Cecil to be less of a problem, they might best accomplish their goal by a show of compassion. Finally, it was agreed that he could travel to Dallas's Presbyterian Hospital in the company of a guard. Shackled and handcuffed, he would be allowed only a ten-minute visit with his mother before returning immediately to prison. The guard, initially skeptical about the trip outside the prison, was amazed by Cecil's perfect behavior and let the visit stretch to two hours before beginning the return trip to Huntsville. Thereafter, Cecil was a model prisoner.

Eventually he was paroled, but unfortunately, he wasted little time in returning to his criminal ways. He became an arsonist-for-hire and an enforcer for a loan shark. Soon after he'd broken a man's legs with a baseball bat, his parole was revoked, and he was returned to prison. This time, however, his residence would be the infamous Eastham Unit, where the system's most dangerous inmates were kept.

I had not thought of Cecil for some time when his wife telephoned my office one morning to tell me that his mother had died. Was there, she asked, some way I could get word to him?

I drove out to Eastham, explained the purpose of my visit to the warden, and asked that Cecil be brought to an interview room. When he arrived, he was shackled and in handcuffs. The guard expressed surprise and concern when I asked that the chains and cuffs be removed. "I know this guy," I explained. "He's not going to hurt me." Reluctantly the guard did as I asked.

That afternoon I informed him of his mother's death. Then I sat there, looking across the table at a man judged one of the meanest in the entire Texas penal community, and watched as his shoulders slumped and tears filled his eyes.

Later in the day, as I made my way back to my office, I wondered what events in Cecil's life had turned him down the angry, criminal road he'd been traveling so long. He had proven himself a danger to society and therefore would not likely ever again be free. And, intellectually, I could not argue with that decision. Yet questions persisted: What mixture of genes and emotions, social climate and educational process, could allow a man to show absolutely no remorse over taking a baseball bat to the knees of a stranger yet cry uncontrollably at the death of his mother? Had society somehow failed him at a critical time in his life? Or were his problems simply of his own making?

What, I wished to know, had turned Cecil and so many like him into the hopeless cases they had become? Had there been a time in his life, long ago, when he too had dreams of a more positive kind of life?

It was difficult to watch prisoners' hope erode, to see strong men grow weak of spirit despite one's best effort at encouragement. In my choir was a man whose tenor voice was remarkable. The solo hymns he sang filled the chapel like summer sunlight. Yet I doubt that he ever really heard the words.

He had come to prison for assault on a brother-in-law who he learned had sexually molested his three children. Upon finding out what his relative had done, Bill, crazed with anger, encouraged his pregnant wife to help him as he avenged the crimes committed against his children. While she helped hold her brother down, her husband had beaten the child molester so severely that for a time it was feared that he might die. Bill and his wife were both convicted of assault and sentenced to lengthy prison terms.

Not long after being sent to the women's unit in Gatesville, Bill's wife gave birth to a child that immediately became a ward of the state. Despondent, she soon filed for divorce. The children he'd tried to avenge refused to visit him. The only person who continued to offer any kind of support at all was a sister living in Alabama, too far away to visit.

Repeatedly, Bill's case had been reviewed and turned down by the parole board. And with each turndown, any hope of rebuilding his life slipped further away. He remained convinced that he'd done nothing but respond to a horrible evil. "I shouldn't be here," he often told me.

Bill eventually began the slow process of ending his life, literally eating himself to death. I constantly pled with him to lose weight and begin exercising. "What for?" he asked.

He weighed almost four hundred pounds by the time he suffered a fatal heart attack one afternoon as he stood alone in the yard, watching others play basketball.

Suicides in prison are commonplace, prompted by everything from a "Dear John" letter to depression fueled by the boredom of being confined to a five-by-nine cell day after day. It is impossible to describe the claustrophobia. Even when he is free of a cell, the inmate's entire world exists within the boundaries of four walls that hide all else from view. Even knowing that at day's end I could walk out, returning to a world of colors dictated by the seasons and to the sights and sounds of freedom, I too fought the depression that awaited, sinister and constant, inside The Walls.

The lone venue from which one could look beyond the prison to the outside world was the fifth floor of the hospital unit. One day, as Blue accompanied me on my visitation rounds, we stood at a window, and I pointed out such landmarks as the downtown area and the college campus and my old church, as well as where I had once lived. He stood there, childlike, as if viewing a wonder he'd never expected to see.

The holiday season was always the most difficult. Though I made certain to provide special services on Passover, Thanksgiving, and Christmas, even having inmates help decorate the chapel with the traditional lights, wreaths, and even a tree, it was difficult to defuse the sadness that overwhelmed many of the inmates.

One Sunday afternoon in December, I sat in my office, not expecting anyone to visit. With the football season in full swing, many watched television while others awaited their turns to be escorted to the visiting room to see friends and family. From my window I could see that the yard, generally teeming with prisoners, was empty.

It was shortly after four when I received an emergency request from a prisoner who had been a regular in my office.

"I just had a bad visit," he explained as he slumped into a chair. He was crying. "My wife just told me she's involved in a relationship with another man," he said. "She's sleeping with him. She told me she was feeling guilty about it and had to tell me."

"Is she asking for a divorce?"

"No."

"Is she pregnant?"

"No."

He would not look at me as he clipped off his answers, and I felt certain there was more that he wanted to tell me. But, for whatever reason, he couldn't bring himself to tell it. I'd heard his story repeatedly from so many other inmates, most often after they had received letters from wives who had announced that they had found someone else or on the dreaded Tuesdays when warrant servers routinely delivered divorce papers to the prison. Rarely was there anything I could say that would soften the blow felt as another part of life was severed. I was simply a handy shoulder to cry on.

My visitor was still in tears as he politely thanked me for listening and turned to leave. I suggested that we talk again on Monday, and he nodded.

He had been gone only a few minutes when I received a call from a guard assigned to the yard. An inmate, he said, had taken his life by draining antifreeze from one of the prison trucks and drinking it. It would be my responsibility to notify his nearest kin.

It is a difficult task, best done straightforwardly. Calling his wife, I said only that I had some bad news to relate and asked if she had someone at home with her or if there might be someone I could contact for her. When she said that her sister was visiting, I proceeded to tell her what had happened. For what seemed like several minutes, I heard only a series of painful screams on the other end of the line, and then she composed herself enough to ask the question I'd so often heard: "Why did he do it?"

I could have told her that the loneliness and isolation had simply become too much to bear. That he'd seen the last shred of hope disappear. That he'd simply reached that point where death had seemed easier than living. Instead, I gave her the only honest answer that I knew. "I don't know," I said, and I told her that I would be back in touch soon to discuss funeral arrangements.

Suddenly, I was anxious to return home, to get away from the prison and the sadness that surrounded it. Two distraught men, one tortured by infidelity, the other dead for reasons I didn't specifically know, had dramatically dimmed all holiday spirit.

It would only get worse.

Shortly after the ten o'clock head count had been completed, my phone rang. The young man who had visited me only hours earlier had been found dead in his cell. He'd hanged himself.

When I arrived in the cell block, his body still dangled limply at the end of knotted bed linens. I looked through the bars at his empty eyes, recalling the tears they had shed. I silently prayed that the end had come quickly and with a minimum of pain.

I would soon be the bearer of tragic news for the second time in only a matter of hours. Again I would hear the question: why?

From a nearby cell an inmate called out to me. Only minutes before taking his own life, I was told, the prisoner had walked to the wooden box at the end of the hallway and left a letter to be mailed.

Certain that it offered a more complete explanation of the man's state of mind than the one he'd shared with me in my office, I asked the major's permission to retrieve the letter. I knew that it was against regulations to in any way tamper with a prisoner's mail. I argued that since it had only been placed in the box to await pickup the next day, the letter was not yet officially in the possession of the mail room. I suggested that it might not only help me in considering what I could say when I phoned his next of kin but might also shed light that would benefit prison officials in their attempt to determine whether there had been any foul play involved or if his decision to kill himself had been triggered by something that had occurred in the prison. I was, I knew, splitting hairs, but I finally persuaded the major to allow me to retrieve the letter from the box.

I took it to my office and read it before placing the call. In a shaky hand that was barely legible, he had, in fact, written an angry explanation for his suicide. The letter was addressed to his wife. In it, he described the pain he'd experienced earlier in the day when she had admitted to him that she was involved in a sexual relationship with his father.

Checking the records, I was relieved to find that the person I was to notify was his mother. Even before dialing the number I knew I would plead ignorance when she asked the reason for her son's death. Grief has its limitations.

Before returning home, I went back to the cell block to thank the inmate who had alerted me to the letter. By the time I got there, the cell adjacent to his was empty, the lifeless body cut down and removed. Only the pin-drop silence among the inmates signaled that anything out of the ordinary had occurred.

I had been there only minutes when the walkie-talkie of a sergeant who had accompanied me crackled with an urgent message. I should report to the hospital as quickly as possible, he said. There had been yet another suicide.

An inmate confined to the psychiatric ward had fashioned a weapon from the tiny blade of a disposable razor and a toothbrush handle, then slashed deep cuts all over his body before finally cutting his own throat. The cell was a pool of blood. The nude body that lay on the concrete floor was covered with wounds.

It was after midnight when I finally made the short walk home. Even in the crisp winter air, my nostrils remained filled with the foul smell of death, my thoughts consumed by the dark despair that had caused three suicides in a single evening. A full moon lit my way, and I was reminded of the warning I'd heard from several guards since my arrival at the prison: "It's when there's a full moon that things get really crazy around here."

Once inside, I turned on some music and made my way to a recliner in the living room. Sitting there, I closed my eyes—not to sleep, but to pray for the lost souls, and for the strength to return for another day.

FOUR

On a late November afternoon in 1982, I received word that the warden had summoned a staff meeting for the following day. Certainly it was not unusual for such gatherings to be called, but in this case everyone had been notified by phone rather than by the written memorandum that was normally circulated. It was obvious that something out of the ordinary was to be announced.

Well before Warden Pursley entered, whispered questions swept through the room. I turned to a security officer seated next to me and asked, "What's going on?" He replied with the same shrug I was seeing throughout the room.

Generally, such meetings were conducted in a relaxed atmosphere, the business of the day mixed with good-natured banter, coffee, and doughnuts. This time, however, there were neither amenities nor warmth. The warden entered the room, clipboard in hand, a grim look on his face.

An all-state football player for Huntsville High School during his teenage days, the warden had remained fit with weekend work on the small cattle ranch he owned. Always dressed in a western suit and boots, rarely without a cowboy hat, he fit the image of a Texas prison warden to perfection.

Placing his Stetson on the desk in front of him, he went straight to the point: "We will soon be having an execution," he announced.

The news was met with a stunned silence. The last time that a death sentence had been carried out in Texas was in 1964, when a convicted murderer named Joseph Johnson was electrocuted. He had been the 361st Texas prison inmate put to death since the state had, in 1924, assumed the responsibility. Prior to that, the law of the Old West had generally applied to cattle rustlers, bank robbers, murderers, and whoever else was judged to be a blight on the community. Authorities of the county in which they committed crimes—or were unfortunate enough to be arrested—wielded swift justice at the nearest hanging tree. Mercifully, those ugly days were long past.

In 1972 the U.S. Supreme Court ruled the practice of capital punishment to be cruel and unusual, and many breathed a sigh of relief, assuming our culture had at long last advanced beyond the mentality of death-penalty justice. The sentences of prisoners residing on Death Rows throughout the nation—including forty-five Texas inmates— were quickly commuted to life in prison. Even after the Texas legislature revised the Texas Penal Code two years later, attempting to satisfy the "humane" guidelines demanded by the Supreme Court and allowing courts to continue assessing the death penalty in the cases of capital murder, there seemed no serious move to follow through with such sentencing. Only when political pressures increased, applied by dissatisfied family members of murder victims and sympathetic justice organizations who made clear their feelings that men should die for their crimes, had the debate resurfaced.

And even when a convicted killer named Gary Gilmore stood before a Utah State Prison firing squad to die in January of 1977, signaling a return to the ultimate punishment, there was no strong feeling nationwide that a wholesale revisit of the death penalty was on the way. Yet now, like Hell's special delivery, it was coming to Texas. I could feel the knots forming in my stomach.

Among those hearing Warden Pursley's chilling announcement, there was not a single employee who had worked for the prison when the last execution had occurred. The days of a condemned man "riding Old Sparky" to his death were little more than fodder for the history books and for the spit-and-whittle tales traded by old men sunning on the town square benches. (Among the favored legends that continued to circulate was the one claiming that lights in homes and businesses throughout the community would dramatically dim as the current was turned on in the nearby death chamber, thus alerting everyone that the life of yet another criminal was ending.) Now, however, we were being told that each of us would be required to play a role in a new chapter of prison history. To adhere to the absurd notion that there was, in fact, a way of putting someone to death that was neither cruel nor inhumane, the upcoming state-ordered execution would be done by lethal injection. Instead of strapping the prisoner into a chair and sending high-voltage electrodes through his body, he would lie on a gurney while a mixture of sodium thiopentothal, pancuronium bromide, and potassium chloride was pumped into the veins.

It would be the first such execution ever done, and only medical theory promised that death would come swiftly and without pain. "I don't know a thing about what we've got to do," Pursley said. "All of us have a great deal of learning to do in a short period of time."

The execution, he said, was scheduled for December 7. And with that he looked down at his clipboard and began calling out the responsibilities each of us would be dealt. There was no call for volunteers, only assignments to serve in capacities that ranged from security to membership on what would come to be called the "tiedown team." The warden called my name last. "We'll discuss your role later," he said.

At that moment I had the distinct impression that he had no idea what part I might play, yet already I was questioning whether I could bring myself to participate at all.

The Presbyterian Church, I knew, had long held a firm stance against capital punishment. In a strongly worded policy statement authored by its general assembly, it noted that the Bible demanded that "as Christians we must seek the redemption of evildoers and not their death." Further, it had noted that "the use of the death penalty tends to brutalize the society that condones it." And while my feelings were mixed, still colored by the cruelties committed on the final night of the 1974 prison siege, deep in my heart I knew my church was right. Despite the fact that I'd felt anger and the need for some manner of revenge in the wake of the deaths of Judy Standley and Yvonne Beseda, despite the absolute distaste that I'd felt toward the men who had caused their senseless, unforgivable deaths, I held to the belief that the death penalty was nothing more than a legalized violation of the biblical commandment that we should not kill.

A task force on criminal justice, organized by the Presbyterian Church, had studied the issue and warned that if we ignored God's own order, we did so at our own peril.

Even before the warden suggested that we visit the long-abandoned "death house" to view where the execution would occur, my stomach was churning.

Out of the meeting room, past the visitation waiting area and the parole office, then through a series of winding halls, we silently followed the warden, two abreast. There were two heavy iron doors to be unlocked and to pass through before finally arriving at a scene few had ever visited. The original Death Row of the Texas prison system, with its thick layers of drab gray paint that had been applied over the years, was the closest thing to a medieval dungeon I'd ever seen. Until someone opened the push-out windows along the walkway, it felt that all the air had somehow been sucked from the room. Air-conditioning, obviously, had not been among the comforts afforded those scheduled to die. Slowly walking along the narrow corridor, I counted seven small cells, testament to the fact that the original planners had never anticipated having more than seven prisoners on Death Row at any one time. Even as we made our grim tour, 150 candidates for capital punishment were locked away on a new, more modern Death Row in the maximum-security Ellis Unit, fifteen miles away.

One could almost hear the exhalations of surprise when it was pointed out that a large wooden crate sitting at the end of the run stored "Old Sparky," the legendary oak electric chair that medical science was now prepared to replace. In a far corner sat the generator that had been used to power previous executions.

To one side another metal door led into a small exercise yard surrounded by brick walls topped with tangles of razor wire. Long vacant, it was now nothing more than wasted space.

As we stood silently, each attempting to grasp the gravity of what was soon to take place in these surroundings, the warden nodded to his major. On cue he opened yet another steel door.

We crowded into the death chamber.

A gurney, bare except for the large leather straps that lay across it, sat in the middle of a twelve-by-sixteen room that was brightened by a bank of lights anchored in the white latex ceiling. The mixture of colors was an assault on the eyes. The polished linoleum tiles on the floor were a dark green, the walls the ever-present redbrick. Overhead was an exhaust vent, painted white, its purpose no longer suitable. In the days of electrocutions, the vile odor of death had made it a necessity. Now, through the miracle of science, we were promised that death would not only be painless but odorless as well.

Only a few feet from the gurney was a waist-high brass railing that would separate those who would be allowed to witness the grim event. On the north wall were three small windows framed in mint green. Behind them, we were told, the chemical mixtures would be prepared. Then they would be infused into the inmate's veins through plastic intravenous tubes connected to his arms. Somewhere back there, hidden from view, his identity never to be known, would be the executioner.

Testing all irony was the fact that two phone lines—one connected to the governor's office, another to the attorney general—ran into that same room, there to alert attending prison officials in the event of some dramatic last-minute stay (or to pass along word the execution should proceed). Behind those windows, draped by curtains made from hand towels, would hide both death and last hope.

If all went according to plan, however, the first injection would begin soon after midnight on the day designated by the state. The first drug would sedate the inmate, the second would relax his muscles, then collapse the diaphram and lungs, and the third would stop his heart from beating. The entire process would last no more than a few minutes.

For the first time since becoming a chaplain, I felt a strange and discomforting kinship with the inmates. Sweat soaked my collar while my throat was absolutely dry. I wanted to run, to be as far from this dark and ugly place as possible. But I couldn't. The heavy steel doors had been closed behind me, locking me in. I, too, had become a prisoner.

In time the warden dismissed all but the assigned members of the tie-down team and me. "We're going to walk through this," he said. "Then we'll do it again tomorrow and the next day." The tone of his voice made clear his concern. If an execution had to happen, it was to be carried out perfectly.

There was a macabre atmosphere attached to our daily practice sessions. The tie-down team, men assigned to place the leather straps on the prisoner's arms and legs and across his chest, debated everything from whether to secure the feet or hands first to how to determine if the straps were tight enough. Questions abounded. Who would insert the IV needles? Would doctors from the prison be called on to participate, or would some special team be brought in? What was to be done if difficulties developed in finding a suitable vein? How would the warden, who would be in the death chamber, signal that the procedure should begin? And since I would be with the prisoner from the time he arrived at the death house until he breathed his final breath, where should I position myself? In a manner of speaking, we were making it up as we went along, trying one thing, then another, until we were comfortable that we had decided on the best way to handle a bad situation. Just as everyone was beginning to feel that the routine was workable, the warden added a new twist. For days a young lieutenant recruited to play the role of the condemned man had quietly followed instructions. When I notified him the time had come, he joined me in the hallway outside his cell and, in the company of the guards, made the short walk into the death chamber. There, he climbed onto the gurney. On this particular day, however, he erupted into a full-scale panic attack as we entered the chamber, fighting the guards and refusing to cooperate. After a few seconds of surprised hesitation, the guards subdued him and, soon bathed in sweat, managed to force him onto the gurney, where the restraints were quickly applied.

The warden had secretely instructed the lieutenant to put up the fight. "A scene like that," he said, "is always a possibility. We've got to be ready." That afternoon it was decided that an additional man would be added to the tie-down team.

Then he looked over at me. For several days my only instructions had been to stand and watch. I had been told where I was to be standing when the prisoner arrived and also that, as chaplain, I would be with him throughout the wait, then accompany him into the death chamber. Otherwise, I knew precious little. Pointing to the drapes that hung on a track between the death room and the small area reserved for witnesses, he said it would be my responsibility to pull them closed in the event that anything went wrong.

"But your main job," Warden Pursley said, "is to help see that something like what just played out doesn't happen. You're going to be with the inmate all day, and it is important that you gain his trust as quickly as possible. Talk to him, listen to him, comfort him as much as you possibly can. But, above all else, I want you to seduce his emotions so he won't fight."

Sleep became increasingly difficult as the days leading up to the execution passed. While I understood the warden's request, the idea that my only purpose was to provide whatever calming effect I could troubled me. There had to be more I could do.

In a meeting in his office, the warden expanded on my role. The prisoner would, he explained, be transported from the Ellis Unit to the Death House on the day the execution was scheduled. The route the guards in charge of the inmate would take would be known only to them. The time of departure would also remain secret in an effort to divert the attention of the media.

Upon his arrival, I would be there to greet him. During the hours leading up to his death, I would help with paperwork that needed to be completed, aid in writing letters and arranging visits with anyone okayed by the prison authorities, and even help with the construction of whatever final words the prisoner might wish to say before dying. In essence, I would be there to offer whatever simple kindnesses I could.

What was soon to come was rarely out of mind. Though I attempted to remain focused on my normal routine in the chapel and in my office, I could not escape from the thought that I would be ministering to a person not terminally ill but nonetheless scheduled to die. I struggled with the philosophy of my church and my own convictions. And I wondered how, despite the sanctions of the state, what we were preparing to do could be judged as anything but murder.

Such thoughts overwhelmed me. How could I be a party to something that I judged so un-Christian, so barbaric? For all the dark feelings that had haunted me since the prison siege, I realized that my thoughts of retribution had never extended to the boundaries that I was now being asked to cross. And, I asked myself, was it possible that even by ministering to a condemned man, I would be viewed as a willing participant in his death?

One recurring thought enabled me to stay the course. Throughout my career as a minister, I had held strongly to the belief that a person's need for comfort is never so great as when he is forced to deal with the realities of death. If, in fact, God had provided me a gift, it was to help those in their final hours. No one, I had long believed, should face dying alone. Not even a hardened criminal about to be executed.

Weighing the options, I knew that I could not lift my voice to a pitch that would reverse the decision of lawmakers. With or without me, the execution would proceed. Gradually, my attitude turned from doubt to resignation, then finally a determination to make whatever positive contribution I could to the process.

I made up my mind that I would try to do more than seduce the condemned man's mind as suggested by the warden. In the Death

House as in the chapel. I would minister as best I could. If it meant reading Scriptures or prayers or singing hymns, I would do it. If it meant nothing more than trying to keep the fear of the inevitable at arm's length, I would do that. If my only role was that of listener and escort for visitors, that too would be done as best I could. Rather than continuing to dread the event, I began to plan.

Paying a visit to my old friend Jim Estelle, I shared my thoughts with him in hopes that he might have advice to offer. I felt duty-bound, I explained, to do whatever possible to make the best of a bad situation, including trying to befriend the prisoner. "I don't care what crime brought him to this point," I said. "I will stand with him, not in judgment."

Estelle smiled as he nodded his head. "I know this is difficult for you, for all of us. I can't even imagine how hard that day is going to be or what kinds of nightmares we're all going to have to endure. But we've been given no choice in the matter." And with that he offered the only advice I ever received about dealing with a Death Row inmate: "Follow your heart," he said. "Never promise anything that you can't deliver, and always deliver what you promise."

As the execution date crept closer, a tension fell over the entire city. Inside The Walls, prisoners went about their activities in a subdued manner. From all parts of the world the media began to arrive, some curious about the new technique of death that was to be debuted, others—particularly members of the European press—to try to explain to their readers why we Americans continued with an ancient ritual that they deemed uncivilized. As requests for interviews piled up on my desk, I decided not to respond to any of them for the simple reason that I knew full well the first question I would be asked: did I believe in the death penalty?

Another decision I'd reached was that it would be in the best interest of all concerned that I not make my feelings known. How could I possibly hope to comfort someone facing execution if he knew that I was opposed to what was taking place? Or, for that matter, that I felt it was just? If I was to be effective at all, I had to remain non-committal.

In those days before the prisoner was to arrive, I prayed the strangest prayer that I'd ever spoken. I knew that once the prisoner was escorted to his Death House cell, where I would be waiting, we would be locked inside, there to remain until those minutes past midnight when the end finally came.

"God," I asked, "please don't make me want to run."

FIVE

Charles Brooks, Jr., had been on the Ellis Unit's Death Row for 1,687 days—just over four and one-half years—when he was transported to The Walls on a cold and pitch-black December morning. Shackled and handcuffed, dressed in his prison-issued white jumpsuit, he sat silently in the backseat of a van, his head rocking slightly, keeping rhythm with the bumps and turns of the blacktop road that wound toward Huntsville. Along the way, rural homes twinkled with predawn Christmas lights but were of no interest. Charles's eyes remained closed throughout the trip. The meager belongings that he'd collected during his years of incarceration had been packed into two cardboard boxes and rested on the seat next to him. The only things he'd really wanted to make sure to bring were a small clock radio and a dozen cans of Dr Pepper that he'd purchased from the commissary earlier in the week.

Just forty years old, he was on the final leg of a wasted life filled with alcohol, drugs, and thoughtless violence. Charles Brooks had not been a discarded child of the streets but, rather, the pampered son of a churchgoing Fort Worth meat cutter. He was only fourteen when his father had first purchased him a car. When the elder Brooks later died of a heart attack, he left behind a small pension that would assure that Charles had money in his pockets. The youngster squandered that and his life. By his own admission he traveled the Fort Worth mean streets with a swagger and a sizable chip on his shoulder. He had scars from knife and gunshot wounds proving that he didn't back away from confrontation. He dropped out of school, shoplifted, began drinking heavily, and used whatever drugs were available to him. In time he married and fathered two sons, who saw him all too rarely.

By 1962 he'd pled guilty to a burglary in Baton Rouge. In 1968 he was convicted on federal firearms charges after authorities caught him with a sawed-off shotgun. No sooner was he out of prison than he was charged with burglary and theft and sent to Huntsville.

Then, after being released in 1975, he had committed the crime that led to the ride he was taking from Ellis.

On a December morning in 1976, a Fort Worth prostitute and heroin addict named Marlene Smith had visited a Fort Worth, Texas, used-car lot and traded sexual favors for a test drive. From the car lot she drove to a liquor store on Rosedale Avenue, where she picked up boyfriend Woodie Loudres and Brooks. The three then went to the motel where Loudres and the woman lived. There they injected heroin. Later they moved their party to the home of Brooks's mother, where they drank beer for several hours.

Finally out of booze, dope, and money, the woman suggested a trip to a shopping center on the south side of the city, where she could shoplift items that might quickly be converted into cash to buy more heroin.

On the way, however, the "borrowed" car vapor-locked. Pushing it into a nearby service station, they tried without success to get it started. Brooks, high and angered by the turn of events, walked to a nearby car lot, where he asked to test-drive another car. Since company policy required that an employee of the dealership accompany customers on any test-drives, a paint and body repairman named David Gregory was asked to go with Brooks as he drove around the block.

The next time Gregory was seen, he was being released from the trunk of the car in the parking lot of the New Lincoln Motel at around six that afternoon and escorted into the room rented by Marlene Smith and Loudres. Soon thereafter, shots were heard.

Police, summoned by a motel employee, arrived to find David Gregory, husband and father, alone in the room. He was gagged and bound with adhesive tape and clothes-hanger wire and had been shot in the head.

Brooks and Loudres were later arrested and charged with the kidnap-murder of Gregory—a capital crime, punishable by death. Tried separately, both had been sentenced to die despite the fact that it was never determined which man actually fired the shot that killed Gregory. The weapon used in the murder was never found. Several years later, Loudres got lucky. An appeals court overturned his death penalty conviction, and in October of 1982 he was able to plea-bargain for a forty-year sentence.

Thus, as Charles Brooks would count away his final hours in the Death House, Loudres looked ahead to the distant day when he would be paroled.

I knew none of this as I reported to my office at six o'clock on the morning Brooks was to arrive. I was convinced that if I was to counsel and befriend him during the next eighteen hours, I could best do so with as clean a slate as possible. When the warden had asked if I wished to read Brooks's criminal file before meeting him, I declined.

Thus, the man I saw walk into the Death House was, by my choice, a virtual stranger to me. Small and fit, he looked younger than his age despite the few flecks of gray sprinkled along his temples. His body was marked by the ugly signature of many inmates, jailhouse tattoos that ran along both arms and peeked from the exposed portion of his chest. In all, I would later learn, there were seventeen amateurish messages that had been pierced onto his body. Among them was one that prophetically read, "I Was Born to Die."

He only nodded as I introduced myself, then entered the cell.

Part of the information I had requested in the days leading up to his execution was his religious preference. Brooks, I learned, had first embraced Christianity shortly after arriving at the Ellis Unit, but, after determining that it did not provide the comfort he sought, he began to study other religions. The one that had most appealed to him was

Islam. For the past three years, then, he had been a practicing Muslim, adopting the Arabic name Shareef Ahmad Abdul-Rahim, and praying daily to Allah. Though he professed remorse for the life he'd led, he stopped short of admitting to murder. Still, he had come to believe that all wrongful deeds of his past were forgiven. Thus, Charles Brooks was, from the moment he entered the last cell in which he would be confined, confident that he would soon be leaving for a better place.

And since it was clear that a Presbyterian chaplain wasn't likely to be able to meet his spiritual needs, Akbar Nurid-Din Shabazz, an American Muslim Mission chaplain for the prison system, had agreed to be on hand to serve as muezzin—the religion's listener and prayer leader—to Brooks. Meanwhile, I would stand ready to deal with any other needs that might arise.

Somber and obviously nervous, Brooks immediately joined Shabazz in a brief prayer, then asked the guard if he would get the small radio he'd brought with him from Ellis and try to find a local news station so that he might hear any report that came in on the papers his lawyers had filed, seeking a stay of execution. For years he had unsuccessfully fought the judicial system through nine hearings in five courts and before twenty-three different judges, yet now his fate rested in the hands of a three-judge panel of the Fifth Circuit Court of Appeals, which was scheduled to meet later in the morning in New Orleans. There were higher courts to appeal to, he knew, but in the event the Fifth Circuit ruled against him, the others, right up to and including the Supreme Court, were likely to follow suit. I sensed no real optimism.

Noticing the small refrigerator at the opposite end of the hall where the two assigned guards sat, he asked if his soft drinks could be placed in it to cool.

Then, seating himself on the small cot, he smiled for the first time. "Anybody play chess?" he asked, providing my first challenge as Death Row chaplain.

Neither Shabazz nor either of the guards played. I knew the game, but played on a child's level. Brooks, meanwhile, had wasted no time boasting that he had reigned over the entire Ellis Unit, defeating fellow inmates and guards alike with great regularity. I placed a call to the warden's office, asking if there was a guard on duty who fancied himself an expert at the game. If so, I needed him.

Eventually a tall, bookish-looking employee of the security department was ushered into the Death House, carrying with him a collapsible board and a box of plastic chess pieces. It was not difficult to see that he would have preferred being elsewhere. On a small table moved close to the bars, the two men silently played a series of games as Shabazz and I watched. The guard was no match for Brooks and soon remembered other duties he had to attend to. Brooks made no attempt to persuade him to stay.

The only hint of anger I would see in him came shortly after the prison cook arrived to ask what Charles wanted for his final meal, which would be served later in the day. He asked for fried shrimp and oysters but was told that, despite the impression Hollywood screenwriters and crime novelists had long perpetuated, condemned men could be served only what the prison kitchen had in stock. "I thought the rules were that I got my choice," he fired back. Then, in an instant, a smile returned to his face, and he was back in control. He ordered a T-bone steak and French fries with peach cobbler for his dessert. "And a toothpick," he said.

Looking over at me, he shrugged. "Hey, I know the difference," he said. "In prison you've got rights, and you've got privileges. I guess shrimp and oysters are considered a privilege."

"I guess so," I acknowledged. "This is all new to me."

"Both of us," he replied.

Shortly after noon, a newscaster announced that Brooks's appeal to the Fifth Circuit had been turned down. "Well, that's it," he said.

"I think it is time that we begin your preparation," Shabazz told him.

Outside The Walls, another kind of preparation was already underway. From throughout the United States and several foreign countries, reporters had converged to chronicle the event. In life, Charles Brooks, Jr., had been a nobody, a faceless black man lost in the sea of criminal behavior and court appearances. Now, for the simple reason that he was to become the first man ever executed by lethal injection, he had suddenly gained celebrity status. In prior weeks he had been the subject of countless interview requests. Now, after gathering information on his tattered and unremarkable life from friends, family, and the lengthy list of lawyers who had represented him, the journalists had nothing left to do but count down the hours until he was dead. To pass the time, they photographed and interviewed the growing throng of demonstrators gathered to either protest or praise what was soon to take place.

Brooks expected no visitors. There was an outside chance, he said, that a Fort Worth woman he described as his fiancée might attempt to make the trip, but he wasn't optimistic. He was, he said, prepared to die without final support from family or friends. That, he explained to me, was one of the reasons that he'd felt the concept of Christianity had so failed him. It had not kept his family together. Nor had it kept him out of prison. Nowhere in his reasoning was the suggestion that such failures were of his own making. Even his Islamic faith had been altered to fit his personal needs. He admitted that he had initially committed himself to the Muslim ritual for a six-month trial period without any strong resolve. Rather than facing east when chanting his prayers—as is the Muslim tradition—he chose instead to face the doorway of his prison cell, as if Mecca had the key that would swing it open. He routinely fasted on Tuesdays and Thursdays, but had set the ritual aside on Thanksgiving since he didn't want to miss out on the turkey and dressing that he knew would be served in the dining room. And, while the Muslim faith demanded that its followers speak only the truth, he had never admitted his guilt in the death of David Gregory.

Still, however flawed or misused I judged his faith, it seemed to provide him a remarkable degree of inner peace. And as I continued to silently pray for strength to help me through the long hours before midnight, I was increasingly glad Shabazz was there to address Brooks's spiritual needs. My role was simply to befriend him.

Time dragged eternally, the Death House mood growing increasingly sober as conversation topics were exhausted. I felt a welcome sense of relief when word came late in the afternoon that Brooks's niece had unexpectedly arrived to see him. Brooks's spirits lifted noticeably. "She's really here?" he said, a tone of childlike amazement in his voice.

Despite having arrived a half hour after the deadline for visitations, Berrie Jean Mitchell, accompanied by a Fort Worth Muslim imam, was escorted into the Death House. Standing in front of the cell her uncle occupied, she was obviously unsettled by the surroundings yet spoke of better days in a soft, melodic voice. For an hour she and Charles smiled at each other through heavy mesh wire, reliving childhood memories, moments of laughter even punctuating their recollections. In time, though, there were no more good times to discuss and no more laughter to share. All that remained was the difficult task of saying good-bye. When Berrie Mitchell began to cry, covering her tired face in her hands, the minister who had accompanied her stepped forward and placed a hand on her shoulder. "Maybe," he whispered, "it is time we have a prayer."

A few minutes later they were gone.

The guards, who had remained at the end of the hall, appeared. It was time, they announced, for Brooks to shower and change from his prison whites into the civilian clothes he would wear into the death chamber. Then his last meal was delivered.

I watched as he ate in silence, thoughts of the strangeness of the whole ritual I was involved in speed-racing through my mind. What real sense was to be made of showering and changing clothes in preparation to be put to death? What difference would it really make that he would die in a new sport shirt, yellow trousers, and a pair of blue tennis shoes? How could one have any appetite, even for the most tantalizing of dishes, when aware that it was one's last meal? What frightful images played in the mind as the hours before beginning an eternal sleep passed? And how, regardless of one's faith, does one maintain any vestige of calm and dignity?

I was no stranger to death watches. As a minister and chaplain I had lost count of the bedside vigils in which I'd participated. But this was different. This was the first time that I'd tried to comfort and befriend someone in perfect health, someone with no life-threatening affliction, who was soon to die. His life would not be taken by some fast-spreading cancer; no incurable disease was stealing life away. Charles Brooks was simply going to be killed by order of the state of Texas.

It was nearing 6:00 P.M. when he asked for some privacy. He had letters he needed to write and wanted to do so alone. Alerting the guards to keep a distant watch, Shabazz and I left. As we made our way through the gates and winding hallways that led toward my office, I was suddenly aware that perspiration had soaked the collar of the shirt I was wearing. I noticed for the first time that beads of sweat dotted Shabazz's forehead.

"This," he whispered as we breathed in the clean, cool air of the outside world, "is the most frightening thing I've ever been involved in."

I wholeheartedly agreed.

Waiting in an assistant warden's office was Clyde Johnston, director of chaplains for the prison system. Nearing retirement, he had been chaplain at The Walls before executions were discontinued. On fourteen occasions he had accompanied convicts on their walk to the electric chair. He had come to see if there were any questions he could answer.

I explained that Brooks seemed remarkably calm, even resigned. Johnston nodded as I described the atmosphere and the inmate's demeanor. "He's likely to retain that attitude right up to the time he enters the death chamber," he said. "But, without exception, it was my experience that all poise and pride disappear once the inmate is strapped down. That's when the real fear becomes evident. You're going to see it and feel it deeply, so prepare yourself."

Beyond that, he could offer little insight. "Frankly," he said, "I have no idea what lethal injection is going to be like. We can only hope that it is as quick and painless as the experts say it will be." As he looked at me, I sensed that the long-hidden memories of bygone executions had come rushing back to him, unwelcome pictures that neither time nor effort could erase. And I wondered how he had endured the process so many times and retained his sanity.

"It's important," he said, "that you talk to him about what will happen in the next few hours," he advised. "Even if he doesn't ask, he wants to know. Needs to know. Walk him through it as best you can, tell him every minute detail of the practices you went through, so that there won't be any surprises."

Outside the building, I saw for the first time the carnival-like atmosphere had filled the streets. People carrying hand-drawn placards milled in front of the prison. Some chanted in singsong unison, urging the execution on. Others angrily cried out against it. Still others roamed the crowd wide-eyed, as if being allowed free admission to their first rock concert. In the vernacular of the day, Brooks's execution had clearly turned into a happening, and I swallowed a sudden urge to cry out to those who had come to participate: go home. . . . Let us do this in peace and with some degree of dignity.

Inside, Brooks handed Shabazz a small stack of letters he'd written, asking that they be delivered as soon as possible after his death. The Muslim imam placed them in his jacket pocket along with a statement that Brooks had written to members of the press. It read: "I at this very moment have absolutely no fear of what may happen to this body. My fear is for Allah, God only, Who has at this moment the only power to determine if I should live or die. As a devout Muslim I am taught and believe that this material life is only for the express purpose of preparing oneself for the real life that is to come. Since becoming a Muslim, I have tried to live as Allah wanted me to live. . . ."

• • •

"It's time," I told him, "that we talk about what is going to happen."

In the final hours things had begun to take on a more hurried tone. Results of the legal community's last-minute efforts began coming in. The governor telephoned the warden's office to say that he would not honor the tradition of granting a thirty-day reprieve. The Court of Criminal Appeals and the U.S. Supreme Court both concluded deliberations and decreed that the execution should be carried out. In Fort Worth, Jack Strickland, the prosecutor in Brooks's case, phoned a judge to say that he was troubled by the fact that Brooks was scheduled to die while his coconspirator, Woodie Loudres, had managed to have his death sentence overturned. That one of the men he'd helped convict was to die while the other was ordered to serve only forty years in prison, Strickland argued, was grossly unfair. A new appeal was sent to the Fifth Circuit but quickly turned down.

It was, then, not until late in the evening that all avenues open to saving Brooks's life had finally closed.

At ten-thirty the warden telephoned me to say that a woman named Vanessa Sapp, a vocational nurse from Fort Worth, had arrived and was now asking to see Charlie. She had begun corresponding with Brooks in 1977, and had visited him regularly at the Ellis Unit. They had even had one brief encounter during which they had not been separated by visiting room Plexiglas.

At one of Charles's endless hearings, Sapp had appeared in the courtroom. At the end of the proceedings, Brooks had asked the judge if he might be allowed a few minutes to speak with his "fiancée" before being returned to prison. The accommodating judge had not only agreed to the brief visit but volunteered to marry the couple if they so wished. Brooks thanked the judge for the chance to talk with Vanessa but quietly declined the second offer.

Still, he seemed pleased to learn that she had come to be a witness to his execution. I explained that I would have to go tell her that the time for visiting was long past. "Just make sure she's okay," Brooks requested.

Outside, I had no difficulty locating her. A large woman wearing a polyester print dress, she was surrounded by members of the media. The warden had agreed to allow me to bring her into the lobby, away from the still-growing crowd, where she could wait until it was time to join the other witnesses in the death chamber. I attempted to explain why a visit was impossible and was answered by a look that clearly told me I was viewed as the enemy.

Returning to Brooks's cell, I told him Vanessa was being taken care of. "Is she okay? Is she going to be strong enough for this?" he asked.

"I believe so," I replied.

Word then came that more late-arriving visitors were asking to see him. During the weeks of planning for the execution, it had been determined that certain rules regarding visitations would be strictly followed. Only those Brooks had included on a list he had supplied days earlier would be allowed inside, and no visits could occur after 4.00 p.m. Already, the warden had allowed bending of the timetable to accommodate the surprise arrival of Brooks's niece.

Now, only an hour away from his scheduled execution, Brooks's sons, Derek and Adrian, had arrived, asking to see him.

Charles breathed deeply and shook his head. No, he said, he didn't want to see them. "They had five years to come see me and never did. Not once. Tell them they've waited too long."

He was, he said, ready to go over the final statement he'd begun rehearsing earlier in the afternoon.

Buttoning the tan cotton shirt he had changed into after his shower, Brooks looked at me and smiled, as if he sensed the great apprehension I was trying so desperately to hide. "It's okay," he said. "Really, the only trouble with dying this way is that the state took five years too long to get around to it. The waiting—that's the hard part."

Standing in the doorway of his cell, flanked by the guards, I said the words that had seemed so simple during our practice sessions yet now came with great difficulty. "It's time to go."

Brooks stepped into the hallway, falling in step behind Shabazz and me. The two guards silently followed the prisoner. Inside the death chamber, he climbed onto the gurney without hesitation and lay back as members of the tie-down team began putting the white restraining straps in place with grim precision. The prisoner's arms were extended along flat, narrow boards, his hands affixed to them by adhesive tape. In a matter of seconds the needles through which the fatal chemicals would flow were inserted.

When those allowed to witness the execution were ushered into the small viewing area, Warden Pursley was already in his place at the head of the gurney. I stood at its foot, Shabazz at my side. From my vantage point I could see the fear in the prisoner's eyes that Clyde Johnston had predicted. And, just as he'd warned, I felt it as well. My heart raced, and my breathing had suddenly become difficult.

I placed a hand on Brooks's ankle as Pursley recited the orders of the state that required the execution to take place. Then he asked, "Do you have any last words?"

"Yes, I do," Brooks said, turning his head toward the witness gallery in search of Vanessa Sapp. Seated in the front row, little more than an arm's length away, she smiled and blew a kiss in his direction. "I love you," Charles said.

And then he began a chant from the Koran:

"Ashhadu an la ilah illa Allah,
Ashhadu an la ilah illa Allah.
Ashhadu anna Muhammadan Rasul Allah,
Ashhadu anna Muhammadan Rasul Allah."

Then he translated:

"I bear witness that there is no God but Allah.
I bear witness that Muhammad is the messenger of Allah."

Again he returned to Arabic:

"Inna li-Allah,
wa-inna ilayhi rajiun . . ."

From the gallery, the Muslim imam who had accompanied Brooks's niece from Fort Worth called out a prayer of his own: "May Allah admit you to paradise."

Brooks strained to turn his head so that he might look directly at Vanessa before saying his final words. "Be strong," he told her.

Only after several seconds of silence did Warden Pursley, convinced that the prisoner had said all he wished to, remove his glasses, the prearranged signal to begin the flow of the deadly poisons into the IV line. It was 12:09.

Despite an inclination to turn away, I did not take my eyes off the prisoner. He remained rigidly still and quiet, his eyes filling with tears, the fear no longer hidden. For a moment he tried to flex his right fist, but he was able only to move his fingers slightly, as if to hurry the process along. But soon he was still. He had told me earlier that he planned to say the words of admission to paradise in the final seconds of life, but he managed only the first syllable before his eyes fluttered, then closed. Looking down on his chest, I saw a slight heave; then there was no indication that he was breathing. Beneath my hand, still resting on his ankle, there was no pulse. His head slumped slightly to one side.

At 12:16, Dr. Ralph Gray, the prison's chief physican, entered the room, placed a stethoscope to Brooks's chest, and pronounced him dead. The execution had, as promised, taken only minutes—seven to be exact—and, so far as I could tell, it had been as painless and as merciful as possible.

As I stood there, I was vaguely aware of the witnesses quietly filing out. If there were tears, I did not see them; if there were sobs of grief, they did not reach my ears. All that remained was an air of stunned silence—testimony to the fact that none of those who had witnessed penal history being made had really been prepared for what they had seen.

Shabazz and I remained with Brooks's body until the local justice of the peace completed his inquest and the funeral home came to take him away.

And still it was not over.

. . .

Those who had been participants in the execution had been told to gather afterwards in the warden's office, there to evaluate the procedure just carried out. The meeting had been underway for some time when I arrived. It was, I learned, generally agreed that things had gone "smoothly." And as I heard the word repeated several times, I fought to hold my tongue. Intellectually, I understood what was being said. Emotionally, I wondered how anyone could describe the act of killing someone in terms better suited to making a presentation to corporate stockholders.

Killing, I wanted to say, is not something that goes smoothly.

I quickly excused myself, explaining that I had promised to visit with Brooks's family at their hotel. Shabazz reluctantly followed me from the room.

Despite the fact that it was almost two-thirty in the morning, crowds still filled the streets in front of the prison. "I'm not crazy about getting out in that," he said.

Neither was I. With the help of a guard, we left by way of the prison yard, out a rear gate near the maintenance shop and through the deserted rodeo arena. A half hour later we were in the University Hotel.

Brooks's niece, Berrie Mitchell, answered, forcing a smile on her weary face as she invited us in. In the room was her husband, Brooks's ex-wife, his two sons, and the Muslim imam who had accompanied them on their trip from Fort Worth. Shabazz distributed the letters he'd been given earlier in the day while I answered questions as honestly as I possibly could. Had Brooks been treated well in the hours before his execution? Did he mention any of them? Did I think he felt pain in those minutes on the gurney? When would they be allowed to claim the body and have it returned home for burial? Had I brought Brooks's possessions?

On the other side of the room Shabazz had talked quietly with the family's minister.

As we were preparing to leave, Berrie Mitchell followed me to the door, hugged me, and thanked me for coming. "I know you must be exhausted," she whispered, "but I would appreciate it if you could say something to the boys before you leave."

I nodded and looked across the room at two young men, both in their twenties, who had said nothing during the time that we had been in the room. Both had read the letters written by their father as soon as Shabazz had handed them to them. They sat glaring at me. As I approached, neither bothered to get up.

"Is there anything," I asked, "that you want explained? Anything I might help you with?"

Adrian spoke up. "Yeah," he said. "Why didn't we get to see our father before he was executed?" Looking down on the angry young man, my thoughts flashed back to what his father had said only hours earlier: "They had five years. . . . they've waited too long. . . ."

I considered my reply for some time. In the wee morning hours, with emotions scorched and nerves raw, I opted to avoid a complete truth that might only cause more pain.

"Because," I finally said before turning toward the door, "you got here too late."

SIX

J. D. Autry, a solitary drifter from the Texas Panhandle, was called Cowboy—not because he rodeoed or had grown up on a ranch, but because of his unbridled passion for the twangy, nasal sound of country-and-western music. If there was much else he felt passion for, it had gone unnoticed before he shot and killed a convenience-store clerk named Shirley Crouet during a robbery in the spring of 1980.

The crime had netted him and his accomplice a six-pack of beer.

As 1983 wound down, he was scheduled to become the second Texas inmate executed since the reinstatement of capital punishment.

Autry's life story was one that could be recited by thousands of inmates nationwide. The product of a broken home, he had been a truant and runaway since age ten, spending considerable time in Texas Youth Council juvenile detention centers. By age eighteen he had graduated to more serious crimes, receiving a five-year prison sentence for the assault and attempted robbery of an Amarillo service station. Released in 1975 he took a job working alongside his father as caretaker of a local tennis club but was soon behind bars again after he broke into the place one night and stole liquor and food. In violation of his parole and charged with burglary, he was sentenced to eight more years in prison.

It was just four months after his second release that he'd entered a Port Arthur convenience store where, during yet another robbery, he shot and killed Mrs. Crouet, the mother of five. A customer in the store at the time was also wounded and destined to be a paraplegic for the remainder of his life. Additionally, Autry was suspected of killing a former Catholic priest.

When convicted of capital murder, Autry had glared at the members of the jury and angrily shouted, "I'll get you."

Yet, on an October morning in 1983, he arrived at The Walls virtually unknown to the outside world, just another faceless convict with a lengthy record of criminal behavior and a chip on his shoulder. But before all was said and done, the twenty-nine-year-old, who had spent a third of his life behind bars, would become a full-blown celebrity.

From the moment Warden Pursley introduced us on that morning when he was brought to the Death House, Autry made it clear that his only request was that he not be bothered. He asked that the radio be tuned to a country-music station and that he be allowed privacy.

Though the material I'd received indicated he was a Catholic and had requested that Fr. Joe Sammon be on hand during the day, he quickly pointed out that he had no desire to see the priest. "I was baptized in the Catholic Church when I was a kid," he said, "but I don't believe in what they stand for. As far as Father Sammon is concerned, I barely know the man."

The priest, who was in bad health and had postponed a planned trip to Chicago to be on hand to minister to Autry, remained in the warden's office.

"I just want to be left alone," the inmate said. He told me that he expected no visitors, had no special requests, and had no final statement he wished to practice. Thus, as he paced in his cell, smoking, drinking coffee, and reading a paperback western, I retreated to the far end of the Death House to allow him the solitude he'd asked for.

It was only in the afternoon, as his attorneys stopped in to update him on the status of his appeals, that he gave up his attempt at showing no concern for his situation. I had long since lost count of the times I'd refilled his coffee cup when he finally asked that I pull my chair near his cell and stay. "It's quiet here," he said. "Nothing like Death Row." In the main part of the prison, he explained, the maddening roar never ceased. Constantly, day and night, the mixture of music and loud conversations, the pounding of doors opening and closing, bars being banged against, and nightmarish screams never stopped. In the three and one-half years he'd resided there, he confided, he could not remember a single moment of silence. "I could get used to this place," he said.

When I asked if he wished to make any phone calls to his family, my question initiated a recital of problems he'd dealt with as a youngster. His parents had moved from town to town, job to job, when he was a child. Finally, his father had left without them and filed for divorce. "He put everything behind him when he took off, including me," Autry said. "Us kids tried to take care of my mother, but we didn't do much good."

Life in juvenile facilities, he said, became preferable to that at home.

"You want to talk with your mother?" I asked.

He shrugged and nodded, explaining that she had recently traveled from her home in Colorado to visit with friends in Amarillo. I located the number and placed the call. When his mother came on the line, I asked if she would like to speak with J.D. There was a lengthy pause before she said, "Yes."

Their conversation was brief and, from what I could determine, fairly one-sided. "I'm not afraid to die," Autry told her, "so don't worry. I'm ready. I've been thinking about it for a long time." Only a couple of minutes had passed when he handed the receiver back to me. I sensed that he regretted the decision to make the call.

As evening approached, his mood darkened. Instead of the endless pacing, he sat silently on his bunk, reading. He ate little from the hamburger that had been delivered from the prison kitchen and said nothing as the guards moved him down the hallway to the shower.

An overwhelming sense of frustration settled over me as I awaited his return. Nothing I had said or done had eased the unrest I knew was barely hidden beneath the control and calm he'd displayed. He remained a man angry, not remorseful, bitter at a world he clearly detested. The ugly tattoos on his body spoke loudly of the conflicts he'd spent a lifetime dealing with. On one arm was a devil's head, on the other intertwined snakes. Across his back was a tattoo of Jesus. Beneath it were the words "Born to Lose."

I could not reach J. D. Autry. There was no prayer, no verse from the Bible that he requested, no words I could find that offered comfort. When Father Sammon, who had waited in the administration office throughout the day, appeared to offer last rites, Autry turned his back on him, cursed, and demanded that he leave.

Diabetic and recovering from bypass surgery at the time, the priest later sought me out to say that he would never again visit the Death House.

There was little remaining for me to do but describe the routine that was to come. I explained that at 11:00 P.M. I would tell him that it was time to go. Then, we would make the walk into the death chamber, and he would step up onto the gurney.

"I've got some letters to write," he responded, "so I'd like to spend the last thirty minutes alone." Later, he gave me five envelopes, three to be mailed and two he asked to be hand delivered.

I was soon aware for the first time of the ugly scene being played out in front of the prison. The crowd, I learned, had been building steadily throughout the day. Now hundreds of people roamed the street, many of them chanting angry slogans and demanding a speedy execution. One young man raised a placard that depicted a beer-filled needle being inserted into an inmate's arm. Beneath it were printed the words, "Hey J.D., this Bud's for you." Off to one side a small contingent of anti–death penalty protesters stood, marking time with a candlelight vigil. They were clearly outnumbered by those bent on turning the event into a macabre celebration.

In the original planning for Charley Brooks's execution, it had been decided that it should be carried out as early on the date ordered as possible. To do so, it seemed logical to have the prisoner prepared before midnight so that the process could get underway at one minute past the hour. To assure that all was in proper working order in the death chamber and to allow time for dealing with any problems that might arise, the plan called to move the condemned man from his cell to the gurney at 11:00 P.M. It seemed a humane plan.

Instead, it proved only to emphasize the fact that we still had a great deal to learn.

When the time came, Autry followed me into the death chamber and climbed onto the gurney without assistance. As the tie-down team strapped him down, he silently stared toward the ceiling, rapidly chewing gum. When one of the guards offered him a puff on his cigarette, Autry nodded and accepted. His demeanor did not change as the medical staff quickly inserted the needles into his arms. It was only when it was just he and I who remained in the room that his apprehension showed. He began sweating profusely, and I got a towel and wiped his face.

"Thanks," he said, and smiled for one of the first times all day.

"Anything I can do for you? Would you like me to pray?"

"No."

Then, after several silent seconds, he asked that I straighten one of his pants legs, which had been rumpled when the straps were attached. "Gotta look nice," he joked. "How much longer do I have to live?"

I looked at my watch and told him that it was twenty minutes until midnight. The chemicals that would end his life, I'd already explained, would begin to flow at one minute after the hour.

"Time sure passes fast in here," he said, continuing his attempt at bravado.

It was moments later when the warden entered. "There has been a temporary delay," Pursley said. "Everything is on hold."

Autry waited until the warden had left the room to ask me what a "temporary delay" meant. I couldn't tell him. At that moment I had no idea that Supreme Court justice Byron White had telephoned the governor's office to order a last-minute stay of execution that would allow Autry's team of American Civil Liberties Union lawyers only a half hour to prepare a written motion to be reviewed by all nine Supreme Court judges. Nor was I aware that the Texas attorney general's office was frantically attempting to have the stay lifted so that the execution could go off as scheduled.

It was only a few minutes before twelve when the warden reappeared, this time to say the "delay" had become a "temporary stay." Then, shortly after midnight, he was back again, this time to advise Autry that a "permanent stay" had been ordered by the Supreme Court.

Autry's life had been spared. The saline solution that was already being pumped into his body was shut down, and the needles were removed from his arms. The tie-down team returned, unbuckled the restraining straps, and helped the confused prisoner to his feet.

Back in his cell, he changed into his prison uniform before slumping onto his bunk and quietly staring at the floor.

"Can I get you anything?" I finally asked.

Lifting his head, he looked at me for several long seconds before replying. "I wanted to die, you know. I was ready. Prepared to get it over with. Now I've got to face it all over again, and that's not right. I know there's going to be a next time, and when it comes, I'm not going into that room before midnight. I'm going to fight it, mark my word on that. I'll fight you if I have to."

The anger in his voice was justified. It wasn't right to have forced him to lie on that gurney for over an hour, counting away the last minutes of his life, only because of the convenience it had afforded those assigned to carry out his sentence. If nothing else, a new lesson had been learned. There were still improvements to be made if we were to put people to death in the most humane way possible.

"What should I do with your letters?"

"Aw, go ahead and send them out," he said.

It would not be until the morning guard detail came out that he could be transferred back to the Ellis Unit. I suggested that he try to get some sleep. "Or, you can read the rest of that western you didn't think you were going to get to finish."

He laughed at the irony. "Yeah, I guess I can."

Though he finally dozed off sometime after three, I remained with him.

It was only after he'd had breakfast and boxed up his belongings that he was released from his cell. He reached out and shook my hand. "Thanks," he said. And with that he began walking down the hallway, again shackled and handcuffed, guards at his side. At the doorway he turned, nodded in my direction, and smiled. His big brown eyes had regained their sparkle. "I'll probably be seeing you again soon," he said.

I nodded in response, knowing that he was right. And that he was likely to keep his promise if procedures didn't change. A man who had spent his life in one kind of a fight or another, he would not, I knew, likely hesitate to engage in at least one more.

What I didn't know at the time was that Autry was returning to Death Row to become a martyr and a warring litigant against the Texas prison system.

First, there was a *Newsweek* magazine article that described the tortured day and night Autry had spent while waiting to die. Though I strongly suspected the reporter's information had come directly from Autry and his lawyers, it was so blatantly false that, for the first time in my life, I found myself siding with Warden Pursley in his disdain for the media. As I read the lengthy cover story, I could only shake my head. In time I gave up underlining the untruths, large and small, that were presented as fact.

In addition to the more serious accusations, like those that insisted Death House guards had kicked and hit him and that the warden had allegedly told Autry, "I don't give a damn what the Supreme Court says, you're going to die," the article was liberally sprinkled with make-believe scenes.

Describing the telephone conversation Autry had had with his mother, it said that a guard had ripped the phone from his hand after only a few minutes and hung it up before he could even say good-bye. The last meal he'd requested—a hamburger, fries, and a Dr Pepper—was not, the articles said, prepared at the prison but was purchased at a local take-out restaurant. *Newsweek* quoted Autry as saying that after the needles were inserted into his arms, he could see blood oozing from the wounds they made. I had been only a few feet away and knew that, too, was untrue. And, once the stay had been ordered and we'd returned to the Death House, the Catholic priest was supposed to have called out to Autry, saying, "Well, we prayed that one through," and the inmate had smiled in response, giving a victory sign, and said, "We sure did." The scene described was nothing short of pure fabrication. The priest had left long before the execution process had even gotten underway. There had been no prayer, no victory sign, no such exchange.

The article was a sweeping and unfair indictment not only of the death penalty but of what the writer perceived as a cavalier approach to carrying it out. And, though filled with blatant falsehoods and un-warranted criticisms, it hit a national nerve.

Soon, angry letters were pouring into the warden's office. Protesters marched, and Autry's lawyers fanned the flames.

Meanwhile, Autry was receiving hundreds of letters a day from well-wishing strangers eager to encourage his cause. And he became a mag-net to media representatives from all over. J. D. Autry, once a stranger even to most of his fellow inmates, had become a cause célèbre. Anx-ious to hear the tales of horror from the only man to escape death after actually being strapped onto the gurney, reporters came to record his story. What gruesome details he didn't supply, his attorneys eagerly provided.

And, in virtually every report, the Texas prison system was por-trayed as heartless and mean-spirited. It was the most unfair and un-warranted criticism that I'd ever heard.

The next time I would see Autry, then, was in a packed federal courtroom in Beaumont, Texas. His ACLU attorneys had filed suit against the Texas Department of Corrections, claiming, among other things, that his Eighth Amendment rights had been violated during the death-penalty procedure. The petition charged that being forced to remain on the gurney for over an hour represented an indefensible form of torture. In all good conscience, I could not disagree.

Additionally, he was now charging that his previous counsel had been incompetent. That charge, I learned, had been outlined in one of the letters that he'd earlier asked me to hand deliver. Only later would I learn that one of the lawyers who had visited him in the Death House had suggested he write it on the off chance that his execution might be stayed, so that it could pave the way for future litigation.

Though not named in the lawsuit, I was summoned as a witness. Throughout the day, prison officials were questioned about the execution procedures and the treatment of the defendant during his time at The Walls. It was late in the afternoon when I was finally called to the stand. At the defense table, Autry sat with his hands folded in front of him, staring straight ahead. Throughout my testimony, he refused to look my way.

At the instruction of Assistant Attorney General Leslie Benitez, I detailed the day I had spent with Autry, doing the best I could to separate the facts as I knew them from the fiction that the media, the defendant, and his lawyers had created.

As the time came for the cross-examination, it was clear that the defense attorney was not at all satisfied with the answers I had given. He immediately went on the attack. Was I certain that things had occurred as I said? Wasn't it true that I was a member of the prison staff and therefore interested in protecting the state's interests? Not having been exposed to the adversarial atmosphere of courtroom proceedings, I resented the lawyer's tone and implications but answered his questions.

"Was, in fact, Mr. Autry strapped down to the gurney for over an hour before the decision was finally made to release him?"

"Yes, he was."

"And did it appear to you that he suffered discomfort during that time?"

"Yes, sir, he appeared to be uncomfortable."

"At any time did it occur to you that forcing him to remain there in the death chamber while a stay—even a so-called temporary one—had already been issued was inhumane?"

I acknowledged that I felt it had been cruel to have Autry spend such a lengthy time in the death chamber. At the same time, those in charge had only been following procedure. I explained that though at the time I was not made aware of the legalities involved, I sensed that there had been some confusion. "The warden came in on several occasions to tell J.D. what was going on. He said that things were on hold, then that a temporary stay had been issued. When J.D. asked me what that meant, I had to tell him that I really didn't know. All I could do was remain with him and attempt to make him as comfortable as possible."

The lawyer's questions became increasingly aggressive until the judge interrupted him. "Sir," he said, "I suggest you change your line of questioning. It appears to the court that this witness is making your client's case better than anyone we've heard from today."

"No further questions," the attorney said, glancing at me before returning to the defense table.

It was several weeks before District Judge Robert Parker issued his finding that Autry's case was without merit. The warden and the guards were exonerated, and the stay of execution was lifted. J. D. Autry was again placed in the position of counting the days until his death. The last thing he'd said to me months earlier had been prophetic: "I'll probably be seeing you again soon."

It was not something that I looked forward to.

Yet, in his last self-serving attempt to manipulate the system, J. D. Autry had actually done something good. By calling attention to a major fault in the death-penalty procedure, he assured that no future inmate would be taken into the death chamber before midnight. And, while not guilty of the absurd charges that had been leveled against them, the guards were provided a heightened awareness of the necessity to treat Death House inmates with compassion and respect.

And from it all came a benefit to my ministry that I would not be aware of for some time. In the days to come, men arrived from Death Row talking of things Autry had said upon his return from the Beaumont trial. "He bragged about your honesty," I was repeatedly told.

Publicly, however, he continued to lash out. And even at the Ellis Unit, where he'd enjoyed sudden fame, he boasted that he would ultimately beat the system. As proof of his confidence, he organized a betting pool among his fellow inmates. That no prisoner is allowed to keep cash was no deterrent. The inmates gambled on the exact date and time Autry's death would occur, and the wager grew to $280 worth of commissary merchandise. Only if he avoided execution would Autry himself claim the pot. Of the dozens of fellow inmates who participated, J.D. was the only one to ignore dates and times and place his bet on "stay."

In the parlance of odds-players, it wasn't a good bet.

In mid-March of 1984, on the morning of his second scheduled visit to the Death House, I woke at four-thirty and read a disturbing quote from Autry in the *Houston Chronicle*: "I don't want anyone, particularly any of the TDC chaplains, around me when I get to Huntsville," he had told a reporter. The article went on to note that he planned to keep his word to "fight" in the event that another stay—which he'd said he fully expected to be ordered—failed to save his life.

It was still pitch dark with a biting chill in the air as I made my way toward the administration office. Already, members of the media were in place, awaiting Autry's arrival. A young woman with several cameras over her shoulder sat shivering on the steps as I approached. "Do you have any idea when he'll arrive?" she asked. "I'm freezing."

I could not tell her that her chilly wait would likely be fruitless, that plans were already in place to bring Autry into The Walls through a back entrance in an attempt to avoid her and all other members of the media.

Warden Pursley was in his office when I arrived. Though the day was just beginning, he already looked tired. "He's all yours again," he said as I entered. "He's angry, he's belligerent—and he says he's going to fight."

"I don't think so," I replied.

"What makes you say that?"

I recounted the conversation I'd had with Autry months earlier. "He said he'd fight *only* if we tried to take him into the chamber before twelve o'clock. As long as we don't do that, I think everything will be okay."

Pursley sipped from his coffee and shook his head. "I wish I shared your optimism," he said.

In truth, I was struggling with doubts of my own. What concerned me was Autry's statement that he wanted no chaplains around him. How could I be of any help to him if he turned away from me as he'd done from the priest the last time?

My concerns evaporated the minute he was escorted into the Death House. "There you are," he said, smiling. "I've been looking forward to seeing you."

For a moment I was taken aback. Seeing him again—a small, ruggedly handsome man who looked younger than he was—reminded me of the first thought that had crossed my mind when I'd met him months earlier: he just didn't look like a killer.

In years to come, as men of all ages and color and education, some tall, some short, some overweight, and others painfully thin, were escorted into the Death House, I came to realize the folly of such an observation. A killer, I came to realize, has no look.

"I read where you said you don't want me here," I said. It was important to get whatever problems we were facing out in the open.

He shook his head and smiled again. "That's not what I said at all.

I told that reporter that I didn't want a bunch of chaplains in here. I said the only one I wanted to see was you."

"What about a priest?" I asked.

"Nothing's changed since the last time. I'm still not a Catholic, and I still don't believe in anything they stand for."

Something, however, had changed. This time there was no pacing, no demand for endless cups of coffee or privacy. There were no threats. Finally, I recognized his condition for what it was: resignation. He knew that the game he'd been playing for so long was nearing an end. For all the outrageous statements he'd made to the press and his lawyers, and despite the bravado he'd displayed to his fellow inmates, assuring them that he would somehow beat the system, J. D. Autry had arrived this time prepared to die.

And on this final day of his life there were things he wanted to discuss. Throughout the morning he talked nonstop. He admitted that he had never been completely honest with members of the press but claimed that they had been perfectly willing to embellish his half-truths and innuendoes and build them into something far more dramatic than he'd ever said. His lawyers, he said, had seemed to delight in the same exercise. "There have been a lot of misrepresentations," he said, "like the idea that I didn't want anybody around me today. I specifically said that you were the only person I wanted to talk with— and that was conveniently overlooked. I guess it made a better story to say I didn't want nobody."

Whether he had been shading the truth then or now was of no real importance to me. That he seemed calm and comfortable was all that concerned me. I wanted to ask him why he had lied so blatantly about the treatment he'd received on his last visit but felt it would serve no real purpose. Instead, we went through the same routine we'd gone through before.

This time, he said, he didn't wish to order a last meal. He did, however, expect a visitor. Of the thousands of letters he'd received in recent months, he'd answered one from a Dallas woman named Shirley, and they had begun a correspondence that soon developed into a strong friendship. She would be arriving sometime in the afternoon, he pointed out, and he looked forward to seeing her. Noting that there were several Dr Peppers in the box that contained his property, he asked if they could be placed in the refrigerator and chilled.

"You know, Chaplain," he said, "I never did finish that paperback I was reading the last time I was here."

"Why?"

"Just lost interest in it. Lost interest in a lot of things," he responded.

While we talked, a call came from the warden's office, alerting me that a group of people in the small Colorado community where Autry's mother lived were raising money to have her flown down to see him. Though she wasn't on the visitors' list he'd submitted, I assured him that we could arrange it—if she could, in fact, get there and if he wished to see her.

His response was a mixture of reservation and excitement. "Yeah," he finally said, "I'd like to see her if she can make it."

The issue became moot shortly before noon when it was determined that there were no flight schedules from Colorado that could get her to Huntsville before the 5:30 P.M. cutoff time. Autry only shrugged at the news. "Probably just as well," he observed.

"We can call her," I suggested. He nodded.

Since his mother, Shirley Stucker, had no phone, I placed a call to her next-door neighbor and waited while they went to get her. Identifying myself just as I'd done months earlier, I told her that her son would like to speak with her and handed him the phone.

In retrospect, I wish I'd never suggested the call.

Having made it clear that he had all the time he wanted to say his good-byes, I walked to the end of the hall to provide him some privacy. Even from a distance, however, I could hear Autry repeatedly asking his mother not to cry. Then, after only a few minutes, he was waving me back. "I'm through," he said as he handed me the receiver.

Seeing that he was upset, I asked if he wanted to talk about it.

For what seemed like several minutes it was as if he'd not heard me. With his hands clinched tightly against the bars, he stared into space. Finally, he spoke. "She was drunk," he said. "The last day of my life on Earth, and my mother's drunk."

Thus Autry exposed a side of himself that I suspected had been hidden away for longer than even he could remember. In the somber wake of the disappointing phone call, all pretense disappeared. The cavalier, defiant, don't-give-a-damn cowboy was just as vulnerable and frightened as the next man, suddenly trying in the twilight of his life to figure out where things had gone wrong. "You know," he said, "I missed out on a lot of stuff. I never went to a circus or the zoo. Never attended a wedding or even a funeral. There's a lot about life that I never got to know anything about."

Lifting his head, he smiled weakly. "I've got to get myself out of this mood," he said. "I don't want to be like this when Shirley gets here. She'll cheer me up. She always does."

He had spoken on the phone with his sister ("She's the only one in the family I ever trusted, and I'm sorry for the problems I've caused her. She's accepted the fact that I'm going to die") when word came that his friend Shirley from Dallas was in the waiting room.

Throughout the day her name had been regularly woven through our conversations. She was one of the thousands of strangers who had written to Autry following his first trip to the death chamber, and hers had been one of the few letters he'd responded to. Soon, they were writing each other daily.

Shirley lived in Dallas, he explained, and was married to her third husband. She had three children and had bravely won a battle with cancer years earlier. She had visited him several times on Death Row and, in time, told him she had fallen in love with him. It was not an affection she attempted to hide from her husband. He, in fact, was driving her to Huntsville for this final visit. Shirley would then remain to serve as a witness to the execution.

Perhaps sensing my silent questions—what was it that seemed to attract certain women to men in prison? how could she be married to and living with one man while professing love for someone she hardly knew?—Autry provided an endorsement he no doubt felt I would appreciate. "She's a very spiritual, God-fearing person," he said.

With that he picked up a large Bible that lay on his bunk. "I'd like to give this to her when she gets here," he said.

He had already indicated that she was to receive all of his property following his death, but for him to be able to give her the Bible during their visit would, I explained, require some paperwork the warden would have to sign. "I'll see what I can do," I told him.

Shirley was sitting alone in the prison visitors' room as I approached, small and attractive, her shoulder-length auburn hair shining in the afternoon sun. Before I could say a word, she was on her feet, smiling, her hand extended. "You must be Chaplain Pickett," she said. "How's J. D.?"

"He's waiting to see you," I replied.

They talked almost nonstop, at times giggling like schoolkids. Then they would speak in whispered tones, their hands placed against the wire mesh that separated them. They shared the Dr Peppers that Autry had brought. At one point, Shirley removed her shoes, slipped from her chair, and sat on the floor, displaying no discomfort in her surroundings or in the knowledge that she was involved in the final visit she and Autry would ever have.

She seemed as happy to be there as Autry was to have her there.

I stood at the far end of the hall, watching, and a strange thought began playing through my mind. J. D.'s mother, the cause of his angst earlier in the day, was named Shirley. The convenience-store clerk he had killed with a single shot to the face, resulting in his own death sentence, had been named Shirley. And now, as his final hours ticked away, it was yet another Shirley who helped him pass the time.

I left briefly to see if the warden had signed the papers that would allow me to give her the Bible. When I returned and handed it to her, she broke into tears. In no way did I understand her or what had motivated the relationship, real or perceived, she had with Autry.

The only thing I was certain of was that, for two precious hours, she had succeeded in taking his mind off of what was to come.

It was a little past five when I walked her from the Death House back to the lobby. Outside, the crowd continued to grow. "How can I get out of here without the press stopping me?" she asked, clutching the Bible to her breast.

Calling a guard over to escort her, I explained that the media were being confined to an area just north of the doorway. If she would turn south, the guard could help her through the crowd and to her husband's car.

Then I briefly explained the procedure that would occur later in the evening, telling her where and when she and the other witnesses to the execution would gather. She thanked me and followed the guard out. As they reached the sidewalk, I watched as she took a few steps at his side, then abruptly turned away from him and began walking hurriedly toward a group of waiting journalists.

Suddenly surrounded by microphones, she tearfully described her meeting with Autry. They had laughed and cried, read the Bible together, and prayed, she said. Before leaving, she told reporters, she had kissed J. D. Autry good-bye.

I shook my head, weary of trying to understand the lure of publicity. I had no notion of why she would insist one minute that she wished to avoid the media, only to almost run toward them the next. If she felt some need to become a public part of what was taking place, that was her business; if she wished to invent a kiss that never occurred, I felt no need to dispute her. Standing there, looking out on the shoulder-to-shoulder demonstrators, the rows of television trucks, and the towering floodlights that would soon erase the comforting night-time shadows with their eerie, intrusive glow, I could not help but wonder for whose benefit she had really come to Huntsville. Why, in fact, any of them—some with obscenities on their lips, others with prayers—had come. What had they hoped to accomplish? Was the answer simply that they could return to their homes and say that they had participated in a brief moment of history? I had no idea. At that moment, all I wished was that Shirley had opted to stand above the circus atmosphere that had developed in my city's streets, to walk silently away from it. But the hypnotic lure of playing a role, however small and brief, had overruled.

The sadness I felt as I silently made my way back to the Death House was one I'd never before experienced.

As the evening approached, then stretched into night, a quiet interrupted only by the nearby radio fell over the Death House. The guards, having retreated to the far end of the hallway, said nothing. As he slowly ate his hamburger and French fries, Autry and I discussed what would take place once midnight arrived. Then he showered, changed into civilian clothes, and for a time sat quietly, writing letters.

It was ten-thirty when a radio newsman interrupted the music to announce, "Condemned killer J. D. Autry is inside the Death House, nervous and pacing." Autry shook his head. "How can they say that? I don't want people thinking I'm scared to die. Can we call the station and make them correct what they said?"

I placed a call to the warden's office and was told that he would contact the public-relations officer. At 11:00 P.M., the station retracted its report, pointing out that Autry was "calmly awaiting his fate."

It was only a few minutes later, however, that a new bulletin was aired. "J. D. Autry is now inside the death chamber, strapped to the gurney," the newsman reported.

Autry began to laugh aloud. "Nobody has any idea what really takes place in here, do they?" He asked that I turn the radio off. "There are a couple of things I'd appreciate your doing for me," he said. "After this is over, could you write to Shirley and my mother and let them know that I wasn't afraid and that I felt no pain when I died?"

I promised I would. Then, as the warden and medical personnel began arriving, I rose to stand in front of his cell door. "It's time to go," I said. It was one minute past twelve.

"Don't forget the towel," he said. "I figure I'm going to be sweating some."

As he stepped into the hallway, he said, "Chaplain, we've had two good days together. I'm sorry about the misunderstandings and want to thank you for being a friend." At that moment, as we shook hands, I knew there would be no fight.

Once again he climbed onto the gurney and was strapped down, and once again needles were inserted into his arms. He said nothing as his hands were taped to the boards that extended outward from the gurney. "You won't forget to write those letters," he reminded me.

"I won't forget."

"My hair look okay?"

"Fine."

"Could you straighten the creases in my pants, maybe pull my shirt down a little? I want to look good."

Since his last visit the execution chamber had been repainted and air-conditioned. J.D. noticed. "You tell them I appreciate them fixing the place up for me," he said.

When the warden entered, I moved to the foot of the gurney, and the witnesses began to file in.

Just as before, J.D. had no final words. At 12:26, Warden Pursley lifted his glasses—the signal to begin the flow of the deadly chemicals. "Let us begin," he said. And from the witness area came Shirley's high-pitched voice. "I'm here, J.D.," she yelled. "I love you, Brown Eyes. . . . I wanted to be up there with you, baby, but they wouldn't let me. I'm here, and I love you. . . ."

"I love you, too," Autry whispered between deep breaths.

The young woman's voice continued to ring out through what seemed like an eternity. Concentrating on Autry, watching as his eyelids grew heavy but never closed, I could not shut out her cries.

J. D. Autry, the first man ever to be placed on the death chamber gurney twice, was pronounced dead at 12:40. And immediately Shirley was at the rail that separated the witnesses from the execution chamber. "Chaplain," she said, "let me come hug him. Please let me hold him for a minute." She was crying uncontrollably.

"I can't do that," I said. "If you'll go on back to the visitor's waiting room, I'll be there to see you shortly."

"Could you please shut his eyes?" she asked.

I attempted to do so, but they would not remain closed.

As she was being helped back into the main building, where her husband patiently waited, Shirley, the last friend of a man who never in our hours together expressed a single word of remorse for taking the life of another woman named Shirley, fainted.

SEVEN

The aftermath of J. D. Autry's execution was a nightmare. In the streets outside the prison, death-penalty advocates celebrated as if their favorite team had just won the Super Bowl. Members of the media wandered through the scene, soliciting comments from those whose anger seemed to have turned to frat-party revelry.

It was nearing two in the morning when I finally made my way back to the visitors' waiting room and found Shirley seated on a bench, crying. She told me that she wanted to get Autry's property before leaving for Dallas. And again she was expressing concern that she would have to face the media once she was outside. Though not altogether convinced she really wished to avoid the cameras and microphones, I suggested that while I got J.D.'s things, a guard could help her husband to pull his car to the front of the building. "Get inside as soon as he gets here," I said, "and roll up the windows. I'll be out with the property as quickly as I can."

Under prison guidelines, an inmate's belongings could not be released until they were inventoried and every item was accounted for. A small gold necklace that I'd last seen around J.D.'s neck as he prepared to shower was missing. For almost a half hour we looked everywhere. While a guard went through the property boxes, I returned to the Death House and searched. And, finally, it occurred to me where it might be.

Among the letters Autry had written earlier in the evening and asked that I hand deliver had been one addressed to Shirley. Hurrying out to where she and her husband waited, I knocked on the car window. Shirley, huddled on the floorboard, Bible clutched to her chest, looked up as I motioned for her to roll down the window.

"Let me see the necklace you're wearing," I said.

Pulling the collar of her blouse away from her neck, she revealed the gift Autry had included in his letter. Minutes later, with the necessary paperwork completed, the remainder of his property was placed in their trunk, Shirley and her husband were speeding away toward Dallas.

I felt a sense of genuine relief at watching the taillights of their car grow smaller as it moved from downtown toward the interstate. Shirley's presence had troubled me for reasons I still find difficult to explain. Perhaps she *had* provided a dying man with a few hours of comfort; maybe her outcries in the death chamber had been the product of heartfelt emotion. Yet I lacked whatever wisdom necessary to understand what would motivate a married woman, a mother, to become so attached to someone with whom she had no real kinship. Nor could I understand the seemingly docile acquiescence of her husband to the strange, intense relationship in which his wife had become involved.

In the years to come, I would see similar attachments between convicts and women in the outside world. And always it was far easier to understand the position of the isolated and lonely inmate, starved for female contact, even if in the form of a letter or a few hours of quiet conversation on visiting day, than the position of the women. I could only assume that they developed some kind of strange fascination with a world of which they had no firsthand knowledge, one filled with danger and socially unacceptable behavior. In some way, I suppose, befriending a Death Row prisoner provided a safe, romantic thrill absent in their day-to-day lives.

Trying to untangle the mystery of the relationship between J. D. Autry and Shirley, however, was secondary to another problem that would arise in the wake of the execution.

In the material Autry had submitted prior to his trip to The Walls, he had indicated that arrangements had been made for his mother to claim his body once he had been put to death. Despite calls and letters from throughout the nation from people volunteering to pay for funeral expenses and even provide her son a burial plot, her plan was to have him cremated.

On the afternoon following the execution, the warden called me into his office. "We still have a body at the funeral home," he said. "Find out what's going on."

Back in my own office, I tried to reach Autry's mother, only to learn from a neighbor that she had been hospitalized. Finally, I made contact with his sister. "The doctor has told me that Mother is in no condition to make any kind of decisions," she explained, "so I guess the responsibility now falls to me."

She quickly admitted that she didn't know what to do. "I just want to get all of this over with as quickly as possible. And I can't afford to pay for a funeral."

I had no idea how she might respond to the suggestion I was about to make. "We can bury him in the prison cemetery," I offered.

There was a lengthy pause at the other end of the line. When she returned, it was with a voice that signaled the return of composure. "By doing that," she asked, "would we be able to get it over with quickly . . . today?"

"All I need is your permission in writing," I answered. Explaining the legal wording that was necessary, I suggested that she could send it by telegram.

Again she was quiet for several seconds. "Okay," she finally said, "this is what I'd like: First, I want it done today. Second, I'd appreciate it if you would conduct some kind of graveside service. Third, I want the burial to be done secretly, without any publicity." She paused, as if taking a deep breath before continuing. "And, finally," she added, "I don't want to have to be there."

The raw emotion I heard in her voice was evidence of the fact she had been placed in the middle of an unfair and unbearable situation.

She was not uncaring; she just wanted the nightmare to be ended as quickly and as quietly as possible.

By three-thirty that afternoon, the prison had received her telegram. At four-thirty, Warden Pursley phoned to say that I should be ready to leave for the cemetery at five. We arrived just as the funeral home hearse was coming to a stop near a grave site that had been dug the previous day in anticipation of a funeral for an inmate who had died at one of the other units.

Standing there with a half-dozen inmates who had been called back to the cemetery to serve as pallbearers, I read from Isaiah 51:12, a Scripture that Autry had underlined in the Bible he'd shown me a few days earlier. As a gentle wind whistled through the tall pines that shielded us from public view, I read, "I, even I, am he that comforteth you; who art thou, that thou shouldest be afraid of a man that shall die, and of the son of man which shall be made as grass. . . ."

He'd also told me that during his years on Death Row he'd adopted the Thirty-Ninth Psalm as his philosophy. I read all thirteen verses: "Lord, make me to know mine end, and the measure of my days. . . . And now, Lord, what wait I for? My hope is in thee . . . ," and, finally, "O spare me, that I may recover strength, before I go hence, and be no more."

With that, the only funeral that J. D. Autry had ever attended was over, without public attention or the prying eye of the media, with no friends or family there to mourn him.

For years thereafter, however, his friend Shirley did. Each year, as Autry's birthday approached, she would telephone to say she was coming to Huntsville to "spend the day with J.D." She would be bringing a birthday cake, she always said, and she invited me to join her at the cemetery to share it with her.

Several times I did. After our picnic lunch, she would leave the grave site and retrieve a small battery-powered television from her car. It was my signal to leave. She liked watching her afternoon soap operas in private.

Though I never understood her or her enduring obsession with Autry, she was, in her unique way, as caring a person as I'd ever encountered.

I was no stranger to the prison cemetery. Among my responsibilities as chaplain at The Walls was to conduct graveside services for all indigent inmates buried there. There were stretches of time when it seemed I did a funeral almost daily. On one occasion, I did five in a single day. Many, over the years, were for men I'd come to know in the prison hospital or the Death House. Some were for strangers, convicts who had died in other units, their bodies transported to Huntsville for burial. There were those who died of natural causes, of diseases, and, all too often, at the hand of a fellow inmate.

Now and then there would be family members and a few friends attending the services. Most often, however, they were solitary occasions, watched over only by those inmates assigned to cemetery duty. At the end of the day, prison-made crosses, bearing just the date of death and the inmate's serial number, were put in place. (The decision to not include names on the grave markers had been made long before I arrived at the prison. The reason: the markers of some of the more notorious inmates were often vandalized, sometimes even removed by ghoulish collectors.)

It was always the funerals of men who had been executed that were the most difficult. The conversations we'd shared just hours earlier were fresh in my mind, the troubling sights and sounds of their deaths still with me. To see the sad and shocked faces of loved ones gathered around the grave only added to the somberness of the occasion.

In many instances, they were people I had come to know in the days before their husbands and brothers, fathers and sons, were put to death. Sometimes the relationship had begun with a letter or phone call, sometimes with a visit to my office. Frightened by myths and unwarranted horror stories of what occurs in the death chamber, they wanted to know the truth about the procedure, and I tried to explain it as honestly as possible. In some cases, I think, they wanted nothing more than to learn what they could about the person who would be trying to comfort their loved one during his final hours.

And while the warden subtly discouraged such relationships, I strongly felt a responsibility to include them in my ministry. The families of criminals are, I believe, the forgotten victims of crime, people forced to share guilt that is not theirs, questioning what they might have done differently to avert the horrible crimes their relatives have committed. And, in a society too quick to assign blame to parents and point to their shortcomings, they are often the unfair targets of reproach.

I wanted to help the relatives through the trauma that awaited them on the execution date. I rarely knew what to expect.

On one occasion I met with a family who expressed concern over a father's serious heart condition. While his condemned son had included him on his witness list, they feared that watching the execution might well trigger a fatal heart attack. Even the family doctor had advised against it. After meeting the frail, nervous man, I agreed.

After we had talked for some time, he finally acknowledged that the ordeal of watching his son die might be dangerous to his health. Still, he felt a strong need to know what was to take place and where it would occur. I carefully described the routine for him, detailing the events leading up to the execution.

"Is there some way I can see the place where it will happen?" he asked.

When I explained that the rules forbade anyone other than prison officials to enter the Death House, he was not satisfied. Finally, I told him that I could show him from the outside where his son would be spending his final hours. That seemed agreeable, so I summoned his other son and asked if he would drive us from the Hospitality House, a local facility for families of visiting inmates, so that I might point out to his father where the execution would take place.

Such is the paranoia that accompanies the carrying out of a death sentence that, as we neared The Walls, the son and I in the front seat, the father in back, the major saw us and immediately notified the warden that it appeared that I was being kidnapped by members of the inmate's family.

The paranoia is justified.

Often, the sadness felt by many families arriving to pay their final visit is masked by deep-seated anger. There is an overwhelming need to strike out against someone, and on more than one occasion I was their target. Viewed not as a chaplain but as simply another member of the prison staff, I was judged to be the enemy, and it was difficult to convince a distraught family otherwise. The sister of one inmate, certain that we were putting an innocent man to death, threatened to kill me. Another time, the wife of a man scheduled to die pointed out that her son, an inmate in another unit, was troubled by the fact that he would not be allowed to pay his soon-to-die father a last visit. Would I talk with him? Traveling to the Tennessee Colony Unit on the day prior to the execution, I attempted to explain the long-standing rule that did not allow fellow inmates to visit. The young man, still in his teens, cried and begged, volunteering to make the trip in shackles if only it would be allowed. Prison rules, I attempted to explain, were unbending. Was there some message I might deliver to his father? The frustrated youngster's response was to jump to his feet and lunge at me.

I left feeling relief that a guard had been standing nearby to block the inmate's path. Yet I was also saddened by the disappointing message I'd had to deliver.

Fortunately, however, such instances were the exception. It was generally a mother or a wife or an older sister who managed to quiet the anger of others in the family.

Visiting the large family of an inmate whose execution was scheduled for later in the evening, the mother had introduced me to cousins, sisters, and several brothers who had made the trip from a small South Texas town. "My youngest son," she said, "is very upset, and we are not going to allow him to come to the prison. I'm afraid of what he might do." With that, she pointed him out. A handsome young man with coal black hair and dark, piercing eyes, he stood away from the others. Hands buried in the pockets of his jeans, he glared at me. Clearly, I was his enemy.

It was not until the following morning, as I stood at his brother's grave site preparing to conduct the funeral service that I saw him again. His mother approached me and said, "My son is still very angry." There was a warning tone in her weak, tired voice.

As the family gathered around the grave, he remained in the background, pacing and talking to himself. Beginning the service, I became aware of him slowly making his way toward the small crowd. Then, just as I was beginning the benediction, he began running toward the mound of dirt adjacent to the grave. Just before he disappeared behind members of his family, he picked up a shovel. I was certain that he was planning to attack me.

Crying as he pushed his way through the crowd, shovel in hand, he was only a few feet from me when he spoke. Defiantly, he announced that he alone would shovel the dirt into his brother's grave. Inmate trustees, normally assigned to such duty, stepped away. And for the next half hour, the family stood in silence as the sweat-drenched youngster filled the grave. His task completed, he waited as his mother returned to the car to get a small flower arrangement. Then, with her arm around her sobbing son, she directed her grieving family to the parking lot.

For some, a funeral was a troubling mystery. A family from Dallas arrived with a "professional mourner," a woman who had been hired to advise them and help them through the experience. Dressed in bright colors and wearing a wide-brimmed hat, she began to wail and chant as the body was being unloaded by inmates. Parading among the family members in a strange gypsy dance, she cried and chanted, then began to sing. I had heard of such people—the Bible even refers to "professional weepers and wailers"—but this was my first experience with one. In short order, she had the family crying and chanting along with her.

As I viewed the unconventional proceedings, I felt like an entertainer standing in the wings awaiting completion of a warm-up act might. Only when the woman felt that she had urged the family into a state of mind she deemed proper for a funeral did she nod toward me. It was my cue that the service could begin.

Afterwards, as I spoke with members of the family before their departure, I mentioned that I had three more funerals to conduct. Sadly, I said, there would be no family in attendance at any of them. The professional mourner, overhearing our conversation, stayed after those who had hired her left. Without a word, she followed me through the cemetery to the other grave sites.

Only when I was done did she approach me, a business card in hand. "For these poor souls who have no one," she said, "you need a mourner. I would be pleased provide my services at no charge."

I never called her.

Unusual requests were fairly common. As we were preparing to bury one inmate on his forty-second birthday, family members asked if it would be okay for them to bring forty-two helium-filled balloons to the cemetery. Their plan, they explained, was to release them one at a time. "They will signify that he is on his way to Heaven," his wife explained. They would perform the ceremony at the end of the funeral and stand in wait until each balloon had floated out of sight.

All went well until several became entangled in the branches of the pines that surrounded the cemetery. For quite some time, members of the family stood, eyes shaded against the bright morning sun, waiting for the trapped balloons to make their symbolic way skyward. I had no idea what to say to them.

Finally, it was a family member who lightened the mood. "Each balloon represented a year of his life," she drolly observed. "Obviously, he had some good years and some bad years."

As do we all.

I will not even venture a guess at the number of funerals I conducted during my years as a prison chaplain. Besides officiating at those of indigent inmates who died in custody and were buried in the prison version of a potter's field, I was often asked to accompany inmates' bodies to their homes and conduct funeral services on the premises. Too, on numerous occasions I was called on by families of men whom I'd come to know while they served their sentences and who had died in the free world.

To this day, however, there is one prison cemetery burial that stands out above all others.

Doc Broeckel in no way fit the profile of a convict. For years he had worked as a missionary doctor, traveling throughout South America setting up clinics and providing medical assistance to the poor and uneducated. He was in his fifties when he returned to Texas and opened a free clinic that he made available to a predominately Hispanic population on the state's southern border. He told me of once delivering twenty-five babies in a single day.

Following a divorce, he had remarried and was happily going about his career when his ex-wife went to the local police with charges that he had molested children under his care. Convicted, Doc was sentenced to serve his time at The Walls.

I've never met a nicer person. He was a faithful regular at chapel services and lent a marvelous bass voice to our choir. Though he chose to work in the prison print shop, he was always ready to offer medical advice to any fellow prisoner who asked, and he made regular stops by my office to discuss theology.

And through the years I knew him, he vehemently denied being guilty of the crimes for which he was imprisoned. His new wife, who worked for the Salvation Army, visited him regularly. His sons—both successful doctors themselves—were supportive, as was a brother who was a minister in California. I was convinced that Doc was one of those who should not have been in prison.

Yet he was serving a lengthy sentence, and despite his good nature and upbeat disposition, the toll began to show. I watched as age lines began to crease his cheeks, his temples grayed, and the sparkle faded from his eyes. In time, he began to suffer from heart problems that drastically limited his activities. Eventually, his ongoing battle with shortness of breath made it necessary for him to resign his place in the choir.

Doc was dying.

Visiting the chapel one afternoon, he asked if we might talk. "I'd like to be buried in the prison cemetery," he said. He was aware that its plots were reserved for inmates whose families could not afford the expense of burials and wondered if there might be some financial arrangement that would allow an exception to the rules. He was aware that the state had a contract with a local funeral home that provided burial preparation and a casket for eight hundred dollars. "I can arrange to have that paid directly to the funeral home or the prison," he said.

No doubt sensing my surprise at his request, he continued. "I know this might be difficult to understand," he said, "but before coming here I devoted myself to my work and as a result made very few close friends along the way. My only real friends are the people I've met since I came to prison. And I'd like to be buried among them if at all possible."

Though I did not tell him so, I already knew I would do everything I could to see that his wish was fulfilled.

"Will you want your brother to conduct the funeral service?" I asked.

"No," he said. "I'd like for him and the rest of my family to be here—if they want to—but I'd appreciate it if you could officiate at my funeral. You're my minister."

It was less than a month later when a guard rushed into my office shortly after noon, pale and out of breath. "Doc needs you," he said.

Following him into the yard, I saw one of the hospital nurses bent over Doc's body. Basketball games had been halted, and exercise came to a standstill, as prisoners stood silently watching the nurse's vain attempt to revive him. He had suffered a heart attack and was dead before I could reach him. He was sixty-three years old.

∙   ∙   ∙

Doc's entire family came to Huntsville for the funeral. His brother, the minister, arrived a day early and paid me a visit. "There are things I'm at a loss to explain," he said, "but after my brother came here, he seemed happier than he'd ever been. He wrote regularly, and his letters were always cheerful and filled with humor. He talked of the friends he'd made, of how the idea that everyone in prison was a bad person was far from true. And he wrote about you and your chapel. You made a great impression on him."

"Your brother," I responded, "touched a lot of lives while he was here."

From the moment news circulated that Doc was dead, virtually every inmate trustee at The Walls volunteered to serve as a pallbearer. Those who were allowed to perform the duty made no effort to hide their tears during the brief service that was held under a warm, blue morning sky in the prison cemetery.

Doc's sons, dressed in suits, walked among the trustees, clad in their prison whites, and they shook hands with each of the men their father had called a friend. His brother said a prayer. And his wife hugged me and lightly kissed my cheek.

"This is what he wanted," she whispered. "God bless you for helping to make it happen."

EIGHT

In time, the efficiency with which the Texas prison system had carried out executions was not lost on officials from other states. For all the public criticism of the frequency with which inmates were being put to death, the outcries from anti–death penalty organizations and human rights groups, it was generally agreed that we were handling a distasteful job about as well as it could be done. Difficult though it might be to equate what we were doing with almost any other workplace responsibility I can think of, the fact remained that there was a proper and professional way to approach the procedure. When reduced to the generally accepted basics of job performance—a concept I could never personally bring myself to consider—we were doing what we had to quite well. In fact, we were the model that other prisons being forced to enter the legal death march chose to follow.

Routinely, officials from throughout the United States visited Huntsville as legislation decreed their return to capital punishment. I met no one who relished the task, spoke with none who showed the slightest eagerness for what they were preparing to do. Instead, I saw a steady stream of grim-faced men who only wished to carry out the death penalty as humanely as possible.

Among them was Daniel Vasquez, the warden of California's fabled San Quentin.

Since the reinstatement of the death penalty, he had presided over the execution of one inmate and had been severely troubled by the manner in which it had been carried out. At the 150-year-old prison, they had resumed gas-chamber executions after a 23-year hiatus. With the advent of lethal injection, a move to allow condemned prisoners a choice was underway. Vasquez was convinced that lethal injection more closely met the humane guidelines set forth by the courts, and thus he wanted to learn as much about the Texas procedure as he could. Contacting Jack Pursley, a longtime friend, he asked if he and members of his staff could come and observe an execution.

I found it easy to understand why his peers throughout the nation had recently honored Vasquez as Warden of the Year. A physically impressive man who dressed like a member of the Fortune 500, he paid close attention to even the smallest details of the execution routine. He interviewed everyone from the correction officers who delivered the prisoner to The Walls to members of the tie-down team. He asked questions about the mixture of the deadly chemicals, wanted to know what training those assigned to insert the needles into the inmate's arms had undergone, and toured the Death House, constantly making notes as he went.

On the day of the scheduled execution of Justin Lee May, a man convicted of the murder of the husband-and-wife owners of a Western Auto Store in Freeport, Texas, that he had robbed, Vasquez spent time with us inside the Death House, standing quietly with the guards at the end of the hallway to observe the routine of the prisoner on his final day. And then, just as unobtrusively, he entered the witness area to watch the final procedure being carried out. In the late night aftermath he studied the manner in which the public relations officer dealt with questions from members of the media. It seemed that no detail was too insignificant to include in his notebook.

The day after, he came into my office for a final visit before returning to California. I could tell that what he'd observed and would soon orchestrate at his own prison troubled him. "I still don't know how you people have managed it," he said as he sat across from me, "but what I've seen here is a remarkable team effort, a seamless coordination under the most difficult of circumstances. We don't have that at San Quentin, and, honestly, I'm not sure how to achieve it. But it is obvious to me that we've got to."

It was for that reason, he said, that he'd asked Pursley that we travel to California and help train his staff. "I'd like you to speak with my chaplains," he told me. "Make them aware of the importance of their roles. Explain to them the relationship you have with your warden."

The use of several chaplains was, I believed, part of the problem he was dealing with. Unlike Pursley, he had not adopted the "one butt to kick" philosophy that had been outlined to me the first day I'd reported for work at The Walls. Under Pursley's guidelines, a specific task was assigned to a single person, its success that individual's sole responsibility. The fewer individuals involved, Pursley felt, the better the system was likely to work, and the more confident everyone involved would be. By limiting involvement to those absolutely necessary, the chance for conflicts of interest, arguments over methods, misunderstandings, and questioning of purpose was dramatically lessened.

His selective method also insured a bond of loyalty that was crucial.

In the weeks leading up to the April 1992 execution of Robert Alton Harris at San Quentin, the controversy being fanned by the media had found its way into the prison itself. Despite the fact that a recently published poll indicated that 82 percent of those residing in California approved a return to the death penalty, resistance within the prison system persisted. Each of the seven chaplains assigned to the prison had insisted on ministering to the man who was to die. One had participated in an anti–death penalty march, another had taken out an ad in the nearby San Francisco newspaper, demanding that the execution be halted. Several staff members had made it clear that they would in no way participate, even if ordered to do so.

I could not count the times I'd wished to speak out myself; how often I'd reached the verge of refusing to be involved in yet another death. But to what good? Until some legislative mandate changed things, the executions would go on. That, I had absolutely no power to change. So long as they continued, whatever calming service I could provide to the condemned was all that really mattered. By speaking my mind on the issue I would only hinder the effort I felt duty-bound to put forth. My own feelings were best kept secret.

How effective could I be if the person sitting across from me in the Death House was under the impression that I believed he deserved to be killed? Or that I felt what was to take place was unjust? Already I'd had to repeatedly answer an unfounded rumor, spread by an inmate who had received a stay of execution after visiting the Death House, that I had angrily cursed the late-night announcement that prevented his death. No sooner had he been returned to Death Row than he told his fellow convicts that it had been clear to him that I was staunchly in favor of the death penalty. Which is to say that things were difficult enough without my publicly announcing my feelings. At the same time, how would I explain my being there if the condemned man knew that I was morally and spiritually opposed to what the state had ordered?

Neutrality, I strongly believed, was my only chance at earning an inmate's confidence. In those frightening final hours, my responsibility was not to judge the legal system any more than it was to judge the inmate to whom I ministered. I was there simply as God's spokesman—as a friend if the inmate so wished, as a confidant if he wanted one.

I would be there to assure that no man went to his death alone.

These were among the things that I had tried to explain to visiting officials from prisons in places like Colorado, New Mexico, Alabama, Kansas, Missouri, and Indiana. They were what I would also tell the chaplains of San Quentin.

"Your warden and I have discussed the fact that there is no manual on the procedure," Vasquez had pointed out, "and I believe one would be useful." Pursley, he said, had suggested that I prepare one before we visited California.

Up to that moment it had never occurred to me that there was nothing in writing about the responsibilities and sequence of events involved in an execution. Our step-by-step procedure had simply evolved from experience, and from refinement and improvements suggested at staff meetings. Over time, those of us involved—prison officials, guards, doctors, members of the tie-down team, the public-information director—had managed to function as a well-coordinated unit—each aware of his responsibility, each determined that his input contribute to the dignity and professionalism of the task. The more I thought about it, the more remarkable I realized it was. And I felt a pride in the fact, despite being aware that very few could ever under-stand how one could look positively on what we had been required to do forty-eight times in the past ten years.

Thus, in the weeks before our scheduled trip to California, I began preparing "The Team Concept of Execution." Little did I know as I spent late nights in my office, writing and revising, that I was creating an outline that would eventually serve as a guideline for execution procedures throughout the United States.

As I worked, it occurred to me that my essay might well be the most important sermon I'd ever prepared.

Though I detailed the laws and social climate that had led to the renewed application of the death penalty, and outlined the execution procedure and manpower involved, it was the psychological aspect that seemed most important to me. In my years as chaplain, I had often been asked point-blank how I, as a Christian and ordained min-ister, could, in good conscience, involve myself in the process. It was a question that I knew other chaplains were constantly being asked. There was no simple answer that everyone would deem satisfactory.

With that in mind I dealt at length with my own purpose, mentally retreating to that day, years earlier, when it had been announced that Texas would resume executions. In weighing the burden that I felt had been placed on my own shoulders, I had with great difficulty reached a spiritual decision that allowed me to involve myself in the state-authorized death of another human being. I had made no laws that led the way to such an act. I held no power to determine who lived and who died. Though officially a member of the prison staff, I was not charged with the duty of inserting needles into an inmate's arm and gave no order for the chemicals to flow. Those were the responsibilities of men with a strength and dedication to duty that went beyond my understanding.

My purpose in the process was not to see that laws were carried out or that social payback was accomplished. Others, I hoped, could benefit from the mapless road I'd traveled. Yes, it was important that we be committed to our philosophies of life and death, that we hold firmly to our faith and belief in the Scriptures. At the same time, if we were to effectively minister to a man sentenced to die, it was essential that for those few hours during the death watch, our own misgivings and pains of the heart be set aside. We had to call upon strength from a higher source, ignore our own feelings, and focus on the needs of others.

To do so, I hoped to explain, had required the difficult acceptance that I was a part of the chain reaction begun when an individual committed a crime that was punishable by death. The police, the court system, the lawyers, and the prison officials were all simply following the unbending dictates of man's law. Many had righteously argued that the death penalty was the only method of checks and balances available to assure maintenance of a civil society; others passionately labeled it the lone avenue to justice; some insisted it was the best manner by which to send a dramatic warning that would provide safety for law-abiding members of society.

After it was all done—the arrests, the legal warfare, the convictions, the sentencing, the cries for vengeance and appeals that all life, however spoiled, was too precious to take—there would eventually come a day when a frightened man in chains and cuffs was escorted into the hidden corner of prison where the Death House was located and heard the words, "I'm Chaplain Pickett." From that moment on, my primary purpose was to help him through the dark hours that lay ahead.

That, I needed to make them understand, was the isolated world in which our responsibility began.

. . .

Located on the north shore of San Francisco Bay, the pre–Civil War facility is more fortress than prison, a relic from some old James Cagney movie. Time had passed San Quentin by—it was crowded and lacking in many of the modern conveniences I'd become accustomed to at The Walls. It was dark and cold, and its proximity to the Pacific made lockdowns necessary every time the thick fog rolled in. Its death chamber was located on the same cell block that housed its Death Row. There, almost a quarter century earlier, what many had hoped would be California's last execution had taken place. As sodium cyanide gas steamed from the cast-iron bucket at his feet, convicted murderer Aaron Mitchell had gone to his death screaming that he was Jesus Christ.

I found the place a depressing eyesore, a throwback to the days of medieval dungeons.

We toured the facility, met members of the staff, and listened to a series of concerns and complaints. There was a discomforting level of tension in the air. Pursley was a picture of self-assuredness, offering blunt criticism and thoughtful encouragment with confidence and great poise. "We have made our share of mistakes," he assured his audience, "but we've learned from them and corrected them. We don't necessarily like what we're doing, but we've learned how to do it well." He made it clear that the only way he could help was to offer an honest evaluation of the San Quentin procedures. During a meeting attended by the chaplains, he brought a silence to the room with his answer to a question about the prisoner-chaplain relationship in the final hours before an execution. "The thing that is absolutely essential," he said, "is that you have only one chaplain in charge on that day. If there is any hope that a positive, trusting relationship can be developed over the course of those short but very tense hours, it lies in a one-on-one situation."

I felt the eyes of everyone in the room turn toward me. "Chaplain Pickett is my representative, my pipeline to the prisoner from the moment he arrives at the Death House until the execution takes place," Pursley said. "He's there to make decisions, to meet needs, and to deal with whatever problems might arise. It is a tremendous responsibility and not one that can be carried out by committee. Chaplain Pickett has been assigned to be with the condemned prisoners for the simple reason that he is best qualified to handle what I consider the most important job in the entire execution process."

We spent most of a week there. For several days I talked with the chaplains, in groups and individually. I toured their chapel, sat in on services, and listened to their choir. I accompanied them on visits to the prison hospital. And, as best I could, I responded to their concerns about the execution they were soon to participate in.

One afternoon, as we walked from the main gate into the visitors' parking lot, Head Chaplain Earl Smith stopped and breathed deeply of the cool, salt air that wafted in from the bay. It was as if he were inhaling the smell of the free world for the first time. For several seconds he silently stared out toward the end of the peninsula before turning to me.

"I have one last question," he said. "You've been through this so often, walked so many men to their deaths. I can't imagine it. How have you managed to insulate yourself from it all, to not feel the pain and suffering that go on?"

It surprised me to learn that he thought I might have found some magic way to do so, that in the repetition I'd someway managed to shield off the fragile emotions attached to ministering to someone scheduled to die. It took me a minute to decide on my answer.

"When I agreed to be the Death House chaplain," I finally said, "I made a single promise to God, the prison director, the warden, and myself: if the time ever came when I no longer felt anything, I'd quit."

Following the second execution performed at San Quentin State Prison, Warden Vasquez did. So did several of his chaplains and security officers. Unable to reconcile the law they were obligated to carry out with their personal feelings that the death penalty was morally wrong, they sought new directions for their careers. Vasquez continued to work in the penal system, taking a job as warden of a privately owned prison in California. Once away from San Quentin, he became an outspoken advocate of doing away with the death penalty.

His decision was not an isolated occurrence. As executions became increasingly frequent throughout the United States, several prison staff members whom I had met during their visits to Texas had tendered their resignations after seeing the death penalty carried out. In Florida and Alabama, wardens and chaplains announced their retirements and walked away.

Such decisions provided me with new questions to ponder. What fueled the willingness of one warden to continue while another opted to resign? And what of my fellow ministers, no longer able to deal with the concept of state-ordered killing? Were they more committed to their vows; had they received some divine signal that had passed me by?

The answers, I came to believe, were buried deep inside the heart and were more complex even than the eternal conflicts of right and wrong, strength and weakness. I knew only that I believed in my role and its purpose. And in that I found my own comfort.

So long as I was needed, I would continue.

NINE

In the early eighties Texas's Rio Grande Valley was a breeding ground for the violence and corruption that go hand in hand with the illegal drug trade. The predominately Hispanic population was—and remains—dirt poor and desperate. The limited educational opportunities that existed were often ignored in favor of the survival needs of large and struggling families. The per capita income hovered at or below the poverty level, and criminal activity became part of the region's troubled legacy, passed from father to son, brother to brother. All of which contributed to the fact that an unusually large number of inmates in Texas prisons listed the hardscrabble border communities as their previous homes.

Among them was an Edinburg roofer–drug smuggler–high school dropout named Leonel Torres Herrera, charged with and convicted of murdering two law-enforcement officers within a ten-minute span on a night in September of 1981.

According to court records, Herrera had been stopped for speeding by a Texas Department of Public Safety trooper named David Rucker. After approaching the car and asking the driver for identification, the officer was shot and killed. Herrera sped away and, just minutes later, was again stopped, this time by a rookie patrolman with the Los Fresnos Police Department. Officer Enrique Carrisalez was shot in the chest. He lived long enough to tell fellow officers that it had been Herrera who shot him.

The evidence seemed overwhelming. In addition to the eyewitness statement of the dying policeman, Herrera's Social Security card, which prosecutors argued he'd shown when asked for identification, had been found lying near Carrisalez's body. When he was arrested in his home, bloodstained pants were found in the washing machine. There was also blood found on his wallet. In both cases, forensic testing matched the blood to samples taken from the dead officer. From his car, investigators seized the sawed-off shotgun used in the murders, ammunition, and traces of marijuana. Herrera was soon convicted of capital murder in the Carrisalez case and sentenced to die. Later, he pled guilty to killing Rucker and received a life sentence.

At the time, the deaths of two officers and the imprisonment of Herrera were judged by many as little more than just another tragic episode in the state's ongoing drug war. There was nothing in Herrera's background that would earn him sympathy. He was, after all, a man law enforcement had been after for some time. Virtually everyone who knew him was aware that he regularly hired himself out to help smuggle drugs across the border, then delivered them to dealers waiting in Houston and Dallas. In 1980 he had been tried on, and acquitted of, charges that he fired shots at a Cameron County deputy sheriff who had responded to a disturbance in a bar. He was also considered the prime suspect in the unsolved murder of a deputy constable in Hidalgo County.

Even during his brief service in the navy, Herrera had earned a reputation as a man with an uncontrolled temper. He'd been dishonorably discharged after striking an officer and knocking out several of his teeth. His commander called him one of the most violent men he'd ever encountered. Following his arrest on murder charges, Herrera had threatened to kill the troopers who were guarding him and attacked a television news photographer assigned to film a pretrial court hearing.

Violence, it seemed, flowed through the genes of the Herrera family. Two years after Leonel was sent to Death Row, his brother was shot and killed. Raul Herrera and his twelve-year-old son had visited the home of a drug-world associate named José Lopez, and, as they walked away, Lopez fired a fatal shot into Herrera's back. Despite the cold-blooded nature of the crime, Lopez had received a ten-year probated sentence for involuntary manslaughter after his lawyers argued that the purpose of Herrera's visit had been to threaten to kill him and his family.

It was not altogether surprising, then, that Raul, Jr., would add to the disquieting family legacy and ultimately find his own name on the court dockets.

As a child he had looked on as his father beat his mother with his fists and pointed guns at her. By the time he was a teenager, he had severely beaten a man with a baseball bat during an argument over an unpaid drug debt and been convicted of aggravated assault and sentenced to twenty years in prison.

Still, despite the shattered lives left in the wake of their crimes, public awareness of the Herreras would normally have quickly faded; they would have been remembered only by loved ones and those victimized by their alleged wrongdoings. There were other crimes and criminals to take their places on the front pages. Despite Leonel's constant insistence that he was innocent of the crime for which he was to die, he became little more than another sad and angry face among the Death Row population.

Raul Herrera, Jr., however, would change all that when, a decade after the courts had found Leonel Herrera guilty of murder, he signed an affadavit swearing that his uncle was not the man who had killed the two police officers.

The man who committed the crimes, Raul insisted, was his own father. He said that he had been in the car that night and witnessed the murders. (He was nine years old at the time.) Soon there was an avalanche of new information that created doubt about Leonel Herrera's guilt.

His sister, Norma Rodriguez, long fearful for her own life if she spoke out, came forward to say that on the night of the crimes Raul had brought Leonel to her house early in the evening "so messed up on cocaine" that she had immediately put him to bed. It was, she said, hours later when Raul returned with news of the highway murders. If anyone asked, he told his sister, Leonel was to say that he had committed the crimes.

An investigator for the elder Raul's attorney said that he had been told by several people that his client had, in fact, confessed the murders to at least three associates and, shortly before he died, had considered turning himself in. His defense attorney even came forward to say that his client had told him that he killed the officers.

Raul's death at the hands of José Lopez, family members insisted, had been a desperate effort to prevent the authorities from learning the truth—that Lopez had been in the car with Raul and his son on the night of the murders.

Polygraph tests administered to Raul Herrera, Jr., Norma Rodriguez, and Ruben Rodriguez, Raul Sr.'s former attorney, indicated that they had responded truthfully when questioned about their statements.

In short order, a team of lawyers with the Texas Resource Center, a federally funded agency that provided legal assistance to condemned inmates, began working to block Leonel Herrera's execution. From the office of Texas governor Ann Richards to the Supreme Court, they pled Herrera's innocence. Suddenly, the case that had been short-lived local news was the subject of national attention as reporters from *Newsweek* and the *New York Times* arrived to investigate the possibility than an innocent man might soon be executed. Anti–death penalty activists like actor Danny Glover and members of Amnesty International were soon traveling to Texas to speak at rallies.

They warned that the state was about to put an innocent man to death.

After all the tumult, after legal filings and court rulings, Herrera's execution date was set.

There is a phrase in the state-issued death warrant that indicates that on the date the sentence is to be imposed, the execution must take place "before sunrise." No one ever explained why to me. It was just one of those rules.

And, for a time, it appeared that deadline alone might temporarily save Herrera. Instead, the courts beat the sun by thirty-nine minutes. Having arrived at the Death House in the early morning of the previous day, Herrera received a stay at 6:20 the following morning. I had been with him for almost twenty-four hours when he was escorted from his cell and returned to the Ellis Unit.

It was one of the most exhausting and draining experiences I'd ever been through. Much of the night had been spent receiving reports from attorneys who rushed in and out of the Death House to say that an appeal had been denied and that it looked as if the execution was on, only to return soon thereafter to say that there was new reason to be optimistic that a stay might be ordered. And, as the activity swirled, I could not help but think that what I was observing was cruel and unusual punishment at its worst. Long after the midnight hour had passed, Herrera sat in his cell, being told one minute that he should prepare to die, then that his life might be spared.

That night I rode along with him on the emotional roller-coaster, perspiring so badly that my dry cleaner's would later tell me that there was nothing they could do to remove the stains from the suit I'd worn during the ordeal.

It was one of the few instances when the convict displayed more calm than I myself could muster. Amid the steady stream of lawyers who visited the Death House to advise him on the progress of appeals that had been filed, he spoke softly on the phone with his mother and sister. He had, he told them, asked that his body be cremated and the ashes sent to them. And he assured them of what they were already certain—that he was innocent of the crime for which he was being put to death.

And, while he did not dwell on it in conversations we had, he told me the same thing. "God," he said, "has forgiven me my sins. I've done wrong things in my life, but I didn't do what they've put me here for."

It was just after ten in the evening when the warden notified me that it was time to begin preparing the inmate for his trip to the death chamber. As I'd done so many times before, I described the procedure. As I spoke, Herrera stared silently at the huge steel door that led to the gurney.

Soon, however, I was notified that the execution would be delayed. Though the Fifth Circuit and the Supreme Court had denied their request for a stay, his lawyers continued their nerve-wracking battle for their client's life.

At a few minutes past 2:00 A.M., attorney Phyllis Crocker arrived to tell Herrera that things didn't look good and that he should prepare himself for the worst possible news. Herrera simply nodded. "When you're innocent," he replied, "you shouldn't fear death."

We began to discuss what his final words would be. Those who had gone before him had wanted to bid farewell to their loved ones, apologize for the pain their crime had caused, finally admit their guilt, or profess their innocence one last time. I anticipated the latter from Herrera.

"Straight Sierra. Let's make contact," he said. "That's all I want to say."

I asked that he repeat it, then questioned what it meant.

"You don't need to know," he replied.

It was two minutes after six in the morning when I told him that the time to go was only minutes away. "I'm ready," he said. "And I want to thank you for staying with me all night. I know it's been a hard thing for you. I want to tell you good-bye here, not in there." Again he turned to stare at the nearby doorway we would soon pass through. "I'll never forget what you've done."

I looked for fear or anger in his eyes but saw only resignation.

And then, at 6:20, word came that Texas Court of Criminal Appeals judge Sam Clinton had granted a stay to the execution. Suddenly, the long night was over, and arrangements were being made to transport Herrera back to the Ellis Unit.

The sun had just begun to peek over the walls of the prison as I made my way to my office, bone weary and troubled.

Though his life had been misguided and filled with wrongdoing, I had serious doubts that Leonel Herrera was guilty of the murder that had sent him to Death Row. Yet he had come within minutes of dying.

What bothered me even more was the knowledge that one day I would probably see him again.

At the time I had no way of knowing the effect he would have on my life in the months before his next execution date was set.

I was in the chapel, making preparations for a late-morning choir practice, when word came that the warden wanted to see me. "It's urgent," said the correctional officer who delivered the message.

A much-traveled letter had arrived from the Texas attorney general's office that left me speechless as I read it.

Samuel Hawkins, also a Death Row inmate, had written to a woman in France named Dominique Malon, criticizing my behavior on the night Leonel Herrera had spent in the Death House. The letter painted me as uncaring and angry over the fact the execution had not been carried out. In part it read:

> He [Herrera] said Chaplain Pickett told him why not go ahead and get it over with? He does not believe Pickett is a minister, and nor do I believe. The man is such a sad terrorist and he terrorizes people deliberately. This mad man has a position. He loves to torture people. Herrera and I had a 3 hour long talk. He is a very proud man but I see his tension, fear, nervousness, torture . . . .

It also made clear that Herrera did not want me present on his next visit to the Death House. Malon and lawyers with the Texas Resource Center had made the same request. I didn't know what to think. Over the years, I knew, there had been vile rumors spread among the Death

Row inmates about what occurred during the execution process—bizarre stories of men being buried alive or their bodies being unceremoniously tossed into the creek that ran behind the prison after they were killed—but I thought they had been put to rest. Always keenly aware that if an execution was stayed, the inmate would return to Ellis to provide great detail of what occurred at The Walls, I had made every effort humanly possible to be sure that whatever he had to report was positive in nature. And now this.

I agonized over the false charges, praying for guidance. Why, I kept asking myself, would Herrera make such accusations? Had he, in fact? Or was Samuel Hawkins lying in the letter he'd written to Dominique Malon?

I had met her during one of her trips to the United States and had been impressed with the genuine concern she expressed over the cruelty of the death penalty. She, like many Europeans, had viewed a documentary that had aired on the life of inmate Charlie Bass, who had been executed in 1986. Bass had been convicted of murdering a Houston city marshal following the armed robbery of a nightclub. And, while he had gone to his death saying that he deserved to be executed for his crime, the story of his troubled life became a rallying point for the anti–death penalty movement abroad. The Charlie Bass Society was formed to lobby against what it deemed the barbaric custom of capital punishment in the United States.

I did not fault their passion. But, as I agonized over the accusations that had prompted Malon's letter, I could not help but wonder why the word of a man like Hawkins, convicted of the rape and stabbing death of a pregnant woman, carried more weight than that of a minister and chaplain. Feeling wounded, for a time I let my own ego get in the the way. Finally, it seemed the only thing to do was step aside and allow a religious advisor of Herrera's chosing to counsel him on the day he was scheduled to be executed.

It was a decision Warden Pursley did not immediately embrace. "You are the Death House chaplain," he argued. "You are *my* representative, and I have every confidence in your abilities to help this man through his ordeal. The lies of an inmate with an ax to grind won't change that.

"As far as I'm concerned, the choice is not his."

While I was grateful for the vote of confidence, my response was that the choice *was* his. On the witness list Herrera had already prepared was the Ellis Unit chaplain, Fr. Bob Zawacki. If Herrera wished him to be there instead of me, I strongly felt that his wish should be granted.

Reluctantly, the warden offered a compromise. "I want you standing by that cell door when Herrera arrives," he said. "Show him the letter and ask him if he actually said those things. If he says he doesn't want you there, we'll deal with it."

It was only one of the things that weighed on my mind as Herrera's new execution date approached.

While no student of the law, I could not help but wonder at the strange logic that moved the process along. In Texas, the law requires that any new evidence relative to a case in which a trial and conviction have occurred must be brought before the court no less than thirty days after sentencing if it is to be considered. Thereafter, too late and too bad.

However, it was the ruling of the United States Supreme Court on the matter that most troubled me.

After hearing arguments, Chief Justice William Rehnquist issued a ruling that, in layman's language, said that if a person received a legally fair trial, one in which all appeals had been exhausted, the sentence issued should stand.

Simply put, Leonel Herrera, guilty or innocent, was subject to the death penalty.

Even before Herrera arrived at the Death House, I had Father Zawacki in my office in the event he asked for him. Though neither of us voiced our feelings, we shared a common anxiety. I was soon to face a condemned man who had allegedly judged me less than godly; the priest was, for the first time, facing the possibility of going through the ordeal of ministering to an inmate scheduled to die.

"I'll pray for you," the father said as I stood to leave.

"Pray for us all," I said.

As guards escorted Herrera toward the same cell he'd occupied a year earlier, I did not even have the opportunity to pull Sammy Hawkins's letter from my coat pocket before he spoke. "I'm sorry for the things I've said about you," he said. "It wasn't right, but I had to say them. You don't know what it's like over there. You've got to act tough and angry at the system all the time. It's part of getting along. But I'm sorry."

"Leonel, my only concern is whether you want me to be here or not. It's your call. Father Zawacki can be over here in just a few minutes."

Herrera shook his head. "No," he said. "You stay. Father Zawacki is a good man, and I put him on my witness list. But I don't want him. You stayed with me before; I'd like you to stay again."

Thus, the problem over which I'd agonized for weeks was quickly resolved. And, as the final hours passed, we never spoke of it again.

Instead, he talked proudly of the high school equivalency diploma he'd received while in prison. And he spoke of loved ones who had stood by him over the years and of his concern that a disproportionate number of those he'd come to know on Death Row were minorities, poor and uneducated—men whose courses he felt had been set by their heritage. I listened as he shared a philosophy he'd arrived at during the past eleven years. Involvement in drugs, he readily admitted, had been his downfall. They were, he feared, going to be the ruin of the nation unless drastic measures were taken. "The thing that holds everything together is family," he said. "I believe that with all my heart. And I see that being torn apart. I've watched what's on television, what the kids today are seeing, and it's all about hate and violence and drugs. Same with the music they're listening to. They see or hear nothing that tells of the importance of family."

And, between telephone calls to his mother and sister and messages delivered by his lawyers, he spoke of his life in prison. "I don't want to go back to Death Row," he said. "I don't want to spend one more day in that lousy cell. People don't understand that a life sentence is worse than death. I'd rather die tonight."

Even in the years that I'd observed the culture of prison life—its boring sameness, its ever-present dangers, its hopelessness—I still found it difficult to grasp a despair so dark and devastating that one would choose death over another day of life. Yet the words I heard from Herrera were not new to me. I'd heard them on numerous occasions, spoken from the very same cell where he sat.

Still, his legal team battled long into the night, well beyond the midnight deadline, urging the courts to reconsider. It was four-thirty in the morning before I finally accompanied him into the Death Chamber.

I watched as he climbed onto the gurney and was strapped down. I watched as a needle was inserted into his left arm. When no suitable vein could be found on his right arm, the second injection was done in the back of his hand. It was not until the tie-down team and the medics had left the room that he looked in my direction, his eyes finally showing the fear that he'd long hidden. "I'm so sorry for the things I said about you," he said. "I judged you wrongly. Thanks for being with me."

I placed my hand on his ankle and nodded. "I'm not going anywhere," I said.

Soon, the witnesses were quietly led into the viewing area and heard his final words: "I am innocent, innocent, innocent," he said without anger. "Make no mistake about this. I owe society nothing. Continue the struggle for human rights, helping those who are innocent. . . . I am an innocent man, and something very wrong is taking place tonight. May God bless you all. . . ."

And with that he turned his head to the warden. "I'm ready," he said.

Ten minutes later—the same short span of time that had elapsed between the two horrible murders he'd been accused of—Leonel Tor-res Herrera, forty-five, was dead.

Was he innocent? Had something very wrong taken place, as he had stated? There is no way I can say for certain. Was he, at the time of his death, the same angry and uneducated man who had first entered prison? I have no reason to believe so. The simple fact that such questions play in my mind to this day is reason enough to seriously ponder their answers—and to deplore the irreversible act that had finally been performed in those early morning hours ten years ago.

There are times, generally in the wee hours of my own restless nights, when the voices of the Leonel Herreras whom I've met still visit me, crying out their innocence. And I am doomed to forever wonder.

Samuel Hawkins, a man who fought the system at every opportunity during the sixteen years he spent on Death Row, was finally executed in February of 1995. Labeled by the media as "the Traveling Rapist," he had been sentenced to death for the rape-murder of a nineteen-year-old pregnant woman. Stabbed more than twenty times, she had been almost decapitated by her attacker. He'd also been found guilty of raping and killing a twelve year-old girl. Authorities believed that Hawkins had been responsible for as many as forty rapes committed in four states.

Having been on Death Row longer than any other inmate, he had made a game of firing lawyers with such regularity that it aided him in achieving three stays of execution. Over the years, we had become well acquainted.

On his first visit to the Death House, he had been unrepentant and cocky, not only bragging of the horrendous crimes for which he'd been convicted, but delighting in describing to me fourteen other rapes he'd committed. His father, he explained, had taught him that the best way to get back at the evils of the white man was to rape his women. He had, he told me, been looking for yet another victim on the night he was arrested. It didn't matter who, he said, so long as she was white.

Sammy Hawkins was a difficult man to like. And it went beyond the arrogance he displayed, the lies he had told about me, even his refusal to discuss any possibility of forgiveness and salvation. He was a man constantly in search of new ways to victimize others.

There had been a time when he'd gotten the addresses of local churches from the local paper and written a series of plaintive letters in which he sought donations to finance his appeal. Unaware that I pastored the Shiro Presbyterian Church, he'd even sent a letter to me. I wrote him a reply, suggesting that he stop the deceptive practice. Hawkins thought it humorous that I'd caught him at his scam.

On his final trip to the Death House, however, he did not speak of past crimes and lies or the racial hatred that had been instilled in him since childhood. From the moment he was escorted in and called me by name, I sensed that he was resigned to his fate. This time, he knew, there was not likely to be a reprieve.

Nor was there. Shortly after midnight, on February 21, Sammy Hawkins was strapped onto the gurney. From behind the horn-rimmed glasses that he insisted on wearing, he looked up at the warden and thanked him for allowing him to speak with family and friends earlier in the evening. Then he turned to me. "I love you, chaplain," he said. "You're a great guy."

He had no final words to the witnesses gathered nearby. At 12:21 A.M. he was pronounced dead.

The execution of Sammy Hawkins stayed with me. But for a different reason. Though I had attempted to put all things past aside and offer him whatever comfort I could, the honest truth was that I felt far less remorse than I should have at his passing. He was, by any definition, a bad person who had filled his life with bad deeds. The pain he had inflicted on so many people defied description and would forever remain.

Dominique Malon had traveled all the way from France to visit and befriend Hawkins in his final hours, "He is not a monster," she had told members of the press shortly before his execution. "He's a human being."

All I had been able to see was the monster. And that troubled me greatly.

TEN

David Ruiz was only twenty-nine, a small, sour-faced man who had spent his life robbing, stealing, and living behind bars, when he suddenly became a bigger-than-life legend. He'd done four stretches in reform school before ending his formal education in the seventh grade, then as an adult had spent more time in prison than on the streets. He'd first been convicted of armed robbery in 1960 and served eight years before being paroled. He'd not been out a year when he returned, convicted of two additional counts of robbery and assault. He was also wanted for questioning about a murder in Ohio, where he'd spent his brief seven months of freedom between prison terms. While incarcerated, he'd been placed in solitary confinement on fifteen occasions, most of which occurred when guards found him in possession of handmade weapons. By his own admission he'd stabbed "three or four" fellow inmates. Once he'd even slashed his wrists while in solitary—little more than a grandstand play to get himself out of isolation and into the more comfortable surroundings of the prison hospital.

Hardly the resumé of a hero. Yet in the minds of many he became just that; the diminutive David who rose up to slay Goliath. With a handwritten document, printed in ballpoint ink on an ordinary piece of onionskin paper—prison legend has it that his original draft was actually written on toilet tissue—he launched a legal campaign that would make prison-reform history. His lawsuit—*Ruiz vs. Estelle*—would, over a period that stretched from the early seventies into the late eighties, cost the taxpayers of Texas several billion dollars and bring about wholesale changes in the manner in which things were run.

There are those—myself included—convinced that David Ruiz in-itiated a downfall in the prison system that is still being felt today. The crime he committed against the system was, many will argue, far worse than any for which he stood before a judge and jury.

It began as a criticism of the treatment he'd received while placed in administrative segregation. The isolation, the small ration of food, and the confining space of the cell, he wrote in his lawsuit, amounted to unconstitutional and inhumane punishment that was in violation of the U.S. Civil Rights Act.

That's what got the litigious ball rolling. And it didn't take long for it to pick up speed. Ruiz's petition found its way to the chambers of Eastern District Court judge William Wayne Justice. Colorful and controversial, the federal judge not only took Ruiz's complaint seri-ously but attached seven others he'd received from writ-writing in-mates who had petitioned his court to look into perceived shortcomings of the Texas Department of Corrections.

Long praised by many for his pro–civil rights stance, Justice had an impressive track record for making the human condition better. In 1970 he had set forth the order for desegregation of public schools in the state. A few years later he ruled that Texas schools should provide free education for the children of undocumented aliens. The son of a lawyer and friend of such influential political stars as Lyndon Johnson and Ralph Yarbrough, Justice curried little favor with the state's con-servatives, who were routinely critical of his decisions. Justice made his decisions without the support of the majority in Texas, and some charged that his motivation was to gain the applause of the Eastern liberal establishment, with which, they claimed, he was enamored.

He seemed to thrive on the controversy he created.

And now, he determined, the time had come for a wholesale reform of the prison system that had long been judged the safest, most eco-nomic, and best run in the United States. He summoned the U.S.

Department of Justice to speak for the state and appointed a number of the nation's best-known prison litigation attorneys to represent the inmates in a class-action suit. He not only wished them to conduct fact-finding missions on the claims by those who had filed suit but also wanted a wholesale evaluation of the prison system.

In time, he would hear the angry testimony of 349 inmate witnesses.

And, even before the lengthy trial took place, he had begun issuing orders that systematically disempowered those charged with keeping order inside Texas prisons.

In a 248-page opinion, the judge faulted everything from over-crowded conditions to the quality of meals, work demands, and crea-ture comforts. To a layman, much of it seemed ridiculous. When Justice decreed that the dayroom space where inmates gathered to watch television in the older Walls and Darrington Units did not offer enough square footage per prisoner, the only solution, since expansion was impossible, was to provide each individual cell with a small tele-vision as well as headphones for every inmate. That seemingly simple demand created a domino effect of expense and manpower. In addition to the cost of thousands of new television sets, a workforce became necessary to keep them repaired so that inmates' favorite soap operas and game shows were not missed.

No longer would those placed in solitary confinement be served sandwiches in a brown bag. Instead, they were to receive the same meal that other prisoners ate in the dining room. Correctional officers delivering them were provided with thermometers with which to mea-sure their heat before they were served. If food did not meet the spe-cific temperature requirements, it had to be returned to the kitchen and reheated.

Prior to Judge Justice's intervention, our medical staff was primarily composed of inmates—doctors and nurses who had come to prison with extensive experience. Except on those rare occasions when the need arose for an outside specialist, it had been inmates caring for inmates, and I routinely saw lives saved, wounds mended, illnesses properly diagnosed and cured. And, most important, there was trust between patients and caregivers. I would have had no reservation whatsoever in allowing prison doctors to care for my own family. Even those who lacked a medical degree often reached a level of expertise that would have been the envy of hospitals and clinics throughout the country. I recall one who, despite little outside-world training, became so proficient that when his parole date neared, we contacted a California doctor who was in search of an office assistant and recommended that he hire the inmate. Paroled to California, he took and easily passed a required exam and immediately went to work as a surgical assistant.

Under the new guidelines, however, taxpayers were called on to pay salaries for licensed doctors and registered nurses. In all too many instances what we got were practitioners who made little attempt to hide their dislike for the work or their patients. The trust that had formed between the hospital staffs and the inmates eroded dramatically and quickly.

After hearing the complaint of an asthmatic inmate that he was not allowed to keep an inhaler in his cell, the judge quickly issued a dictate to change the procedure, despite argument from officials that the rule had a logical purpose. His decision remained in place even after a bomb, fashioned from one of the plastic asthma inhalers, was exploded in one of the cell blocks.

After several prisoners complained that the uniforms they were issued were not as white as they once were, the use of more laundry detergent was ordered.

Programs that had been in place for years went by the wayside.

In special situations, "medical reprieves" were given to terminal patients who had shown no indication that they would be a risk if released. If it was clear that an inmate was dying and had a place in the free world to live, a doctor willing to provide whatever care necessary, and a hospital that would see to his needs, a reprieve could be granted.

I remember an inmate named Charles Duckworth, dying of cancer, who was allowed the leave. His family arrived from Dallas to pick him up, and we rolled him out the front door of the prison in a wheelchair. Weak but smiling, he managed to get into the backseat of the car and wave happily as he was driven away. Twenty-eight miles up the highway, he died. But not in prison.

Bill Shipman, the patient who had stood over his fellow inmate, holding that small reading light so that his friend might not die in the dark he so feared, was another who ultimately received a medical reprieve. He went home to a small town in West Texas, visited with his family, then checked into a motel, where he was found dead the following day. I can only imagine how precious those final hours of freedom were to him, breathing the air of his heartland, seeing the smiles of loved ones, touching them for the first time in years. And, perhaps most important, dying a free man. That, to me, was a shining example of humanity and civil rights.

Yet such opportunities were eliminated by the Ruiz ruling. No aspect of prison life went untouched.

The only way the overcrowding issue could be handled was for the system to simply refuse for a time to accept new prisoners while groundbreaking for additional facilities got underway. The Catch-22 to that solution quickly surfaced when the prison system was ordered to pay millions to the suddenly overcrowded county jails where convicted felons remained in lieu of being transferred to prison. Another method by which officials attempted to keep the inmate population under control was to hand out paroles in record numbers. The joke that made the rounds was that an incoming prisoner entered the front door and was processed into the system, handed his parole papers, and ushered out the back door.

When it was ruled that no inmate should be allowed access to confidential material related to another prisoner, the positions of clerks were eliminated. Blue McComb, my trusted helper who had also become my friend, was sent back to his cell, disappointed and angry, describing the new reforms in terms that I prefer to spare you.

I also received notification that my chapel was in violation of a number of newly arrived orders. If it were to remain open, a second door—an "emergency egress," the order called it—would have to be installed. I could allow no more than 288 inmates at any service. Any more than that, I was informed, created a health hazard. A federal marshal appeared in my office one day to deliver a paper stating that I was in contempt of a federal court order since no fire-hose reel had been installed in the chapel. There was nothing in the order stating that we had to have a fire hose; we just had to have a reel for one.

The most absurd, order however, had to do with the summer temperatures. Since the chapel was not air-conditioned, an edict had been issued that if the temperature and humidity reached a certain level, no services could be held. Thus, I had to purchase a thermometer and barometer.

Since I'd begun conducting services inside The Walls, I had never once heard a complaint about the heat. Most of those in my congregation had spent the day outside, working in the fields, or in the non-air-conditioned shops, yet had eagerly attended church services. Which, I wanted badly to remind the judge and his political allies, was done on a voluntary basis. Instead, I kept my mouth shut, read my thermometer, and on several occasions during the heat of the long Texas summers had to cancel services and choir practices.

Even those inmates who relished the idea of the system being slapped down by court orders soon came to the realization that for every benefit they were gaining, several others were being lost.

The most dramatic change prompted by Judge Justice's ruling had to do with the manner in which discipline had been kept in the prison system for decades. Traditionally, those inmates who had demonstrated leadership abilities and were trusted by the administration were assigned the role of building tenders. Within the cell blocks where they resided, they were viewed in much the same manner as a squad leader in an army barrack. If problems arose, they solved them. And, yes, there were times when it was neither pretty nor subtle, but they were the men who saw to it that the convicts under their watch lived as close to a democratic lifestyle as prison would allow.

In exchange, the building tender enjoyed special privileges. The door to his cell was never locked. He was allowed free rein, day and night. He had the ear of prison officials. And, with the help of a small group of fellow inmates whom he trusted, he had the unspoken okay to address problems in the manner he felt suited the situation.

On occasion I was called to the hospital when a badly beaten inmate was brought in from one of the other units. His jaw might be broken, teeth missing, ribs cracked—all in the name of the drastic discipline a building tender had deemed necessary. Almost without exception I would eventually learn that the injured inmate had sexually assaulted a younger prisoner, tried to kill a cell mate, thrown urine or feces on a passing guard, or stolen from others.

In my early days with the prison, I was admittedly concerned that such practices drew no reaction from the guards, the majors, or even the warden. Heads turned away, and eyes shut tightly. It was, I would learn, simply judged as the way by which order was kept in a disorderly society populated by men who recognized justice only at its most basic level. And, brutal though it might have been at times, it worked.

It was an effective way of assuring that the Texas prisons were as nonviolent as possible. Fewer prisoners died at the hands of fellow inmates than in any prison in the country. Riots did not occur. Because attendance was mandatory, classrooms were filled with prisoners working toward their GED or taking vocational and college-level courses. Old-timers insisted that discipline and calm were the product of the fear factor instituted by those who walked the halls of the cell blocks. In the idiom of the day, the building tenders—street-smart and themselves no strangers to violence—kept the lid on. But, in the wake of Ruiz vs. Estelle, the situation changed drastically.

Judge Justice ruled the building-tender concept unconstitutional and demanded that it immediately end and that an additional five hundred prison guards be hired to deal with whatever problems occurred.

If one only read news reports of the laundry list of prison shortcomings outlined in the Ruiz lawsuit or heard just the observations of the parade of inmate witnesses, one formed an image of the building tenders as a group of hard-core thugs given permission to deal out whatever punishment they deemed fitting. I find it troubling to this day that the good done by these men was never recognized. The truth was that building tenders were subject to their own loss of status and privilege if officials determined that they had taken unfair advantage of the authority given them.

The majority of the building tenders I became acquainted with attended chapel services regularly and showed a genuine interest in the well-being of those they were assigned to look after. They were, within their unique social environment, the leaders, more respected than feared. Their primary concern, it seemed to me, was to see that the more troublesome prisoners did not harm others.

Routinely, they would come to me for help in solving problems that they saw developing on their cell blocks. They would tell me of a convict who had begun "messing" with some of the younger inmates. "He's looking to make somebody his punk," I would be told. "Maybe you can talk to him and get him straightened out. If you can't, we will."

If an inmate became extremely depressed and was feared to be suicidal, word got to me quickly. On my visits into the yard, tenders would seek me out and say, "Over at my place I've got a kid in Cell Twenty-six who was crying all last night." That would be my signal to pay the prisoner a visit. Such alerts were triggered by any number of problems: receipt of a "Dear John" letter from a girlfriend or divorce papers from a wife, a death in the family, or maybe just the cold terror that accompanied the first realization by an inmate that he was destined to spend years, perhaps the remainder of his life, in a cell. It was generally when the tender had no explanation for a prisoner's sudden display of grief and anxiety that he was most anxious to contact me.

Many suicides, I'm convinced, were averted by alert and caring building tenders.

Which is to say that I found their input invaluable and their presence a benefit to my role as chaplain. I came to depend on their knowledge and insight.

On one occasion I'd received word that the son of a convict had died of a heart attack, and I was faced with the duty of passing along the bad news. It was a building tender who alerted me to the fact that the father also had serious heart problems, and who suggested that I have one of the prison nurses standing by when I told him of his son's death. In fact, the man did suffer a heart attack in my office that afternoon as I spoke with him. Only the presence of a nurse and a stretcher, waiting in the hallway outside my office, saved his life.

One morning, a BT (building tender) came to my office to express concern for an inmate who had received a letter about a death in his family. The youngster, new to prison, had been hysterical since receiving the news, crying, cursing, and threatening to end his own life. I phoned the hospital immediately, suggesting that a sedative might be in order, then asked that the inmate be sent to my office. Even when he arrived, he was still so upset that he couldn't compose himself enough to tell me who had died. Finally, I asked if there was someone I could call, and he gave me the number of his wife, who lived on their small West Texas ranch.

It was only after speaking to her that I learned it had been the inmate's favorite horse that had died.

Still, I was grateful that I'd been alerted. In such situations, those keeping watch had learned to take no chances.

It was a building tender who, early in my tenure at The Walls, had come to me with the suggestion that I cancel a Sunday chapel service because he'd heard that an angered inmate, who regularly sat in the front row during services, had told several of his fellow prisoners that he planned to kill me. The man had decided that I was the cause of all the problems he'd encountered since his arrival.

When word of the BT's warning reached the administrative offices, it was strongly suggested that I either cancel the service or conduct it under the watchful eye of a small army of guards stationed along the walls. I opted for neither solution. On that Sunday, however, there were more building tenders in the chapel than I'd ever before seen. The service went off without a hitch.

With the disappearance of the building tenders, critical pipelines ceased to function. And, I felt, my ministry suffered greatly.

In their absence a new level of anger soon arose within the prison community. So many inmates were stealing silverware from the dining halls and fashioning it into weapons that it became necessary to spend thousands of dollars on the purchase of disposable plastic utensils. The ceramic commodes in cells were vandalized so routinely that a half-million dollars were spent replacing them with stainless-steel facilities. Metal detectors were installed in the hallways of each cell block to ferret out weapons suddenly being carried by a large portion of the population. In 1984 and 1985, a horrifying fifty-two inmate-on-inmate murders occurred, and there were seven hundred stabbings. Rapes escalated. The number of suicides increased. Shakedowns of cells turned up hundreds of weapons. Prison gangs were formed and declared war—whites against blacks, blacks against Hispanics.

Among the victims of the "reform" was a twenty-eight-year-old first-time offender named Charles Marx. He was serving the first day of a five-year sentence when four gang members approached him in the dayroom and demanded that he make the choice between paying them for "protection" or becoming their sexual servant. When Marx responded that he wished only to quietly do his time and get back home, he was beaten and stomped by the steel-toed shoes worn by the gang members. He was unconscious by the time a guard reached him. Thirty-one days later he died from the head wounds he'd suffered during the beating.

A good BT might have prevented the attack.

The inmates who caused his death were placed in solitary to await their trial and served their hot meals daily.

On another occasion I was called over to the East Building after an inmate had fallen to his death from the third-floor landing. His body had landed on the concrete floor between two tables where men sat playing dominoes. No one, it seemed, had seen him fall. No one, in fact, had even left the game to see if he might still be alive. In time, prisoners would shrug and suggest that it was an infamous "ghost" that was said to haunt the building that was responsible for the man's death. Though it will never be proven, he was pushed—something that would never have happened in the days of the building tenders.

Refusal to report to work or attend classes was met with frustrated shrugs by officials who knew full well that with nothing to burn off excess energies and frustrations, inmates would become increasingly unruly.

To the majority of inmates I'd come to know, work was their salvation, a daily escape from the drudgery and boredom of their cells. For those who had gained trustee status, it even promised a few hours outside the prison walls. For years, supervised prison work crews had been dispatched to city parks to mow, prune trees, and do general maintenance. Under the new order, those duties were returned to Huntsville city employees while the inmates remained inside, watching *Days of Our Lives*.

For years, the demands of work and education had served as an incentive to the prisoners. Work hard and keep your nose clean and you could count on being elevated to a better job, maybe trustee status. Fulfill the academic requirements set forth, and it would earn you not only "good time" that shortened your prison term but also a kind word to the parole board. Many of those benefits disappeared, all in the name of civil rights.

In time, it seemed, the inmates had more rights than their keepers. And there were those who quickly took full advantage.

In a misguided effort to make prison life better, the courts had created a brand of chaos for which there was no solution. I saw prison officials' frustration grow, and watched guards become so fearful for their own well-being that they dreaded reporting to work. With spirits broken, control stolen away, and fear reigning, many walked away.

And it was not only those charged with maintaining order who were affected. Most of the inmates viewed the wholesale changes with disdain. A growing despair settled over the entire Texas prison system that defied description.

What most puzzled me throughout the legal process was the fact that those making the rulings had absolutely no firsthand knowledge of the daily problems of running a prison. The best-intentioned politicians and lawmakers simply do not understand the unique social structure that exists behind the bars and brick walls. To my knowledge, Judge Justice, throughout the years of litigation he directed, never once set foot inside the prison system he was so determined to criticize.

Had he done so, he would have seen that prison life bears little resemblance to free society. Certain civil rights are, out of necessity, forfeited when one is convicted of rape, murder, and assault. While, granted, violence wanders our nation's streets, it pales in comparison to that along a cell block that houses angry and hopeless men already proven to be threats to others. To expect self-motivation and a new attitude triggered by a few more square feet of elbow room is, in most cases, an exercise in pure fantasy. Throughout my tenure at The Walls, I searched desperately for the good in all men. In truth, I daily encountered convicts always eager to take a mile if given an inch and constantly devising new ways to show their contempt for the penal system and those assigned to run it. Such was the truth of prison life.

I became convinced that in a world designed for punishment, any real attempt at democracy is doomed to failure. Certainly, I encountered good men in prison, inmates genuinely remorseful for past behavior and determined to quietly serve their time and rebuild their lives. But without exception they had resigned themselves to the rigid rules and regulations that not only determined their daily behavior but helped insure their safety.

Yet experts assigned by politicians and lawmakers to judge Texas's prison system lashed out against virtually everything that had once made it a model. The demand that prisoners work and attend school, said one, was "the best example of slavery remaining in the country." The respect shown by inmates toward the staff was, suggested another, nothing more than a by-product of their being "completely cowed by autocratic rules and regulations."

How, I found myself wondering, could these so-called experts expect perfection in a world so imperfect? How did they expect that discipline could be maintained without reward and punishment? How could order be fashioned from the disorder they were orchestrating?

Such are the questions I still ask, since many of the problems created by habitual criminals and misguided federal courts remain to this day.

I finally had the opportunity to meet Ruiz. He'd once again threatened the lives of several inmates at the unit which he was assigned and had been moved to The Walls and placed in administrative segregation. One morning, as I was making my rounds in the hospital, I received word that he wanted to see me. My first thought upon hearing the news was neither charitable nor Christian. In the landslide of new rulings was one that said the response time of prison chaplains to the requests of inmates in administrative segregation had to be immediate.

Ruiz, I assumed, was testing me.

Normally, when visiting isolated prisoners, I made it a point to take a few stamps and envelopes along. To my meeting with Ruiz, I went empty-handed.

On the third floor of Four Building, I found him waiting at the bars of his cell. "Do you know who I am?" he immediately asked. And, despite my acknowledgement, he made a point of telling me that he was responsible for all of the changes that were occurring in the prison system. For a half hour he alternately boasted of his accomplishments and of the publicity that they had generated and criticized the treatment he'd received since his arrival at The Walls. Had I heard, he asked, of the latest lawsuit a fellow solitary-confinement inmate had filed? The warden was being sued by a prisoner who had decided that his scrambled eggs hadn't been cooked to his liking. As Ruiz laughed, I wondered what I was doing there.

"You know," he finally said, "that by law you aren't allowed to tell the warden anything we've talked about."

"David," I responded, "I can't think of anything you've said that the warden might be remotely interested in." His smile quickly disappeared.

It was a few weeks later when I received a request that he be allowed to make a phone call. Normally, it would have been denied since he'd only been at The Walls for a short period of time, but almost as quickly as I submitted the request to the administrative office, it was okayed. There was little doubt that Ruiz, now viewed by prison officials as a political time bomb, was being granted special favors.

I notified security and asked that they bring him to my office. When the guard who had escorted him asked if I wished him to stay with the prisoner, I assured him that it would not be necessary. As he walked into the foyer, closing my door behind him, David smiled and nodded. "That's good," he said. "I have a right to make a private call, you know."

"No," I replied, "the rules say that I'm to place your call—which will last a maximum of five minutes—then remain here with you while you talk. The rules also state that your conversation is to be in English."

For one so keen on regulations, Ruiz was obviously selective. After I'd dialed the number he'd given me and reached the family member he wished to speak to, I handed him the phone and listened as he immediately began speaking in Spanish.

Over the years I'd developed a procedure whereby I would count down the time for a caller, holding up my fingers to indicate how many minutes remained. Then, when the five minutes had elapsed, I would hold up an index card on which I'd written "time's up." In an attempt at leniency I made a habit of giving the inmate an extra thirty seconds or minute so that the conversation would not end abruptly. Ruiz continued talking at least five minutes past his deadline. More testing.

Beneath my desk was an emergency button, seldom used, that I could push to alert the guard standing outside my office if there was a problem. It had been installed years earlier after an incident that I'd not been insightful enough to anticipate.

On that day, I'd had a young inmate brought to my office so that I might break the news to him that there had been a death in his family. I can't even guess how many times I was the messenger of such bad news, but the reaction was generally predictable. There would be shock and tears and, ultimately, a quiet conversation about the lost loved one. On this particular occasion, however, the prisoner had responded with a sudden, violent rage. Jumping from his chair, he began knocking things from my desk and bookshelves. He started beating his head against the wall, then repeatedly hit himself with a metal nameplate he'd grabbed from my desk. My office was bloody and in disarray before guards entered and subdued him.

That's when it had been decided that an alarm button would provide a safeguard I'd never anticipated needing. And, moments before Ruiz finally ended his call, I was contemplating reaching beneath the desk.

Handing the receiver to me, he again smiled, as if awaiting some response. I said nothing.

"Can we visit for a while?" he asked.

"David," I said, "I have several other calls lined up for inmates. Now's not a good time." He only shrugged. The test was over.

Today, almost three decades after the longest-running civil suit in American history began, David Ruiz, now fifty-nine, is back in prison. Paroled in the early eighties, he enjoyed just over a year of freedom before being convicted of yet another armed robbery, judged a habitual criminal, and sentenced to life.

He now resides in a prison system that has expanded to seven times the number of facilities that existed when he set the reform process in motion. The prisoner-guard ratio is now six-to-one. In fact, today there are more prison guards than there were inmates when the lawsuit was initially filed. With 146,000 inmates, crowding remains a serious problem. Discouraged criminologists who compare the prison community of three decades ago to that of the present say that today's inmates are younger, angrier, and far more violent than their predecessors.

And so, the question is begged: what has really been accomplished?

Recently, the U.S. Fifth Circuit Court of Appeals made a dramatic move toward reversing Judge Justice's ruling and finally returning to Texas the control of its prisons. To the surprise of many, the judge, now in his eighties, deemed the system "vastly improved" and relinquished much of the federal control. In his written opinion, however, it was clear that he did so reluctantly. Some aspects of the system, he insisted, still demanded federal overseeing. He wrote that constitutional violations continued in the areas of administrative segregation, the safety of inmates threatened by assault and abuse, and excessive use of force by correctional officers. He criticized the practice of subjecting mentally ill inmates to extended stays in solitary confinement and wrote that prisoners still faced the threat of physical and sexual abuse from other inmates. And he was critical of the threat of force by guards as a method of control.

Even in those areas where he returned control to the state, he did so begrudgingly. "While the court remains deeply disturbed by the current subpar level of medical treatment being provided, a system-wide deliberate indifference to health needs has not been shown to exist," he wrote.

After three decades, he continues to demand perfection in the most imperfect of worlds.

ELEVEN

One of Judge Justice's demands, made in the name of inmate safety, was that a fire escape be installed outside The Walls's five-story prison hospital building. The spiraling stairway was built and never used. Until one morning in the mid-eighties.

For many reasons, Sunday was my favorite day at the prison. It was my routine to get up early and visit with several of the older inmates who worked in the dining room. Then there would be choir practice and services in the morning, and in the afternoon I would wander through the exercise yard and the visitors' room, talking with inmates and meeting members of their families. On the Sabbath, it seemed, a more relaxed atmosphere settled over the place. The steady stream of fresh-scrubbed faces arriving from the free world, rest from the regimentation of work schedules, and the gentle wafting of hymns from the chapel brought prison as close to Main Street U.S.A. as it was ever going to get.

Spirits seemed lifted, and a tangible warmth spread throughout The Walls.

On the particular Sunday morning that remains with me above all others, I was walking from my office toward the dining room when an inmate, well into his seventies, stopped his sweeping near the exercise area and waved. "See you in church," he yelled out as I passed.

He was among my regulars, a gentle man whose crimes had been rooted in his addiction to alcohol. A string of DWI offenses, one of which resulted in a tragic accident, had initially landed him in prison. When I first met him, he had been returned for parole violation. And now he was hoping that the Board of Pardons and Parole would see fit to allow him another chance. Just the Wednesday before, he had stood at the close of evening chapel services to ask for prayers that his parole would soon be granted.

I had waved to him that Sunday morning as I walked to breakfast, confident that I would not be seeing him much longer. I had a good feeling that his prayers would soon be answered. A model prisoner, he had religiously attended Alcoholic Anonymous meetings in an effort to defeat the addiction that had plagued his life.

And then, suddenly, he was dead.

I had just walked onto the steps leading to the dining hall when I heard a female guard scream. She was running toward the corner of the hospital building where the man who had minutes earlier told me he would soon see me in church lay.

He had climbed to the top of the fire escape and jumped. As he neared the ground, his head struck the edge of a brick-rimmed flower garden, killing him instantly. The guard reached him before I did and knelt, cradling him in her arms, tears streaming down her face.

"I didn't notice him until he was almost to the top," she said. "He just stepped off into space." Blood from the inmate's crushed skull was staining her uniform, yet she continued to hold him as doctors arrived from inside the hospital. "He was my favorite," she cried, her voice strained and grief-stricken.

Finally, she was gently pulled away, and the inmate's lifeless body was covered. Soon a justice of the peace and the coroner arrived and, after examining the body and hearing the story told by the guard, declared the death a suicide.

The promise of a glorious Sunday had disappeared. Guards ordered inmates to clear the yard and return to their cells, announcing that there would be a lockdown for the remainder of the day. I canceled choir practice and morning services and turned my attention to the grim task of notifying the next of kin.

At my desk I sat for some time, staring at the file that would tell me how to contact his wife. Though I'd made similar calls more often than I liked to remember, it was a responsibility that always caused my stomach to knot.

I felt the tightening as I dialed a number in California. It grew worse when a lilting voice, filled with warmth and energy, answered.

Early in my ministry I had determined that bad news was best delivered straightforwardly. Despite all wishes to somehow deflect pain and soften the blow, there is really no way to accomplish such a goal.

"Ma'am," I said, "my name is Chaplain Carroll Pickett. I'm calling from the Huntsville prison."

There was only a faint hint of surprise in her response. "Oh, yes, I know who you are," she said. "My husband has often mentioned you in his letters." I felt as if she had somehow expected my call.

I told her what had happened.

"He can't be dead," she finally said, her voice suddenly weakened by shock. "I've just been packing a suitcase. I was coming to Texas to get him tomorrow. I thought that was why you were calling."

I wasn't sure what she was talking about.

"His parole was granted two weeks ago," she explained. "I got the papers in the mail yesterday." She was now crying. "Didn't anybody tell him? Didn't he know he was coming home? This can't be. I've been telling all our friends that he would be here soon."

I felt my body go numb. On the other end of the line I heard only sobs. And finally, a faint, heartbreaking observation: "It's so unfair," she whispered.

Indeed, it was. The papers she had received, I later learned, had been mailed out on that same Wednesday evening he'd asked members of the chapel congregation to pray that his parole would be granted.

How had such vital information—in retrospect, literally a matter of life and death—been allowed to slip through some bureaucratic crack? How easily it could have been to turn suicidal despair into hope and optimism if only a timely message had been delivered.

No anger is more frustrating than that for which there is no specific target. There had been, I was certain, no malicious effort to keep the parole board's decision secret. No one individual was to blame for the unnecessary death. It was "the system"—the ever-growing piles of paperwork, rules too numerous for anyone to even know them all, the often illogical pecking order of responsibility, demands for trivialities like eggs scrambled to satisfaction—that had failed.

I hung up the phone and sat looking out the window. It was several minutes before I could get to my feet. Walking back into the morning sun, I could feel no warmth as I made my way toward the hospital. Two guards stood near the cloth-covered body, awaiting the arrival of an ambulance that had been summoned.

Kneeling beside the dead inmate, I said a brief prayer. Then, to no one in particular, I echoed the observation of a woman who, until minutes earlier, had looked forward to seeing her husband return home. "This just isn't fair," I said.

Overhearing my comment, the guards silently nodded their agreement.

Much of society, it seems, holds tightly to the once-a-convict-always-a-convict myth. And while I would be the first to agree that the great majority of those behind bars are there for good reason, and that many of them should never return to the free world, there were men I met whose crimes did not match their punishment. And there were those who I felt had no business in prison; and others who, while guilty of criminal behavior, were remorseful and had evolved into responsible human beings deserving of second chances.

I've often been asked what percentage of those I visited in the Death House were genuinely sorry for the crime they committed.

Though I have no science to back my claim, I'd estimate that 60 percent demonstrated genuine remorse. Quite often, the man I met in the final hours of his life was in no way the same person who, in some impulsive and mindless moment in his teen years, had committed a murder. Throughout The Walls, populated by inmates serving sentences that would not end in executions, the percentage of the remorseful and rehabilitated was considerably higher.

For every dark soul I encountered, there was someone who gathered the pieces of his shattered life and moved forward. They were examples of restorative justice that worked.

My longtime clerk Blue was nearing parole after twenty years in prison when he confided his future plans to me. A man who had shown a voracious appetite for learning throughout his incarceration, he wished to add a master's degree to his academic portfolio. In an effort to somehow thank him for the education he had provided me—I learned far more from him than he ever did from me during our years together—I began exploring any scholarship possibilities that might exist for an ex-convict. I wasn't surprised to find that there were none. Finally, however, I did learn of a grant offered by the University of Texas in Austin that would provide twelve thousand dollars annually to assist an individual who was "socially disabled." Not even aware of the defining boundaries of such an obscure grant, I suggested he apply. And he received it.

Back in the free world, he flourished. He got his master's, then a good job with an electronics company. He married. On occasional trips to Austin, I would visit him, recalling old times and getting updates on the progress he was making in his new life.

Then, as the years passed, time and pressing responsibilities swallowed both of us up. Though I thought of Blue often, I heard from him less frequently. Time, unfortunately, does that even to the best of friendships. Then, one spring morning in 1992, I opened a letter that had been postmarked in a small Montana fishing village.

Blue was there, on the first vacation he'd ever taken, trekking through the Cabinet Mountains. He wrote:

What am I doing here? Hunting black bear. But all this big critter I've been tracking for the past few days is doing is taking me higher and higher into the mountains—each day bringing me closer to your God than I've ever been before. Which, as I recall, is a feat you so patiently sought to achieve so many years ago.

Did you fail? No, not by any means, because in working for you and close to you I learned much-needed lessons in life, lessons that continue to allow me to function in society. Your example and patience taught me to accept and overcome disappointment and failure not only in myself but in others. You probably didn't even realize it, but you taught me how to succeed. And for that I will forever be thankful.

I reread his eloquent words several times before folding the letter and replacing it in its envelope. And felt better than I had in a long time.

Al, another of my clerks, had been a highly successful Dallas businessman, leasing fire trucks, ambulances, and hearses, before he was convicted of murdering his wife. Suspecting that she was having an affair, he had returned home one day and confronted her. Panicked, she burst into the front yard and began running down the street. She was knocking on a neighbor's door when Al caught up to her and shot her.

When assigned to work for me, he made it clear that he was not pleased with the job. When I explained that he had no choice, he'd only shrugged. "I'm stuck with you, and you're stuck with me, huh?"

"That's about the size of it."

Like Blue before him, he made it clear that he would not be attending chapel services. His reasoning, however, was different. "It only makes me feel more guilty about what I did," he explained.

In time, he became a trustee and was assigned to drive one of the prison trucks. Making deliveries to other units, he spent a great amount of time on the open road, unsupervised. And with the help of a supportive brother back in Dallas, he managed to keep his leasing company in operation. Eventually, he even found his way to the chapel.

When the time finally approached for his parole, he explained that he had been studying real estate and planned to go into the field upon his release. Would I, he asked, consider writing a letter of recommendation to the licensing board?

I did so with neither hesitation nor reservation.

Today he is again successful, this time in commercial real estate. I hear from him regularly. His brother continues to operate the leasing company, and for years it wasn't unusual for me to look out the window and see an ambulance or hearse in my driveway. When making a delivery to some nearby destination, he would stop by to assure me that my old clerk was doing well and brag of his brother's post-prison accomplishments. Whatever the case, it's always good to see him.

When I first agreed to go to work for the prison, I was repeatedly warned against getting too personally involved with the inmates. Trust, I was told, would only be exploited. Friendships were impossible. I wondered how anyone could expect a minister to abide by such guidelines. Considering myself a reasonably good judge of character, I chose to ignore the warnings.

For many inmates, I soon learned, a friend was the most treasured possession.

When Joseph Robicheaux, a career welder with a thick Cajun accent, first came to my office, he was the loneliest man I'd ever encountered. Since I made it a point never to read an inmate's jacket, I never knew what crime had led him to The Walls. He never discussed it. He had no family on the outside and stayed to himself inside. Visiting my office one morning, he explained that he knew nothing about the church or Christianity. "Can I try it?" he asked. He was a man searching, desperately reaching out for any helping hand.

It was only a few days after his visit that I received a letter from a woman who was the director of nurses at a hospital in nearby Livingston. As many before her had done, she asked if I could recommend an inmate who might benefit from an occasional letter or card. I replied, giving her Joseph's name and mailing address.

In time they began to correspond. Then she began driving to Huntsville on Sundays to visit. And when he was paroled, she was waiting for him as he stepped back into the free world. Soon, I received an invitation to their wedding.

They were married fifteen years ago. I received a call from them just recently, and they're doing well.

Over the years, I was called on to perform numerous weddings for released inmates. And, sadly, too many funerals. Even those occasions, however, provided a feeling of warmth that is difficult to explain. All I can say is that there is something intimately rewarding in being asked to conduct the funeral of a friend.

Bobby Bell was the inmate who had long ago threatened to kill me on Christmas Eve (for simply threatening to have him removed from choir practice because of his horseplay), then spent years afterwards apologizing. After twenty-three years in prison he was finally paroled, and he enrolled in Texas Tech and earned a degree. As is the case with so many inmates, however, he had returned to the free world infected with hepatitis. As his illness grew worse, he moved to Lewisville to live with his brother. He called me regularly in the final months of his life, and each time his voice sounded weaker. Finally, even talking on the telephone became difficult for him. In the last conversation we had, he could only whisper. "Chaplain," he said, "can you do me one more favor?"

"Whatever you need."

"I'd like for you to do my funeral," he said.

In no way will I ever be able to divine what was going through Roy Villanueva's mind that long-ago day in Houston when he made the fatal mistake of offering an undercover police officer three hundred dollars to kill his wife. I don't know what demons suddenly possessed a man with a master's degree, a good job, and a loving family to plot such a crime. All I know for certain was that it robbed him of ten years of his life. Frankly, it never made a great deal of sense to me. Roy's wife—still very much alive—came to Huntsville regularly to visit him.

The man I first met on the steps of the prison chapel in no way fit the profile of a convict. During the decade when I saw him on an almost daily basis, he was always pleasant, eager to help his fellow inmates, God-fearing, and resigned to the fact that he owed a debt to society. A gifted musician, he served as director of my Hispanic choir for years.

His mother, who visited him almost every Sunday, arranged her trips from Kenedy (where I'd done my apprentice ministry years earlier) so that she might attend church services in my little Shiro church before her afternoon visits with Roy.

When I first went to work for the prison system, there was a rule forbidding any employee to get involved in the parole process. By the time Villanueva became eligible, however, that rule had been relaxed. Feeling strongly that any more time spent in prison would be a waste of Roy's time and of the taxpayers' money, I wrote the board, urging that they consider his release.

Today, on frequent drives to Austin for visits with fast-growing grandchildren, I schedule a stop at a popular roadside restaurant in a small town on the edge of the Texas Hill Country. There, I visit with Roy, the manager. He talks of the local church he's actively involved in, of how he and his wife both sing in the choir.

Several years ago he enrolled in a program for those wishing to do prison volunteer work and today regularly visits convicts who are nearing their parole dates and have no outside support from family or friends. When one of those he's befriended gets out, it is Roy standing outside on the sidewalk, waiting to usher him back into the free world. He helps the parolee shop for new clothes, then takes him out to dinner, where they discuss what lies ahead.

There are many others: the certified public accountant who embezzled $250,000 from the company for which he was working is a good example. Though convicted and sentenced to serve a ten-year sentence, he'd never spent any of the money he'd stolen. Even before being released from The Walls, he had returned it to his former employer, along with the considerable interest it had earned while hidden away in an account he had opened.

Released from prison after two years, he was hired back by the same company that he'd stolen from. He works there to this day.

When Lenny Miller came to prison for committing murder, he was one of twenty-six of the Jewish faith residing at The Walls. The chapel had little to offer in the way for Jews. With Lenny's help, we changed that.

A highly regarded chef before coming to prison, he even helped me with the planning for the first Passover celebration ever conducted in the Chapel of Hope. He detailed what materials were needed for his faith's most important night of the year, including the Seder, during which a lengthy meal and prayer service trace the story of his people's departure from Egypt.

Every Jew in the unit showed up for the ceremony. Clearly Lenny was proud that he'd played a vital role in restoring Jewish services in the prison. I gained a friend for life.

Years later, following his release, he returned to his hometown and opened a deli. And he called me often to tell me of his new life and ask about friends still at The Walls.

One evening, just as I was preparing to leave the office, I answered the phone to hear his voice. "Chaplain," he said, "I've got a problem that I need to come talk with you about."

"Are you in trouble?"

He laughed. "Oh, no, it's nothing like that. It's *good* problem."

The following day he appeared at my office, an attractive woman at his side. "I want to get married," Lenny explained, then introduced me to his fiancé. "She's not Jewish," he explained. According to the doctrine of his religion, no marriage ceremony that involved someone outside the faith could be conducted in a temple or synagogue.

"We'd like for you to do our wedding in your church," he said.

As time continues to distance me from those days spent as a prison chaplain, I find myself more drawn to the warmth of such memories. Along the way I met men good and bad, all scarred by some manner of misdeed, fragile and imperfect, some with remarkable inner strength, others with souls bitter as bile. The long days and nights in the Death House are the ugly ghosts that haunt me. It is those who overcame their mistakes, who rebuilt their lives, responding to the helping hands of strangers, returning to family, friends, loved ones, and their faith, who continue to give me strength.

TWELVE

Even prison has its heroes, men respected not for past evil deeds but for the quality of life they fashioned for themselves within the narrow boundries of their confinement. O'Neal Browning was such a man.

Since the early thirties, the annual Texas Prison Rodeo, staged each Sunday afternoon during the month of October, was eagerly anticipated not only by the prisoners but by thousands of fans who traveled to Huntsville to watch. The competition was open to any inmate with a clean record and the courage to mount a bucking bronco or bull that had no interest whatsoever in being ridden. Others whose behavior had earned them the coveted privilege were bussed to the arena weekly to sit in a well-guarded section and watch and cheer the performers on.

Featuring all the events one might expect at a professional rodeo, including celebrity entertainers—from Western movie star Tom Mix in the early days to country music legends like Loretta Lynn and Willie Nelson in later times—it had a variety of purposes. Not only did it provide fun and diversion for inmates and prison officials, but the money it earned provided a badly needed subsidy for the education and recreation funds. By the time I had begun working for the prison system, the rodeo was earning almost a half-million dollars yearly.

Even the inmate competitors enjoyed the promise of winning small amounts of prize money for their efforts. One of the most popular events, in fact, was that in which a small sack of money, sometimes

several hundred dollars, was laced to the horns of a Brahma bull that
was turned loose in the arena. Then the "Hard Money Scramble"
would begin. The bravest and most agile inmate would grab the money
sack away and claim it for his own. And at each rodeo's grand finale
a panel of judges would award a silver belt buckle to the Best All-
Around Cowboy.

I was amazed to see the collective effort that went into the staging
of the event. Farm inmates were assigned to round up the wildest steers
from the nearby river bottoms and see that they were trucked to the
rodeo pens. Women prisoners housed at the Goree Unit busied themselves sewing the zebra-striped uniforms that the competitors would
wear. Those who worked on the monthly prison newspaper doubled
their journalistic efforts, writing copy and collecting photographs for
the program, which would be printed and sold each Sunday. Others
busied themselves with the leather crafts and artwork that would be
offered for sale alongside the food booths and souvenir stands set up
on the "midway" established along the blocked-off street in front of
The Walls. In all respects, a lighthearted atmosphere prevailed, blur-
ring, for a time, the dismal day-counting routine of prison life.

My job each Sunday afternoon was to join members of the medical
staff in keeping watch over any injuries that might occur. In the event
a rib was busted here or a bone broken there—it was, after all, a
rodeo—I would speak with the injured performer to see if he had
family members watching from the stands. If so, I would locate them
and relay information on his condition as quickly as possible. In the
occasional extreme cases where a contestant was taken to the hospital,
it was my assignment to accompany him so that I might pass word
along to those he wished me to contact.

That's how I came to know the legendary O'Neal Browning.

He had come to prison in 1949 after receiving a life sentence for the
ax murder of his father. A farm boy whose two chief interests in life
were competing in amateur rodeos and hard drinking, he'd been introduced to the cowboy life at age sixteen when he was hired to put

out hay for the stock contractor's animals at the annual Houston Fat Stock Show and Rodeo. "They would bring the stock in several days ahead of time so they would be rested," he recalled. "Then, a couple of days before the show was to open, they'd hire cowboys to ride the bulls and broncs to make sure they were in a properly foul humor before the performances got underway. The pay was five dollars a ride, so I started watching how the cowboys got down on the animals, how they held the rigging and all, then went over and told the foreman I was ready to ride."

He was scared to death, but five dollars was big money in those days. One afternoon, he boasted, he rode twenty bulls.

Soon thereafter he began slipping away from home to compete in jackpot rodeos in nearby communities. And while he was enjoying modest success, he could expect a stern reprimand upon his arrival home. His mother demanded that he give it up, fearful that he might get hurt; his father said that his help was more sorely needed on the family's hard-scrabble farm.

The fears of Browning's mother were realized one long-ago summer evening after her son had slipped away to a nearby ranch to practice roping steers. "As I was roping," he said, "my left thumb caught in the loop. When the steer jerked, it pulled my thumb completely off. It happened so quickly that I didn't even know what had happened— until I saw all the blood."

The ranch owner's wife had hurried him to the hospital for medical attention, and later Browning had returned home, his entire hand heavily bandaged. Only when the bandages were finally removed did his parents learn that he had lost the thumb.

O'Neal would laugh as he told the story. "I was really pretty lucky," he would say. "If it had been my right thumb, I'd never have been able to grip the rigging when I was riding bulls."

By the time I met him, he had established himself as the most celebrated inmate ever to compete in the prison rodeo. In 1950, less than a year after his arrival in Huntsville, he'd won the belt buckle awarded the event's premier performer. In the years to come he would repeat the accomplishment six more times over an incredible span of three decades. Other prisoners would hang on his every word as each year's tryouts neared, listening as he described how to grip the rigging on a bull or maintain balance in the saddle until the last second before lunging forward to bulldog a fast-moving steer. They would talk of how, in 1970, he had suffered a broken leg on a bull ride during the first Sunday but had never missed a performance in the weekends to come.

I'd heard the story from several inmates. On the Sunday following his injury, Browning arrived on crutches, ready to ride. Fellow inmates had helped him onto each animal he was scheduled to ride. And while he would not repeat as the All-Around Cowboy that year, he did manage to finish a respectable sixth in the standings.

It was not, however, the most oft-repeated of the many O'Neal Browning tales.

One October, while watching other competitors as he awaited his next ride, he saw a young cowboy, competing in his first rodeo, thrown from the bull he was attempting to ride. The bull, not satisfied with having rid itself of the rider, began attacking the semiconscious competitor. Browning instinctively jumped from the railing where he was seated and rushed the bull, slapping at it with his hat to draw its attention from the fallen rider.

The bull turned its anger on Browning and chased him to the wall, where it pinned him against the boards with its horns. It never took much persuasion to get O'Neal to take the story from there. "I guess," he would say, his smile revealing a shiny gold tooth, his coffee-colored eyes sparkling, "I was lucky that I didn't weigh any more than I did. That ol' bull's horns took hide off both of my rib cages. If I'd been any bigger around the middle, I'd probably be dead and gone from this place."

Gentle and soft-spoken by the time I became acquainted with him, Browning had, like so many others, encountered great difficulty adjusting to prison life. In his younger days he had been angry, militant, and solitary. He made few friends and little effort to play the role of model prisoner. "I had a big chip on my shoulder," he admitted. "I didn't know any better." Uneducated, he'd dropped out of school after the second grade. "All I ever thought about was getting out," he remembered.

Which, just a year after his arrival, he briefly did. In 1951, while working in the prison cotton gin, he and two fellow inmates made a daring midday escape. While a guard was answering the phone, they had run to a nearby corral and fled on horseback. Three days and two stolen automobiles later, all three were back behind bars.

"That's when I began to realize that I was going to have to make the best of things," he said. He started attending classes and ultimately completed the requirements for a high school diploma. He enrolled in Alcoholics Anonymous classes and began to make friends. And earn a growing respect for his gift as a rodeo cowboy.

In the vernacular of the prison world, O'Neal Browning learned how to do his time.

Eleven years later, he was granted a parole and took a bus to Dallas, where a job had been arranged for him. Yet, after less than a month, Browning had placed a call to prison officials and advised them that there was no way he could continue working for the man to whom he'd been paroled. He asked if he could return to prison.

"I got a lot of kidding when I came back," he remembered. "Some of the guys said the only reason I did was because the rodeo was coming up and I didn't want to miss it. Of course, that wasn't the case. I'd just gotten myself into a situation that looked like it might lead to something bad. So, I chose to come back, hoping that I'd be paroled again later to someone I could get along with."

The following year that hope was realized, and he spent the next twenty-four months in the free world, landscaping, driving a cattle truck, and breaking horses for a rancher near Dallas. On weekends he began to ride in amateur rodeos. Encouraged by his showing, he applied for and received membership in the Rodeo Cowboys Association, earning a permit to compete professionally. In short order he was faring well in some of the circuit's smaller events. Old habits, however, paved the way for yet another downfall.

"I'd started drinking pretty heavily again," he admits. "And in the big city, where there're lots of bars and lots of pretty women, it takes a lot of money to get by. And I never seemed to have enough of it. So, I made the mistake of deciding to get it the easy way."

Arrested and charged with burglary and possession of stolen goods, O'Neal Browning again returned to prison, this time to grow old, with only that one month in October when he would again be a shining star.

It was in the early eighties, as he tried to stretch his incredible winning record into a fourth decade, that a bull named White Lightening got the best of him. Suffering a couple of broken ribs, Browning had managed to get to his feet, tip his hat to the crowd, then wave the medics into the arena before he slumped to his knees. I joined the inmate medical aides as they hurried out to examine him.

Lying in the soft dirt as fifteen thousand people looked on in silence, O'Neal Browning was no longer the supple and steel-muscled cowboy he'd once been. Specks of gray were visible beneath the straw hat he wore. Kneeling near him, I could see the fine web of wrinkles that had begun to form on his once-youthful face. It occurred to me that he should begin to consider retirement, as all star athletes eventually must.

"Are you feeling any pain?" one of the doctors asked.

O'Neal grinned. "Only when I breathe or blink my eyes," he replied.

Later, as he lay in a hospital bed, his damaged ribs tightly bandaged, his eyelids heavy from the painkiller given him, I asked if there was anything he needed. He nodded and began describing an intersection not far from the rodeo grounds. "There'll be a lady standing there, wearing a pretty dress, and I promise she'll knock your eyes out," he whispered in a drowsy voice. "She always waits on that corner to wave and blow me a kiss when the bus goes past on its way back to the unit. I don't want her to worry when she doesn't see me.

"If you could drive over there and tell her I'm okay," he said, "I'd appreciate it."

Finding the location he'd described was not difficult. And, just as he'd said, a pretty woman stood alone at the curb, wearing a newly starched dress and high heels and holding a small handbag at her side. With her other hand she was shading her eyes against the late-afternoon sun.

Her disappointment registered as I explained that O'Neal would not be returning to his unit until later. Then she smiled warmly as I assured her his injuries were not serious. "Can you give him a message?" she asked.

"I'd be happy to."

"Tell him I love him and that I'm doing just fine," she said, then turned away to begin her long trip home.

As I watched her, I found myself wondering at the years of pain and loneliness she had endured, the remarkable patience that no doubt had been tested time and time again. Yet there she had stood, waiting God-only-knows how long for those fleeting seconds when an old prison bus would rumble past, providing her the brief opportunity to demonstrate a kind of love few ever experience.

It occurred to me at that moment that O'Neal Browning had far more to be thankful for than his collection of rodeo trophies.

THIRTEEN

At one time or another there occurs in all of us a disquieting fear of the dark. It first visits in childhood, when imagined noises beneath the bed or the innocent rustle of a window curtain caused by a summer-night breeze creates frightening visions of storybook monsters lurking nearby. For some it is a wariness that lingers well into adulthood, triggered by dire warnings of danger on the ten o'clock news or ill-chosen bedtime reading material. Ultimately it evolves into a concern for the safety of others: our children racing against a midnight curfew along dark streets filled with careless drivers, the knowledge that a loved one must walk across a poorly lit parking lot after a late night at the office. With the arrival of darkness comes the uneasy feeling of vulnerability. Though it is a fact seldom spoken, we agonize over what we do not feel we can control, the unknown hiding in purple shadows. It is in the dark, we've been told all our lives, that bad things happen. Our worst enemies are those we cannot see.

It is particularly true when that enemy is death.

In the Death House there was one small window. When it was open, it allowed in the fresh air. The rays of the sun streaming through it, I believed, helped brighten the dungeonlike atmosphere. Once an inmate settled in for his daylong wait, his attention would inevitably be drawn to the window. Whether talking with relatives, filling out necessary papers, or simply passing the time reading, he would occasionally pause to look toward it, his mood growing darker.

I finally realized why. The small peephole to the outside world offered no comfort, only a grim reminder that time was slipping away. As shadows lengthened and daylight gradually faded to dusk, then dark, I would sense an increasing apprehension that I could only attribute to thoughts of the event that lay ahead. In part, of course, that was the case. But, finally, it occurred to me that the window, through which the inmate could mark the slow approach of the last night of his life, created a level of anxiety that no watch or clock could ever cause.

That it took so long to determine the cause angered me. My job— "seduce the prisoner's emotions, calm him, help in whatever way you can"—had been undermined by my own inability to recognize an elementary problem. Resolving it was easy. I sought and was granted permission to have the panes of the window painted black, hiding away the telltale passage of the day into night.

And thereafter much of the apprehension disappeared. No longer able to monitor the arrival of the dreaded dark, the prisoner was less afraid.

It was only one of the small but important changes we made in procedure.

Early on I realized that the attitude of each inmate brought to Huntsville to be executed was likely to be different. While one might be arrogant and flippant, another would be somber and anxious. Some arrived in a reflective mood. It was important to recognize the state of mind quickly and adapt to it. To do so, it was essential that the guards assigned to the death watch be the most mature on the staff.

At times, I had seen fear cause a cold sweat to appear on the faces of correctional officers who were clearly unsettled by their duty. Adopting a whistling-through-the-graveyard attitude, they would mask their own apprehension with constant joking. In a misguided attempt to lighten the mood, they would only anger the prisoner. On the other hand, if they appeared in a somber mood, it too rubbed off quickly. It was critical that a proper balance be struck, that everyone avoid any attitude or mannerism that might set an inmate off.

It was those prisoners who were mentally retarded who were the most difficult to read. Despite public assurances from the governor's office and the White House that no one lacking the capacity to fully understand what was taking place was ever put to death, I beg to disagree, having spent time with many mentally incompetent prisoners up to the moment of their executions.

When most condemned men arrived from Death Row, their property bag would include toiletries, photographs of family or a girlfriend, letters, legal papers, and maybe a few paperback novels. Johnny Paul Penry first came to the Death House in 1989 with crayons and a coloring book and comics he couldn't read and still believing in Santa Claus. His I.Q. was sixty about forty points below what education experts judged normal.

He could neither write nor read and couldn't recite the days of the week or months of the year.

His life had been almost as nightmarish as the crime of which he'd been convicted. During his trial a sister had testified that their mother had routinely beaten Penry with a belt and broom, had scalded him with boiling water on numerous occasions, and had even forced him to eat his own feces and drink his urine as punishment. When he had wet his bed as a child, she had burned him with cigarettes and threatened to cut off his penis. He would be caged beneath his overturned crib, sometimes going for days without food. By age ten he was diagnosed by the Child and Adolescent Psychiatric Division of the University of Texas Medical Branch at Galveston as being mentally retarded and suffering a number of behavioral disturbances. Two years later he had briefly spent time in the Mexia State School for the Mentally Retarded.

At seventeen, he'd been arrested for arson and was ordered to the Rusk State Hospital, where he was diagnosed with psychoses resulting from brain trauma suffered as a child.

At his 1980 murder trial, his lawyers, arguing that the death penalty was not proper justice for their client, insisted that he had the mind of a six-year-old.

Yet, so overwhelming was the evidence against him that he was sentenced to die. And, indeed, his crime had been abhorrent.

On an October morning in 1979, a young homemaker named Pamela Carpenter was happily cutting out Halloween decorations when a knock came at her door. When she answered, Johnny Penry forced his way inside, then beat and raped her. Then, as she attempted to fight him off, he stabbed her with her own scissors. Thinking she was dead, he ran from the house.

Still alive, however, Carpenter managed to telephone police and identify her attacker. She also told them that during the struggle she thought she had cut Penry with the scissors. Before an ambulance arrived, she died.

Police immediately went to the nearby house where Penry had been living since his parole following an earlier rape conviction. When he responded to their knock, he still had bloodstains on his shirt. Asked about them, he quickly confessed. "I want to get it off my conscience," he said. "I done it."

Over the years, Johnny Penry's case became a battleground issue debated by mental-health and defendants'-rights groups and those organizations embracing the death penalty. Vocal among the latter was a man I had long admired. Mark Moseley, a place kicker for the NFL Washington Redskins, was the brother of Pam Carpenter. In the years following his sister's murder, he had repeatedly made the point that it was time the matter that had shattered his family's life be ended. Penry, he pointed out, had received not one but two fair trials. His case had wound through every court in the land and had been debated by penal scholars and endlessly reviewed by the media. His date with death, Moseley had been saying for years, was long overdue.

Yet, on the night I spent with Penry, trying in vain to make him understand what would happen to him once we entered the death chamber, the Supreme Court intervened, providing him a stay of execution.

And I found myself wondering where the elusive concepts of justice and fairness lay. Certainly, the suffering endured by the victim and her grief-stricken family haunted me. And, in light of the fact that he'd raped twice and taken a life, there was little doubt that Penry was a criminal who posed a continuing threat to society. Clearly, his mind was irreparably diseased, his concept of good and evil clouded by a lifetime of abuse.

Yet the task assigned me was layered with moral issues that I didn't feel lawmakers had addressed. No, I did not want the Johnny Paul Penrys of the world free to stalk other innocent victims, to destroy other families. And, yes, I felt punishment was due. But to order the state-sanctioned murder of someone who had no grasp of the process, someone so childlike that he had no real understanding of why he was to be killed, violated everything humane and Christian I believed in.

On that long-ago night, before the Supreme Court's ruling saved him, the time for entering the death chamber was drawing near when I noticed that Penry, having finished his last meal, was idly thumbing through a comic book. As he studied the colorful pages, lost in a world of make-believe, he would occasionally laugh quietly to himself.

Those innocent, childlike sounds chilled me.

Carlos DeLuna shared a troubling kinship with Penry.

In 1983 he had been convicted of robbing and murdering a twenty-four-year-old Corpus Christi service-station clerk named Wanda Jean Lopez. According to police she had been phoning 911 to provide a description of the man who had robbed her when DeLuna stabbed her. The last word the dispatcher heard from the caller was a plaintive plea for her life.

DeLuna fled on foot with the small amount of money that he'd taken from the cash register. Shortly afterward, police found him hiding beneath a truck parked only a few blocks away.

Though he was twenty-seven when I met him, he seemed much younger. That he'd managed to pass through the first nine years of public school was a sad commentary on our education system. As we talked, I found myself trying to imagine my own children—teenagers at the time—attempting to grasp the concept of their own death.

Upon his arrival at the Death House, he demonstrated the characteristics that, since the Penry case, I'd so often prayed never to see again. Like several I'd encountered before him, he had no real understanding of why he was there.

The signs were always the same. While the inmate of average or above-average intelligence was always focused, those with low I.Q.s seemed disoriented, their thoughts ping-ponging from one subject to another. Despite the popular myth, most condemned men who order an elaborate last meal only pick at it. The mentally challenged always display a voracious appetite. When the time came to describe the procedures that would occur inside the death chamber, most have an endless series of questions. But all DeLuna was concerned with was what pain he might feel when the needles were inserted into his arms.

"It'll be like getting a shot in the doctor's office," I tried to explain.

"You promise it won't hurt?"

"I promise."

"Will you hold my hand?"

That, I told him, would not be possible.

"Why?"

Because, I explained, his hands would be taped down to the gurney. As I'd done on so many other occasions, I explained that when the warden removed his glasses, it would be the signal for the injections to begin, and I assured him that once they started it would be no more than seven to twelve seconds before he was unconscious. Several times before the time came for him to leave the cell, we counted the numbers off together: one . . . two . . . three . . .

Still, as we entered the death chamber, a look of utter confusion swept over DeLuna's face, his piercing brown eyes searching mine. *What's happening? Why are they doing this to me? When can I go back to Ellis?* As members of the tie-down team were strapping him to the gurney, they briefly blocked me from his view. "Where did the chaplain go?" he suddenly cried out in a childlike voice. I immediately moved to a position where he could see me. "I'm here," I told him. "I won't leave you."

He responded with a smile. "It will be over soon," I assured him. "Hold my hand?"

"Carlos, I told you, I can't."

"Why?" Why, indeed?

Standing at the foot of the gurney, I again tried to assure him that only a few seconds would pass before the process was completed. He would, I whispered, be aware when the chemicals began entering his body. "Breathe out," I said, repeating advice that a doctor had suggested I offer. "Clear your lungs of air, and you'll go to sleep more quickly."

With that I placed my hand on his ankle.

Soon, the warden lifted his glasses, the chemicals began to flow, and the seconds ticked away. They stretched into an eternity. Well past the twelve seconds I had promised, I could still feel a pulse beating beneath my hand. Carlos DeLuna's eyes remained open, staring at me, filled with fear and disappointment. I was certain that I could read his thoughts: *You lied to me. You promised. Why did you lie to me?*

I felt my own body begin to shake as several more agonizing seconds crept by before he finally died. His eyes never closed, and as I looked down on his lifeless body, I was overwhelmed by a feeling of failure. He was the thirty-third inmate put to death since I'd become the prison chaplain, and for the first time I felt I'd let someone down.

After everyone had left, I remained with him, awaiting the arrival of the funeral home attendants who would come to take the body. Gone were the warden and the guards, those who had administered the deadly chemicals, and the witnesses, leaving me alone in a silent, sterile world that I badly wanted to lash out against. I wanted to scream out the fact that he'd not even understood what we were doing.

Instead, I only breathed deeply and kept my vigil. Still trembling, I reached out and took his hand.

• • •

In the fifteen years I served as the Death House chaplain, I sought psychological help only twice. Both occasions came in the wake of Carlos DeLuna's death.

For several days after his execution I could not sleep. Shrouded in depression, I went through my routine responsibilities like a zombie, ineffective and racked with a kind of guilt that I had never before experienced. I needed to talk with someone far removed from the world of prison life and criminal justice.

David Erb, the chaplain at Dallas's Presbyterian Hospital, was a man whom I greatly respected. A brilliant Bible scholar and dedicated servant of God, he was aware of my role at The Walls and had extended an offer to provide me with counsel whenever I might need it.

On an early Monday morning I sat in his office, confiding things I'd spoken of to no one else. I told him about the execution of Carlos DeLuna and the oppressive guilt I was unable to shake. I questioned why compassion and human kindness had been so badly beaten down by anger and revenge that, at times, I had begun to wonder if perhaps I was the one out of step with the realities of the world. Had I reached a point where concern for men who had committed unthinkable evil blinded me to the pain and suffering of their victims?

My ministry, I confided, was becoming increasingly difficult.

For several hours he listened as I described the frustrations and the doubts, the sleepless nights and the ever-present lack of hope, that regularly visited my own office. Mostly, however, I talked of the death penalty and the role that I played in it. And, for the first time, I questioned how much longer I could do it.

Finally, it was Chaplain Erb who addressed the issue I'd been reluctant to verbalize. "I have to wonder," he said, "if the basis of all the problems you're describing is your own feelings about a judical system that makes it legal to take a life. Do you believe in the death penalty?" he asked straightforwardly.

There, in the privacy of his office, I felt comfortable in responding to a question that had been posed to me by friends, coworkers, inmates, and the press, but which I had never answered. For the first time I was able to voice my belief without concern over the effect. "No," I responded, "I do not believe it's right. And with every execution that is carried out, that belief grows stronger."

It felt good to say so.

"Then you are wrestling with a dilemma no man should have forced on him," the chaplain said. He invited me to return the following week to continue our discussion.

In the days that followed I did a great deal of soul-searching, pondering the responsibilities that had been given me, tabulating the pluses and minuses of my life's work. And for all the dark and disturbing concerns—the execution of men who were clearly mentally ill, the possibility that innocent men might have died at the hands of the state, the litany of horrible pain and suffering that I'd heard from inmates and families of victims alike—there was one belief that continued to return to my mind. It was my credo, the firm basis of my decision to accept the role of Death House chaplain in the first place: *no one, however troubled his past, however unforgivable his sins, should be made to die alone.*

A man who had never aspired to be anything more than a caring country preacher, I knew, was not likely to dramatically change the world. He could, however, offer care and comfort wherever it might be needed. There was my answer.

I shared it with Chaplain Erb on my next visit. He did not seem surprised by what I had to say. "No one," he said, "not even God Himself, would fault you if you chose to walk away. But the service you provide is of such importance. I'm pleased that you realize that."

With that I returned to my calling.

FOURTEEN

Over the years, my responsibilities as chaplain seemed to constantly broaden, taking me deeper into the mysterious world of prison life than I'd ever anticipated.

One morning, as I sat in my office going over the schedule of inmates who would be stopping in to talk or make phone calls, my clerk, Blue, stood silently at the window, looking out into the exercise yard. Finally, he spoke. "Well, we've got drugs today," he said in a tone so casual that for a moment what he was saying didn't register.

Certainly, I was aware of the drug trafficking that went on inside The Walls (and, for that matter, inside virtually every unit in the Texas system). I'd heard the stories of how visitors managed to smuggle everything from marijuana to heroin past security and into the hands of convicts, and how men inside, with no legal way to have cash or spend it, suddenly had several hundred dollars in their possession. I remember an occasion when a young inmate, a four-sport letterman in high school before he was arrested for drug distribution, came to the chapel and, for reasons I'll never know, pulled three crisp one-hundred-dollar bills from his pocket and proudly showed them to me. He didn't have to tell me where they had come from. It was common knowledge that drug dealing went on behind bars just as it did in mainstream society.

I'd chosen not to pursue the particulars, even when a rumor had spread during the early days of my ministry that an inmate was using a closet in the chapel to hide his stash. On that occasion guards had arrived with drug dogs and literally ransacked the place in an attempt to locate the rumored drugs. I was pleased when they left empty-handed.

Now, however, Blue had piqued my curiosity. How could he know, simply by gazing out my window, that the drug market was open?

"Come over here, and I'll show you," he said.

Pointing to a guard standing near the weight-lifting area, he instructed me to look carefully at the pants legs of the man's uniform. One, I noticed, was partially stuffed into the top of the boot. "Both pants legs down," Blue explained, "means no drugs today. One in the boot means he's got stuff to sell."

It was the sort of thing that I'd just as soon not have known. From the first days that I'd been at The Walls, I had walked a fine line designed to earn the trust of both the inmates and the prison staff members. The only chance my calling had to succeed, I'd believed, was to establish myself as a neutral party. I would snitch neither on an inmate nor on a prison official. Keeping of the law and determining disciplinary action were someone else's business. I was there only to offer balm for the soul, and for some, the stance I'd chosen to take was difficult to understand. On one occasion, in fact, a sheriff had arrived for an execution and immediately asked if I would wear a wire to record anything the condemned prisoner might say to me in the hours before he was escorted into the death chamber. Certain the inmate was responsible for murders other than the one he was scheduled to die for, the sheriff became indignant when I refused his request.

"It might help us to clear up some cases," he argued. "What could it hurt?"

"My credibility," I responded. What he could not understand was that trust and honesty were the only things of value I had to offer those to whom I ministered.

Thus, having weighed the troubling options offered by the enlightenment Blue had provided, I opted to say nothing. The guard, I knew, would soon fall victim to his own careless and illegal activity. In prison, problems seemed always to resolve themselves.

In the case of the drug-dealing employee, it didn't take long.

It was just a few weeks later that I received word that a newly arrived inmate who had been placed in administrative segregation wished to see me. He was, I was told, a very dangerous drug dealer who had encountered trouble at another unit.

Bible in hand, I made my way to the isolated cell where he was kept and introduced myself. Arrogant and mean-eyed, the young Hispanic quickly made it clear that he wished me to serve as a messenger. "I need for you to tell the director I'm here," he said. The reason for his transfer, he confided, was to help with the growing drug problem inside the prison system. I was the only one he felt he could trust not to disclose his secret mission.

With that he launched into a description of the trafficking that was going on at the unit where he'd been, naming guards and fellow prisoners who were involved. And, while the things he told me sounded both legitimate and logical, I had long ago learned to be wary of inmates attempting to curry favor.

"I can't just go knock on the director's door and tell him you want to see him," I argued.

"You don't believe me, do you?"

"Yours isn't the wildest story I've ever heard." I stopped short of confiding to him my concerns about drugs that were coming into The Walls.

"Okay, I'm going to prove something to you," he smiled. "If I show you how easy it is to get drugs in here, will you get word to the director?"

Uneasy, I made no promises. I did, however, know that this was something that flew far beyond the boundaries of chaplain-inmate privilege. Thus, upon my return to my office I placed a call to the office of Steve Martin, the prison system's general counsel, and told him of my conversation. Though guarded in his response, he was clearly aware that the prisoner had come to The Walls to serve as an informant. "Let me know if you hear from him again," he advised. "Otherwise, don't mention this to anyone."

Less than a week had passed when, while making my rounds in the hospital, I again received word that the inmate in solitary confinement wished to see me. It was my routine when visiting segregated prisoners to stand on the walkway in front of their cell, resting my arms on the crossbar of the door as we talked. "Move a little closer," the inmate said. Warily, I did, and he quickly slipped something into my jacket pocket. "Take that to the director," he said, then turned his back on me.

I could hear him laughing as I walked away.

Going directly to my office, I placed a call to Martin and told him what had transpired. Being neutral on prison matters was one thing; finding myself involved in drug matters was another.

"What did he give you?" the attorney asked.

"I don't have any idea. It's still in my pocket."

His suddenly concerned voice dipped several octaves. "Meet me in the garage at your house," he said.

What I delivered to him turned out to be a packet of pure heroin. For the first and only time in my life, I was running drugs—not into the prison but out of it.

"Go back to your office," Martin said. "You'll be getting a call."

In less than half an hour a Texas Ranger phoned to ask where I'd gotten the drugs. I gave him the inmate's cell number. And never heard anything more. But in prison there are precious few secrets. In time I learned that the drug dealer did get his interview with the director. As months passed, a major drug operation in the unit that he'd been transferred from was shut down, and several guards were fired and indicted.

At The Walls, the guard Blue had so casually pointed out to me was never seen again. And, sometime later, I learned that a commendation had been quietly slipped into my personnel file.

• • •

Try though I did, it seemed impossible to limit my duties to religious ones.

One Sunday afternoon, just as I'd completed chapel services, Herbert Scott, one of the assistant wardens, ran up to me. "Come on," he said. "We've got an emergency, and I need your help." As I followed, he explained that a bus full of inmates being taken to the prison hospital in Galveston had broken down on the highway just outside of Huntsville.

In a matter of minutes I was standing in front of a large gun case, arms extended, while he handed me several rifles. "Put them in the trunk of my car," he commanded. "I've got to make a call to be sure another bus is on its way. Then we'll go."

It was obvious that he planned for me to accompany him to the broken-down transport bus. But why?

"We've got to stand guard until another bus arrives and the prisoners are transferred," he said.

He made it clear that there was no time for me to argue that despite having long ago signed an agreement to take up arms when necessary, I'd never really believed that guard duty was among a chaplain's responsibilities. "We're shorthanded today," he said, "and I need some help. You're it."

I hurried to his car and placed the rifles in the trunk.

Shortly, we were standing on the side of Interstate 45. There were four of us: the two guards who had been assigned to accompany the prisoners, the assistant warden, and me—all armed and surrounding the bus. I felt like an idiot. Never in my life had I fired a gun—not even in boyhood days when many of my friends treasured their BB guns and hunted rabbits with the twenty-two rifles their fathers had purchased for them.

There, as drivers slowed their cars to see what was going on, I stood, still dressed in the suit I'd preached in, holding a rifle that I had no idea how to use. Even the inmates on the bus didn't bother to hide their amusement.

Finally, several state troopers arrived, then a sheriff's deputy who relieved me of my post. A few minutes later another bus pulled up, and the prisoners were quietly transferred to it and were put on their way without incident. I returned my weapon to the trunk of the car.

When we were en route back to the prison, Herbert said little. I had the impression that he feared that if he did speak he'd break out in laughter. It wasn't until we pulled into the prison parking lot that he said, "Chaplain, you did just fine."

"Just following the rules," I replied, attempting to make light of what had transpired.

He couldn't help himself. "You know," he pointed out, "that in that agreement you signed, saying that you would take up arms if necessary, there's another important item."

Years had passed since I'd signed it, and I didn't have the slightest idea what he was talking about. "It says," he grinned, "that if you're ever taken hostage, the prison is under no obligation to attempt to save or protect you."

"Well," I said as I climbed from the car, "you've really made my day." I let him put the rifles away himself.

As I began my second decade as a prison chaplain, I began to be concerned that I was no longer effectively fulfilling my purpose. My mission had been to preach, to build the chapel into a peaceful place for inmates, to offer some faint glimmer of hope to those who had lost it and provide a friendly hand and welcome ear to those who could find them nowhere else. I was a preacher, sworn to spend my days doing God's work. But with the passage of each new year, it seemed I found less and less time to do so.

Executions were being carried out at a disturbing rate. During one month alone there were seven. I worried that I had evolved from the minister, choir director, and counselor for the inmates of The Walls into the full-time Death House chaplain. And while I recognized the importance of the latter role, I worried that I'd fallen victim to the old gospel cliché of robbing Peter to pay Paul. Even some of the inmates shared my concern.

One morning as I walked from the chapel into the prison yard, an elderly inmate, one of my piano players and a regular at my services since I'd begun them, called out to me. "Chaplain," he asked, "are you okay?"

"I'm fine. Why do you ask?"

He hesitated, as if uncomfortable with the response he'd prepared himself to offer. "A lot of the men are worried about you," the former high school principal confided. "You've changed, Chaplain. Seems you've been cutting your sermons short more and more. Choir practices get canceled. They don't see you over in the hospital as often. It's the executions, isn't it? They're taking up all your time. We know it's not your fault. We just want to be sure you're okay."

The execution procedure, in fact, had affected virtually everyone residing at The Walls. In the days leading up to one, I could count on dozens of inmates seeking me out just to offer their support. The visits to my office by guards seeking counsel increased dramatically. Moods in the administrative offices turned sullen and tense.

The effect was visible on everyone. One evening, as an execution drew near, I received an urgent call from the warden's office. "I need you here . . . right away," he said. "I've got a serious problem."

Rushing to his office, I found his secretary crying hysterically. For years, her role in the process had been to remain in the office, taking telephoned progress reports on the demeanor of the prisoner and the status of any last-minute appeals. The job had become more and more difficult for her, and on this particular evening she had reached the breaking point. As I embraced her, she began to vomit uncontrollably.

On the night a prisoner was to die, a hush would fall over the cell blocks. Televisions and radios would be shut off, the loud conversations replaced by soft whispers. In those dark hours before the midnight deadline, fellow inmates—though strangers to the condemned man—would offer up their collective show of respect.

Despite my own concerns, I assured the inmate who stopped me that I was fine. At nights I had begun to have dreams in which I was locked away in the Death House, its unique scent so real that it filled my nostrils, and that I could hear voices, faint and far away at first, then nearer and growing louder. They always asked the same question: *where's the chaplain?*

And, in dreams or awake, I knew the answer, and it troubled me: he's busy helping prepare men to die.

I felt I was letting the other prisoners down.

The frustrations that I had once viewed as routine and expected began to gnaw at me. Memories of failures blocked out the successes like storm clouds. I began to worry that the positive relationships I had developed were becoming overshadowed by the isolated incidents of confrontation and disdain.

I had been cursed and spat upon, and had urine thrown on me as I passed the cell of a prisoner angered because I could not allow him to make a phone call. I'd been called into court to answer baseless charges and had endured the absurd rulings resulting from the Ruiz complaints. When I had decided to offer a weekly sermon to those locked away in solitary, preaching from the walkway in front of their cells, I had been barraged by curses and catcalls that quickly proved the idea foolish. There had been the hostile and anonymous letters and phone calls, each with basically the same message: if I were a man of God, I would rip the needles from the arms of a condemned man and wage a Death Chamber battle to save his life rather than stand by and watch the process being carried out.

And my own life had been threatened.

Larry Tucker was serving a life sentence. Had it not been for the fact that he constantly pushed the envelope and stayed on report much of the time, he would have been one of those faceless inmates who went through each mind-numbing day unnoticed. He had no prison friends and seemed not to want any. He never kept any job for long. Only after months of complimenting him on his fine tenor voice had I talked him into joining the chapel choir.

He arrived at my office one day, demanding that he be allowed to make a phone call that he was not eligible to make.

"Larry, you know the rules," I said.

"Come on, Chaplain, you can break a rule now and then."

In truth, I'd done so on numerous occasions when I'd felt the situation merited it. Tucker's didn't. "I can't do it," I explained.

My response set off a tirade of curses, and I told him to leave my office.

Leaning across my desk, his face close enough that I could smell the foul odor of his breath, he said, "You're going to get yours, Chaplain. I promise you that." And then he stormed out.

Threats were nothing new. I had heard them for years, all of them hollow and meaningless. This time, however, the anger lingered.

A few days later, as I walked from the chapel, I felt a blow to my back that caused me to stumble. Even before I could regain my footing, the ever-protective Blue had arrived and pinned my assailant to the wall. He was quickly joined by two other inmates who had rushed over from their cleaning duties in the yard.

As they hurriedly escorted Larry Tucker away, I returned to my office, unnerved by the sudden attack, and removed my jacket. The back had been slashed by a shank fashioned from a razor blade and the stem of a toothbrush. To my relief, I had not been cut.

I was still trying to regain my composure when Blue returned. "You okay?"

"Except for a ruined coat," I said.

"Good," he replied. "Tucker's being taken care of." He offered no additional details. The next time I saw the man who attacked me was when I made my regular rounds in the prison hospital.

And while I felt I had come to an understanding of the inmate mind-set, the frustrations and anger that danced constantly near the breaking point, I could not help but wonder how the simple refusal of a phone call could generate such rage. After so much time in the prison, I still had not completely lost my naîveté. In my early days I

had questioned the process of searching inmates regularly, even after
one had been found to have concealed a shank in the binding of the
Bible that he constantly carried with him.

Yet, if I could not trust in the basic goodness of mankind, even
those imprisoned for the cruelest of deeds, how could I be expected
to serve my purpose?

There were those, I should admit, who made carrying out such a philosophy difficult. Among them was a Death Row inmate named Gary
Graham.

Long before he became a national celebrity, lionized by entertain-
ment world celebrities, black militant groups, and some religious leaders as an innocent man railroaded by the justice system, he had left a
wide wake of criminal behavior behind him—before reaching his eighteenth birthday. He'd been charged with ten robberies in the Houston
area and was the prime suspect in eight others. There had been two
shootings and ten car thefts credited to him before he was arrested
and charged with the robbery-murder of a man outside a supermarket.

The conviction that had sent him to Death Row, however, had
been accomplished largely on the testimony of a single eyewitness who
admitted that she was standing thirty to forty feet away in a dark
parking lot when the shooting occurred. Meanwhile, a store employee
had told investigators that he'd seen the shooter running from the
crime scene and was certain it had not been Graham. Neither finger-
prints nor DNA evidence ever connected him to the crime.

As he spent almost twenty years on Death Row, he became an
international cause célèbre for those in the anti–death penalty movement. In the minds of many, Texas was going to put an innocent man
to death.

On the date set for his execution, the streets outside the prison
were packed with media and foul-tempered protesters. The warden,
clearly concerned about the atmosphere that was developing, had
called me into his office several times to remind me how important it

was that things go smoothly. "Do your best to keep him as calm as possible," Pursley said repeatedly in the days leading up to Graham's arrival at The Walls.

Despite the hostility the inmate registered when we were introduced, things seemed fine until we reached the point where it was necessary to discuss those he'd included on his visiting list. Among them were actor Danny Glover, Rev. Jesse Jackson, and Nation of Islam leader Louis Farrakhan.

I'd seen Farrakhan speaking out in Graham's behalf on television several times in recent days and was aware that he never appeared unless accompanied by a small army of personal guards, each dressed in dark slacks, white shirts, and black bow ties. "Gary," I said, leaning against the bars of his cell, "the warden has said that anyone on your visitors list is welcome. But I'm also to inform you that Minister Farrakhan's guards will not be allowed to accompany him inside the prison."

For several seconds Graham silently stood at the doorway of his cell, his eyes narrowed, glaring pure hatred. And then he spat in my face.

I should admit relief that our time together was cut short by an announcement that then-governor Ann Richards had decided to grant a stay of execution. After only a few hours in the Death House, Graham was returned to the Ellis Unit to continue his appeals and civil lawsuits against the prison system, which would go on until 2000 when, at age thirty-nine, he was executed.

Louis Farrakhan was not among those who visited him in his final hours.

And the inhumane pain wrought by the executions weighed more heavily as each came and passed. The crowds that had gathered in the early days and on occasions when a high-profile prisoner arrived from Ellis had become history. Once front page-news, the carrying out of most of the executions was relegated to a few paragraphs. Court-ordered death in Texas had become routine.

• • •

It was clear, however, that nothing—neither public outcry nor political filibustering—was going to slow the process. The occasional poll results that appeared in the media provided the fuel. Overwhelmingly, the man on the street favored the death penalty.

I wondered how they might feel had they spent time with Juanita Bird.

Her son, Jerry Joe Bird, a fifty-four-year-old mechanic, was scheduled to be the fortieth man to be executed since the reestablishment of the death penalty. And, like so many before him, he had committed an unspeakable crime.

Accompanied by Emmett Korges, Bird had entered the rural home of a retired Harlingen couple with plans to steal an antique gun collection. Inside, the men handcuffed and bound Victor and Jo Ellen Trammell and placed them in separate bedrooms. The wife would later testify that she heard a muffled gunshot from another part of the house before managing to break free from her bonds and flee through a back window. Hiding in a nearby drainage ditch, she watched as her house went up in flames. In shock and suffering from exposure to the frigid January weather, she remained there for twelve hours before a passing mail carrier discovered her and took her to a nearby hospital. Investigators later found the badly burned body of her husband inside the smoldering ruins of the farmhouse. He had been shot twice with a twenty-two-caliber pistol fitted with a silencer.

I had met Emmett Korges years earlier. Having received a life sentence in exchange for testimony that it had been Bird who fired the shots that killed Victor Trammel, he was assigned to The Walls. His health failing even before he came to prison, he was among those who spent their mornings sweeping the yard. In time, he became a regular at chapel services. Then, in May of 1982, he died in the prison hospital.

Bird, too, had myriad health problems during the sixteen years that he spent on Death Row. In fact, just weeks before his sentence was finally to be carried out, he'd suffered a mild stroke and was rushed to the prison hospital in Galveston. There, doctors monitored his condition and after three days informed the warden's office that Bird was well enough to be put to death.

It was not the first time that officials had been forced to wait for such a pronouncement, and on each occasion I found myself flabbergasted by the dark irony of professional healers attending a patient, mending whatever frailty or illness he was suffering, just so that he might be deemed healthy enough to die.

That concern eliminated, the warden's worries turned to another matter. The name of Bird's mother appeared on his list of those invited to serve as witnesses to his execution. Never before had a mother entered the death chamber gallery to watch her son die. "For her own good," Warden Pursley asked, "do you think you can talk her out of it?"

Over the years I had come to the opinion that it was, in fact, a mistake for any family member to put him or herself through the agony of witnessing the actual execution process. The result was always a painful and indelible memory that he or she would live with for life. I never advised anyone against being a witness—the decision was not properly mine to make—yet on countless occasions I found myself privately praying that my explanation of what would transpire might be dissuasive.

Too often I didn't succeed. I remember spending a great deal of time with the mother of condemned prisoner Billy Gardner, killer of a high school cafeteria worker. His mother, insistent that she would witness his execution, had repeatedly asked me if her son would feel any pain when he was put to death. Carefully describing the process, I assured her that he wouldn't.

And, in all honesty, Gardner did die a painless death. Yet as he lay on the gurney that night, his distraught mother was not convinced. Pointing a finger at me, she screamed out, "You're a liar . . . a liar. He is hurting."

Seventy-four-year-old Juanita Bird was determined. Sitting next to her daughter in the parlor of the nearby Hospitality House, she made it perfectly clear that she intended to go through with her plan. "I was with him when he was born," she said, "and I'm going to be with him when he dies."

I told her that we could have a nurse and wheelchair on standby outside the execution chamber if she wished. She declined.

For all the songs and sonnets written of a mother's love, it remains a remarkable and unexplained phenomenon. Juanita Bird's son had, during the course of his misguided life, offered nothing that a parent could point to with pride. He had been expelled from kindergarten for disruptive behavior and finally dropped out of school for good midway through the eighth grade. As a youngster he had cruelly tortured animals, hanging neighborhood dogs and cats from trees until they died. He caught snakes and would cut away at them with his pocketknife, severing an inch or so at a time and delighting in the slow and painful death he was inflicting. Then, as an adult, he had been sentenced to ten years in prison for a 1956 murder, serving four and one-half years before being paroled.

That said, he came to the Death House as the most cooperative and carefree inmate I'd ever encountered. There were no outraged claims of innocence, no real expectations that the last-minute efforts to have his execution stayed would be successful. Weary of Death Row, he didn't want to return. "There's nothing there but boom boxes and basketball on television," he said. "I hate it." His philosophy, he explained, had been reduced to the most common denominator: "Life's a bitch. You're born, and you die. I'm ready to move on."

Bird chain-smoked, shared an endless recital of off-color jokes with the guards (and me), and made it clear that he had no interest in hearing prayer or Scripture. A self-professed agnostic, he said he was going neither to Heaven nor Hell. "I'm going to medical school," he laughed.

Indeed, there was truth to his claim. In the will he had written, Bird had offered his body to the University of Texas medical branch in Houston to be used for research. "When will I get there?" he repeatedly asked me.

If his execution went off as planned, I explained, he would be in Houston by no later than one-thirty in the morning. "That's good," he replied. "See, I've done so many bad things in my life, I'm hoping that giving my body to science will make up for some of them."

That statement was the lone sign of redemption I saw in Jerry Joe Bird during the seven hours we spent together.

Late in the evening, after his appeals had been exhausted, he spoke with his mother on the phone, trying one last time to convince her not to make the short trip from the Hospitality House to the death chamber. "The chaplain tells me it won't hurt," I heard him explain. "He says it's just like when they put you to sleep in the hospital. I believe him, but I still don't know how I'm going to react at the end. I'd understand if you didn't come."

Hanging up the phone, he shook his head. "She's a strong-willed, hard-headed woman," he said. "Always has been."

Juanita Bird was coming to the execution.

As he lay on the gurney, Bird turned his head slightly so that his mother, who sat with her arms resting on the rail that separated the gallery from the execution chamber, might read his lips as he mouthed the words, "Hi, Mom," before he died.

Mrs. Bird waved but did not reply. Later that night, as I visited her at the Hospitality House, she assured me that she was fine. "I've known this was coming for a long time," the former registered nurse said. "In all fairness, this probably should have happened right after he was convicted. I've seen a lot of death in my life. I watched my mother die, and my husband. Seven weeks ago, my little dog died. And now my son. It's all the same; death is death."

They were the last words she ever spoke.

I later received a letter from her daughter, explaining that shortly after their return home, Juanita Bird had gone into what doctors would later diagnose as catatonic shock. In need of perpetual care, she had been placed in a nursing home.

She would never know that her son's final gesture in life had served as an inspiration to another condemned inmate.

Later that same year, twenty-nine-year-old Joseph Paul Jernigan, a convicted murderer, also donated his body to science before his death. And in doing so became internationally famous as "the Visible Man."

Flown to the University of Colorado immediately following the execution, Jernigan's body was frozen in a gel solution. Then a team of doctors sliced it into 1,862 cross sections, which were photographed and posted in cyberspace as the first computerized library of human anatomy.

Bizarre as it may sound, the images of Jernigan's dissected body have, for years now, served as an aid to surgeons in their preparations for difficult operations and invasive diagnostic procedures.

Perhaps in some great master plan too elaborate to fathom, the deaths of Jerry Joe Bird and Joseph Jernigan, men who in life offered nothing but pain and grief to others, may have ultimately helped to save lives.

Such were the mysteries I pondered.

FIFTEEN

The litany of crimes committed by condemned men whose paths I crossed seemed endless: One night I listened as a rapist-murderer told of staking a victim to an ant bed and leaving the horrified young woman to endure a death beyond imagination. Another graphically described how he had raped an elderly nun. I met a man who killed as many people in prison as he had while in the free world. And I met a young man, overwhelmingly disappointed in his life, who had killed his entire family. The condemned men came bearing distressing epithets like "the Good Samaritan Killer" and "the Soldier of Fortune Murderer." Still, the most despised person ever escorted into the Death House was Ronald Clark O'Bryan, a short, puffy man who had been absolutely friendless during the eight-and-a-half years he'd been in prison. In the week before he was scheduled to be executed, in fact, inmates at The Walls had even petitioned to be allowed some manner of organized demonstration to show their disdain for the former optician who had been convicted of murdering his eight-year-old son.

Of the ninety-five men I accompanied into the death chamber during my tenure as prison chaplain, he was the only one who had killed his own child. And, in truth, it was difficult to muster a great deal of compassion for him. I had heard stories of crimes far more gruesome, more savage, than his. There had been men who had confessed to multiple killings, bloody and senseless rampages for which they displayed little or no remorse. O'Bryan's crime was worse in one respect: its cold-bloodedness.

On Halloween evening in 1974, he laced trick-or-treat candy with enough cyanide to kill several grown men and handed it out to his own two children and four others from the doorstep of his suburban Houston home. Fortunately, only Timmy O'Bryan chose to eat from the Pixy Stix given to him. Initially, he complained only of the bitterness of the candy, prompting his father to offer him a glass of Kool-Aid to wash the taste away. Soon, however, Timmy was suffering severe stomach pains and nausea. He died en route to a nearby hospital.

An entire nation grieved at the news that one of the darkest and most enduring urban legends had become a reality. A cruel and sadistic killer, making some insane statement on a holiday when feigned fright was part of the fun and games, had struck. Every parent's worst nightmare had visited the O'Bryan home, and sympathy poured in from all over the country.

What kind of fiendish mind would take advantage of one of childhood's most carefree holidays to commit such an unforgivable act? The culprit, whoever he was, had forever altered the way in which Halloween would be perceived and celebrated.

And the local police had a good idea who that man was. They had watched from a distance as Ronald O'Bryan attended his son's funeral, never shedding a tear, not even looking into the casket as he joined passing mourners paying their final respects. At the cemetery, O'Bryan, flanked by his wife and daughter, fixed his gaze on the attending minister, not once turning his attention to the flower-shrouded grave site.

That he had the strength the following Sunday to stand before the congregation of the Baptist Church he regularly attended and sing a solo—"Blessed Assurance"—in memory of his son was viewed by many as proof of his love and courage.

To those investigating Timmy O'Bryan's death, is was nothing more than a cowardly attempt to hide guilt.

In time, they would make their case and arrest the father. Financially troubled, O'Bryan had murdered his child in an effort to claim twenty thousand dollars in insurance money. On the evening his costumed children prepared to walk the neighborhood with their friends, he had replaced a portion of the sugary powder inside five Pixy Stix with the deadly cyanide. He gave two to his own kids, the other three to random trick-or-treaters. In doing so, he planned to cause five deaths and thus deflect attention from his own motive.

Neatly clipping away one end of each of the packages, he had inserted the poison, then stapled them shut. In doing so, he likely saved the life of at least one youngster who had attempted one last sample of his treats before bedtime.

Alerted to the tragedy that had visited the O'Bryan home, parents in the neighborhood began searching their children's collections of candy, looking for the particular brand police had warned them might be poisoned. In one home parents found their tiny son already asleep, still holding a Pixy Stix in his hand. His fingers had apparently not been strong enough to remove the staple that closed the container.

Though he never admitted his guilt, Ronald O'Bryan was convicted and sentenced to die. The media covering his trial gave him a nickname that he was to live with for the remainder of his life. He would forever be known as "the Candy Man," the person who ruined Halloween for generations to come.

The sentencing judge, in fact, had suggested that once all of O'Bryan's appeals were dismissed, poetic justice would be served if he were executed on some future October 31st.

To this day there are those whose clouded memories summon up the false recollection that it was, in fact, on Halloween that O'Bryan died. That, too, has become part of urban legend. In truth, it was 12:48 on the morning of March 30, 1984, that a prison physician pronounced him dead.

How could even the most evil of men premeditate the murder of his own child, standing by as the most agonizing and painful of deaths gripped an innocent eight-year-old? How could he do nothing as

Timmy, racked in pain, slipped into a coma from which he would never wake?

And how was I going to deal with a day in the company of this man for whom I could summon no real sympathy? I, too, was a parent who had sent children off to knock at friendly doors and gather holiday sweets. At the time of Timmy O'Bryan's death, I also had an eight-year old.

I, too, despised what Ronald O'Bryan had done.

Following a restless sleep, I had been up since before dawn and was sitting in the warden's office when word came that O'Bryan had arrived at the Death House. Normally, I would have been there, waiting, but because of the large crowd that was gathering outside, his trip from the Ellis Unit had been delayed so that additional security might be summoned. For days, calls and correspondence from throughout the world—Australia, the Netherlands, France, and Germany—had arrived at the prison, expressing passionate feelings about the scheduled execution. And while there were those who voiced their disapproval of the death penalty, this time there were almost as many urging that the sentence be carried out.

Finally, Warden Pursley appeared in his doorway and said, "He's here," he said. "He's all yours."

As I made the walk toward the Death House, a major who had accompanied O'Bryan to Huntsville met me in the hallway. "This," he observed, "is a scared man."

I didn't bother to tell him that I was scared too—not because of any physical danger that I might face, but because of my lingering doubts that I could set aside the feelings that I had experienced as I'd read news reports about the inmate's crime. I'd never prayed harder for strength.

He was standing at the doorway of his cell, watching as guards went through the two small bags that contained his property. Even as I approached, I could see that he was nervous and apprehensive.

"I'm Chaplain Pickett," I said.

He extended his hand through the bars and smiled. "I feel like I know you," he replied. "I've heard a great deal about you."

There was a polish and charm about him that was both disarming and disconcerting. Trite though it may sound, Ronald O'Bryan, five-foot-ten, 250 pounds, wearing horn-rimmed glasses, did not look the part of the evil ogre I'd expected to encounter. A quiet loner during his years in prison, he'd only begun to speak out to the media in the months immediately preceding his execution date. He was innocent, he had insisted. Finding anyone who believed him, I'm sure, would have been a monumentally difficult task.

That determination, however, was not for me to make. My purpose was to provide whatever comfort I could in the hours to come.

Almost immediately, he began testing me. He assured me that he and David Autry had been close friends on Death Row. Autry, he said, had spoken of me often after returning to Ellis after his own execution had been stayed. "He says you're an okay guy," O'Bryan said in his best good-ol'-boy manner. For several minutes, he told me of conversations they had had, of things Autry had said about me.

"Let me ask you this: what did David say about me when he was here?"

He was, in a manner of speaking, establishing the ground rules that would set the tone for the remainder of the day. Could I be trusted?

"Ron," I replied, "you know I can't tell you that."

Clearly, it was the answer he'd hoped for. "I think we're going to get along just fine," he said.

Still, he paced nervously as we discussed plans for the day. There were no members of his family on the visitors list he'd filled out before his arrival, just a man he listed as his spiritual advisor and a young woman who was a journalism student at nearby Texas A&M University. The student, an eighteen-year-old named Kim, had begun corresponding with him for a class writing project almost a year earlier, and a strange relationship had developed. O'Bryan had adopted the role of academic advisor to the teenager, suggesting courses she should take and offering career advice.

He said that a former Houston police officer turned minister would arrive sometime in the afternoon. "He's my spiritual advisor," O'Bryan explained.

"You understand," I said, "that the rules allow for only one such visitor."

Just days earlier, I knew, he had spent considerable time with a volunteer chaplain at the Ellis Unit named Perry Barnes. A school superintendent and ordained Church of Christ minister, Barnes had come to my office early in the morning and told me that O'Bryan had requested that he spend the day with him. Checking the paperwork that had been delivered, I found no indication of such a request and asked that he wait in my office while I spoke to the prisoner about the request.

"Naw, I don't want to see him," O'Bryan said dismissively.

The motivation of those who found their way onto inmates' visiting lists often puzzled me. Family members, wishing to say final good-byes, were understandable. So were the appearances of lifelong friends. On the other hand, there were those whose presence defied any logic I could grasp. I'd seen preachers with no ties whatsoever to an inmate suddenly wish to involve themselves in the process; women, young and old, married and single, develop long-distance relationships with an inmate that result in their being welcomed to visit on the final day of his life; and members of the media, aware that prison rules blocked their entrance into the Death House, conspire with the inmate to be passed off as a friend, relative, or spiritual adviser.

On the other hand, for those inmates whose religions were outside the mainstream, I felt duty-bound to see that they received the visits they requested. There was a night when an inmate insisted to me that he was a member of the Church of Wicca and wished to have an ordained witch give him last rites. I was finally able to locate a Wiccan minister who lived near Houston. I explained the situation, and she immediately drove to the prison in a pouring rain to help me fulfill the request.

Then, there was Jean Lefevre, a warm, soft-spoken woman who

ministered from the Church of the White Eagle Lodge in nearby Montgomery, Texas. Organized in Europe, her church had branches throughout the world and offered a spiritual message that ranged from reincarnation, a strict vegetarian diet, and an obligation to care for sick and injured animals. Lefevre visited the prison regularly and became friend and counselor to a number of inmates.

When she asked if I would visit her and her followers to speak about the death penalty, I agreed, in part to return the kindness that she had shown the prisoners, in part out of sheer curiosity about the faith she embraced.

I was not prepared for what I encountered. As the service began, Lefevre sat on a gilded throne, dressed all in white. As soon as the congregation was seated, the ceiling opened, and a huge white eagle was lowered to hover above throughout the ceremony.

I was a long way from the First Presbyterian or even the Chapel of Hope. Yet Lefevre and her followers were obviously strong in their convictions, and I could not help but admire them.

Jean Lefevre, a kind and patient woman, spiritual and filled with a strong belief that there was good in all men, was genuine. Not so others.

In Ronald O'Bryan's case, a reporter attempted entry by claiming to be a preacher. Word came that a woman had arrived at the prison, identifying herself as an ordained minister summoned to visit O'Bryan. She wore a clerical collar and carried a Bible. In truth, she was with a radio station and was turned away, cursing loudly as she was escorted out.

The early afternoon arrival of the spiritual adviser scheduled to visit also raised questions among wary security personnel. Dressed casually in a sport shirt and khaki slacks, he did not even carry a Bible with him. And when the routine search was made, guards found a vial of prescription pills, which the adviser said he was taking for one of several illnesses he was suffering, and a small screwdriver—the kind used to repair eyeglasses—in his pocket. Though hardly ominous-looking, the two-inch screwdriver did meet the prison's definition of a weapon. The adviser seemed embarrassed at its discovery. "It is something that Ron gave me ten years ago," he said. "I can't believe I had it in my pocket today."

After he'd been searched a second time, I was called to escort him to the Death House. "Watch this guy closely," the major whispered to me.

It was an unnecessary warning. Even as we made our way along the corridors and through the succession of gates, he was asking how long he would have to stay. "The only reason I've come," he explained, "is to discuss funeral plans. His family has asked that I conduct the service." By the time the adviser took his seat across from the visiting cell, he was perspiring profusely. An elderly man battling cancer and a heart condition, his discomfort was obvious. It was, in fact, something far worse than discomfort that he was feeling. I sensed that he found the atmosphere I'd escorted him into starkly frightening.

Though I moved to the end of the walk, it was impossible not to hear bits of their conversation. The adviser nervously attempted to make light of the fact that he'd been asked to leave the small screwdriver with the guards who had searched him. For a few minutes they talked of bygone days in their relationship, then briefly of the funeral that would soon occur.

Only fifteen minutes had passed when the adviser rose and walked to where I was standing. "I'm ready to go," he whispered.

I tried to persuade him to stay. "We're not in any rush," I said. "His next visitor won't be here for an hour or so." I thought that perhaps in his role as spiritual adviser he might at least like to have some kind of prayer with O'Bryan before leaving.

"I believe I'd just as soon go now," he replied. Then he added a footnote: "I'll never come back to this place."

After escorting him back to the lobby, I got back to see a suddenly somber O'Bryan being returned to his cell. "How did your visit go?" I asked.

"Not very well," he said. "I think I'd rather just talk with you."

An articulate man, he spoke of his days as an active member of the church, of how much he'd enjoyed singing in the choir. Noticeably absent from his conversation was any mention of his family. The only hint of anger came when he addressed life on Death Row. Like those before him, he hated the constant noise.

He'd had a radio, he said, but had given it to a fellow inmate when he realized that it was all but impossible to enjoy listening to it over the steady drum of boom boxes and the cheering that accompanied the televised sports that most of his fellow inmates enjoyed.

"I kind of wish I'd kept my radio and brought it with me," he said. "It would be nice to listen to some music."

I told him that could be arranged.

Minutes later, as the instrumental sounds from an easy listening station filled the Death House, he lay back on his bunk, eyes closed, as if welcoming the return of some long-ago time in his life when peace and quiet were taken for granted. For the first time since his arrival, Ron O'Bryan seemed relaxed.

Standing near his cell, I silently wondered how one could summon even the smallest measure of peace, even for brief and fleeting moments, when haunted by such an evil deed? Did memories of his son's death visit his dreams? Or had he come to some understanding with God that provided him private comfort? How had he survived the countless hours and days since coming to prison, exiled even in exile, held in such contempt, friendless and alone?

For the first time, the thought occurred to me that to Ronald O'Bryan death might be a welcome end to the unimaginable torture his life had become.

Almost as if reading my thoughts, he sat up and asked a question.

"Chaplain," he said, "in your opinion what is the most unpardonable sin?"

"According to the Bible," I replied, "it is blasphemy of the Holy Spirit."

"And how many sins can God forgive?"

I had never even considered that forgiveness might operate on some quota system. "Ron, I don't have an answer for that."

When a person's life was judged, he pondered, was everything a person had done taken into consideration? Or would the judgment focus on one's frame of mind at life's end?

Not waiting for an answer, he continued. "I think God has forgiven me," he said. "I can't undo mistakes I've made, but I believe I'm going to Heaven. I've been a Christian all my life, you know."

For several more minutes he spoke of his own philosophy of repentance and forgiveness, yet he never once addressed the crime that had brought him to the final hours of his life. Over the years, virtually every condemned man I came to know spoke of his family. Still, he never once mentioned his son Timmy's name. Nor did he talk of his wife or daughter.

Early in the afternoon I received word that his friend Kim had arrived. Walking to the visitors' room, I found a small, frail-looking young woman with an "I don't know what I'm doing here" look on her face. Nicely dressed, she carried with her a Bible, a notebook, and a ballpoint pen.

Explaining the rules, I told her that she would be allowed to visit for two hours. "But Ron told me we could spend all afternoon together," she argued with little conviction.

I could not, for the life of me, understand what interest she could have in a thirty-nine-year-old man sentenced to die for murder. Pretty and childlike, she should have been spending her weekend with school friends instead of being escorted into the Death House. While her relationship with O'Bryan had begun as a journalism project, it had obviously expanded into something more personal. I couldn't help but wonder if this young woman, the same age that Timmy O'Bryan would have been had his life not been cut short, had unwittingly become the substitute family for the man she was there to visit and later watch die.

Once they were settled into the visiting area, I retreated to the end of the walk to join the guards. As I watched from a distance, it appeared to me that O'Bryan was doing all the talking while Kim, her small hands folded in her lap, simply listened.

Then, as their allotted time was winding down, O'Bryan summoned me to the visiting cell. "I'd like to give her some of my things," he said.

I explained that she wouldn't be allowed to accept anything directly from him. Instead, he would have to make a written request that I would then have to take to the warden for approval. "I'll see that she gets them later," I promised.

The bureaucracy that ruled prison life came as no surprise to the inmate.

I escorted Kim back to the front door shortly after four in the afternoon and watched as a familiar routine unfolded. Though she had expressed concern that she would face a barrage of press questions once outside, she made her way directly to the television cameras set up across the street. Later, I would learn that she described how she and O'Bryan had prayed together and how she had read to him from her Bible.

At no time during their visit had I seen their heads bowed or her Bible opened.

"She's a good listener," a rejuvenated O'Bryan said as I returned to the Death House. And then, as if aware of the question I'd been struggling with, he added, "Everyone needs a friend, Chaplain. She's the only friend I have."

It was always impossible to anticipate how swiftly or slowly time would pass in the final hours before an execution. In some instances it seemed to fly past, as if the clock had been set on some merciful fast-forward; in others it seemed at an agonizing standstill. In O'Bryan's case we both felt it speed by.

By early evening we had discussed the procedures that would immediately follow—his shower, his last meal, and preparation for any final statement he might wish to make. He had some letters to write, he said, and would like to spend some time alone. Later, he said, he would like to make a call to his father.

Before leaving I asked him about Chaplain Barnes. "He's been waiting in my office all day," I said. "Wouldn't you like to see him?"

He shrugged. "Maybe later," he said.

Taking that as a positive response, I returned at seven-thirty with the Ellis Unit chaplain at my side. They spoke only briefly. "I'd like to call my father now," O'Bryan said as he shook Barnes's hand and thanked him for coming.

In truth, there is no privacy in the Death House. Only the softest of whispers go unheard, even if all others distance themselves to the opposite end of the walkway. I could not help but hear as O'Bryan stood in front of his cell, alternately speaking with his father, his brother, and his stepmother. Finally, as the conversation began to wind down, I heard him say, "Dad, don't blame yourself for anything I've done. You've been a good father. I'm okay. I'm going to Heaven."

And with that he waved to me, holding out the receiver for me to hang up.

He finished his letters and placed them into envelopes. "I don't have any stamps," he said. I reached into my coat pocket and handed him a book of stamps. "I'll see that they are mailed," I said.

"Can you do me one more favor?"

I nodded.

"I've been thinking about my final statement," he said, "and I was hoping you would help me with it. What I'd like to do is write it out and read it when we go in there. Then, I'd like for copies of it to be handed out to the media."

No other inmate had asked that he be allowed to read a statement. "I'll have to check with the warden about it."

Pursley immediately denied the request. "He'll be strapped down," he said, "and I'm not going to hold any statement in front of him so he can read it. Neither are you." He did agree to have copies made and provided to members of the press.

O'Bryan was again writing when I returned to pass along the warden's message. "You write it," I said, "and we'll rehearse it."

Finally, he read it to me.

What is about to transpire in a few moments is wrong! However, we as human beings do make mistakes and errors. This execution is one of those wrongs. Yet it doesn't mean our whole system of justice is wrong. Therefore, I would forgive all who have taken part in any way in my death.

Also, to anyone I have offended in any way during my thirty-nine years, I pray and ask your forgiveness, just as I forgive anyone who has offended me in any way. And I pray and ask God's forgiveness for all of us respectively as human beings.

To my loved ones, I extend my undying love. To those close to me, know in your hearts I love you one and all. God bless you all, and may God's best blessings be always yours.

"It sound okay to you?"

I nodded. "Let me ask you a question."

"What's that?"

"For years, you've said nothing to the press. Now, lately, you've been giving interviews, and you want this statement distributed to reporters. Why?"

"I just wanted to make people aware that I'm against the death penalty . . . for me or anybody else. I felt I had to express my feelings about capital punishment."

For almost an hour I listened as he read and reread his statement aloud, occasionally changing a word here and there, setting it to memory. And then a quietness so distinct that I could hear my own breathing fell over the Death House. I'd turned the radio off while O'Bryan rehearsed, and the attending guards sat in silence at the end of the hall. The man I'd spent the day with had run out of conversation.

Finally, at eleven-forty-five, he asked if I would get him the piece of Boston cream pie that he'd had me place in the small icebox at the end of the walk. Saved from the last meal he'd eaten earlier, he took two small bites, then flushed the rest down the commode. "Guess I've lost my appetite," he said.

I told him that it was time to put on his shirt.

He nodded and began to dress. Turning his head, he looked at me for several seconds before speaking. "You ready for this?" he asked.

"Ron," I replied, "the question is, Are you ready?"

The digital clock on the nearby radio soon moved to twelve. "Chaplain, are you going to pray when we get in there?"

"Yes."

"What will you pray?"

"A prayer like the one Christ spoke from the cross: Father, into your hands we commit this spirit. . . ."

Extending a hand through the bars, he said, "Thank you."

He would say nothing more until he was strapped down. He asked if I would remove his glasses. "I just want you to know that I appreciate your being here," he whispered.

Though I focused my attention on the gurney, I was aware of the witnesses being escorted in—reporters, the attorney general, the sheriff who had investigated the case, and the young college coed. I could hear her crying.

When the warden asked if he had any final words, O'Bryan recited his statement verbatim, adding a brief postscript. "During my time here," he said, "I have been treated well by all TDC personnel."

Warden Pursley then removed his glasses, signaling the execution to begin. I watched as the inmate's hands relaxed, his eyelids fluttered and closed. He exhaled once, and his lips took on a purplish hue. In two minutes Ronald O'Bryan was dead.

As I stood there, waiting for the funeral home attendants to arrive and take the body away, I could not help but contrast the quick and peaceful death that I'd just witnessed to that of a small child, writhing in pain, foaming at the mouth, and ultimately strangling in his own vomit.

It was early the following morning when the warden phoned. O'Bryan's body, he said, had been delivered to the local funeral home, and its director wanted to know who would be claiming it. Rechecking the paperwork the inmate had filled out, I saw that he had indicated that a member of his family would assume responsibility for his remains. He'd also signed a document donating his eyes to an eye bank.

"Let me call his father," I suggested.

Though he'd never visited his son during the eight years he spent in prison, the elder O'Bryan said he would come to Huntsville and claim the body. When Timmy died, he explained, the insurance company had attempted to deliver a twenty-thousand-dollar check to the child's mother, but she had refused it. Finally, O'Bryan's father, also listed as a beneficiary on the policy, had agreed to accept it and placed it in a savings account he hoped to one day pass along to his granddaughter. He would, he said, use some of the money to bury his son.

It was standard procedure to ask where the burial would take place. "In this case," I suggested, "maybe it is just as well we don't know." The father agreed. There was nothing to be gained by providing future Halloween pranksters a map to the resting place of the man who ruined the holiday.

Thus, Ronald O'Bryan was buried under an alias in a cemetery none of his relatives have ever visited, his casket and headstone paid for by the money he'd hoped to get after causing his own child's death.

SIXTEEN

As the execution toll in Texas continued to mount and critics lashed out at what they viewed as a runaway assembly line of capital punishment, I still had never spoken publicly about my own views on the death penalty. Not to the media or inmates or even fellow workers at the prison. My philosophy remained the same; my opinion simply had no bearing on the responsibilities I had agreed to fulfill. I was the chaplain, plain and simple, not judge or jury or executioner. I was not the avenger for victims. Justice, however defined, was not mine to determine. I had no control over or involvement in the legal process. The planning of an execution had been accomplished long before I met the man scheduled to die. I was there simply to see that no man arrived at death's door alone.

Determinedly, I had maintained a safe (and, I thought, comfortable) distance from the process, walking a fine line that had grown thinner and less defined as the years passed. Yet I felt I had held to my position. And then, on the last day of January 1995, that all changed.

For the first time since 1951, back in the days when they still used Old Sparky, the infamous electric chair hidden away in that ominous wooden crate I'd seen on my first visit to the Death House, two men were scheduled to be executed on the same night.

The prison had nothing to do with it. Rather, it was the result of decisions reached by Texas trial court judges separated by 350 miles and an unawareness of each other's decrees. In Taylor County, Clifton

Russell, convicted of a robbery-murder in Abilene, had been sentenced to die on January 31. In Harris County, Willie Williams was found guilty of similar crimes and given the same death date.

They would be the sixth and seventh men executed that month, and I was feeling mentally exhausted. For the first time since I took over the responsibilities of prison chaplain, days when I had to force myself to report to my office had become increasingly frequent. I began to understand why the warden sometimes didn't return to work for several days following an execution. I too was feeling the drain.

The observant inmates who had spoken candidly to me were right: I was changing.

It had been decided that Russell, who had resided on Death Row for almost fifteen years, would be the first to arrive at the Death House and that the normal routine would be followed. Only when his execution was completed would Williams, who had been in prison for fourteen years, make the trip from the Ellis Unit into Huntsville. It was there that any semblance of normality would end. Though the warden had assured me that I would be allowed ample time with each inmate, I could not stop the ringing of the phrase "assembly line" in my mind as I woke and prepared for the longest day of my life.

As a teenager Clifton Russell had been constantly in trouble with law enforcement before he and accomplace Willie Battee abducted an air-traffic controller named Hubert Tobey from the parking lot of a convenience store. The forty-one-year-old Tobey was later found outside an abandoned house, stabbed repeatedly, his head crushed with a forty-pound concrete block. Russell and Battee were later apprehended in New Mexico, where they had fled in the victim's bloodstained car. They were arrested when authorities were alerted that they were using credit cards stolen from Tobey at a Hobbs shopping mall.

Later, Battee would testify against Russell in exchange for a sixty-year prison sentence. The jury, having heard the terrifying details of the crime, quickly convicted Russell, and he was sentenced to die.

In the days before his arrival at the Death House, Russell had vented his frustration with the system to the press. When he was convicted just shortly after his eighteenth birthday, jurors had collectively agreed he would be a continuing threat to society if allowed to live. "I've been in prison for almost fifteen years," he argued, "and there is not a single violent incident on my record since I came here. What I've done in the past was wrong, inexcusable. I know that. But what the state is planning to do is an atrocity as well."

I fully expected, then, to meet an angry inmate when he was escorted to his holding cell. Instead, I encountered a thirty-eight-year-old man who looked even older, his face weary and resigned, his eyes dull and focused on something I could not see. Clifton Russell, tired of life in prison, was ready to die.

Throughout the day he asked for little except the quick passage of time. He wished to see no visitors, nor would any friend or loved one be arriving to witness his execution. For his final meal he asked only for whatever was being served in the dining hall. There would be no family member, he said, taking responsibility for his body.

From conversations with fellow Death Row inmates who had returned to Ellis following stays of their executions, he obviously knew the routine. "I guess you get to hold my hand today," he smiled, "and bury me tomorrow."

When he did talk, it was of the faith he had found in prison and the comfort it had provided him. And of the long night that was to be played out.

"I know this has to be difficult for you," he observed.

I only nodded an acknowledgment, hoping that the weariness I was experiencing remained secret, that a feeling we shared—our conviction that back-to-back executions were an atrocity—wasn't obvious. "My concern," I replied, "is your needs."

"Chaplain," he said, "they are quite simple. I'm numb. I've been numb for a long time. After a while, that's what you become over at Ellis. All I want is to get this over with."

Through the day and into the evening he drank coffee, wrote letters, and alternately paced and napped. There would be short phone calls to his mother and brothers, and finally to a young woman who had befriended him and pointed him toward Christianity.

"You know," he said after his final call, "it surprised me that I didn't really have much to say. As I've sat around for months—years—thinking about this night, I always thought there would be so much I wanted to do and so little time to do it. It's not that way, is it? In here, time just keeps going by, and you find that all you're really doing is waiting."

Finally, at a few minutes before midnight, the wait was ended. The warden arrived to signal that it was time for us to move into the death chamber.

Russell had felt no need to practice his final words; wasn't, in fact, certain that he would say anything. Once strapped onto the gurney, however, he did thank friends and family who had lent him support during his years in prison and offer words of encouragement to be passed along to his brothers. Then he looked at me and silently nodded. "I thank my Father, God in Heaven, for the grace he has granted me," he said. Closing his eyes, he added, "I am ready."

Clifton Charles Russell, Jr., was pronounced dead at 12:19 A.M. A call had already gone out to the Ellis Unit, ordering that Willie Williams be transported to Huntsville.

As I waited in the death chamber for the funeral home attendants to arrive and remove Russell's body, Warden Morris Jones, who had replaced Pursley after his retirement, returned. The look on his face spoke to the fact that we were deep in uncharted waters. "What we do from here on out is up to you," he said. "I want you to take as much time as you feel you need with this next one. Take care of him. Do things as you see fit."

Even as he spoke, new needles and tubes were replacing those that had funneled the lethal poison into Russell's veins. As soon as his body was removed, the gurney would be wiped clean. I couldn't help but mentally compare the death chamber to a busy restaurant where busboys hustled to a vacated table, cleaning away dishes and silverware and spreading fresh linen so that a new group of customers could be ushered in.

Warden Jones placed a hand on my shoulder and squeezed. He shook his head slowly. "I'll be in my office," he said as he turned to leave. "Call me when you feel like he's ready."

If anything, he was guilty of nothing more than a poor choice of words. But as he walked away, I felt a cold chill run the length of my spine. *Call when you feel he's ready.* What he was saying was that the decision as to when Willie Williams should die was being left to me. And, in that moment, with a nauseous feeling growing in the pit of my stomach, I was suddenly, and without the slightest intent, part of the process, an active participant in the planned death of another human being. There, in the quiet first hour of a new day, with the night outside still as black as a cave, I had been pulled over a line I had long fought not to cross.

I wish I could say that I remember in great detail the time I spent with Williams. In all honesty it is only a blur. For the first and only time in my tenure as chaplain, I accompanied a man to his death with no real idea of who he was or who he had become.

Today, my memories of him come back only in quick snapshots and brief bits of conversation. I do recall that it was obvious the waiting had taken its toll on him. When I first saw him, he was nervous, breathing in short, quick bursts. The hand that he extended to me was shaking, and he had to clear a dry throat just to return my greeting.

Williams was just twenty-three in 1982 when he and a friend named Joseph Nichols had gone on a drug-and-alcohol-fueled crime spree in Houston. Having already committed two armed robberies just hours earlier, the young laborers had walked into a convenience store and ordered corn dogs and a quart of beer from storekeeper Claude Schaffer. As he was ringing up their purchase, they had pulled guns and ordered him to kneel down behind the counter while they took the money from the cash register. Schaffer was shot in the back before the robbers fled.

In the days before they were finally arrested, Williams and Nichols committed two more armed robberies. And while it was Williams who confessed to the murder of Schaffer, both men received death sentences for the crime.

A self-professed Muslim, Williams had not asked that an imam of his faith be present when he arrived. Nor did he wish to make any phone calls. Or, for that matter, to engage in any lengthy discussions. I tried to convince him that despite the late hour, there was no reason to rush things, and I do remember his response: "I had a good visit with my mother and stepfather this afternoon out at Ellis. Since then, all I've been doing is waiting, and I'm feeling really tired," he said. "I just want it to be over."

And so, we almost immediately began discussing the procedure that he was soon to face. I recall wanting so badly to do something that would assure him that his situation was not being taken lightly, to somehow make him know that he was as important as any other who had been delivered to the Death House. At one point he gave out a quick laugh and observed that I seemed more nervous than he was. "And, hey," he added, "you've done this a lot more times than I have."

His body, he told me, would be claimed by his mother. She would also receive his property. Strange that I have no recollection of what he brought with him from Ellis to Huntsville that night, yet to this day I can still remember the amount of money he had in his trust fund account at the time of his death. Willie Williams died with a balance of one cent. A penny.

"Chaplain," he asked as soon as we had gone through the formalities, "how much longer do we have to wait?"

"It's up to you. We can talk some. Maybe there are letters you want to write. It's late, but if there are people you want to call, we'll try to call them," I said.

He shook his head. "I'm ready to get it over with."

"You're sure?"

"As soon as possible."

I placed a call to the warden's office. "He's ready," I said.

And at 1:57 A.M., less than an hour and a half after the death of Clifton Russell, Willie Ray Williams was pronounced dead.

It was soon thereafter that I began to experience abdominal pains for which my doctor, in spite of every test that he could think to perform, could find no physical cause. My problem, I knew, was not of the body but of the mind and spirit. I had watched too many people die in the name of justice and vengeance. My feelings about what was taking place with increasing regularity had grown stronger. It was becoming increasingly difficult to hide my thoughts about the barbaric nature of executions. And I began to consider the possibility that it was time to step away.

Time and time again, condemned men had sat in the Death House holding cell, marking the final hours of their lives, and asked the same question. They were generally not educated, but the simple logic of their question had the wisdom of scholars. How, they repeatedly asked, could the state kill a person to show others that killing is wrong?

It was a question for which I had no good answer. For, in truth, there was none.

As I look back, those days would have been even more difficult had not a new strength come into my life. In June of 1990, I remarried.

I had known Jane since the days when I was the minister at the First Presbyterian. She and her husband had moved to Huntsville in 1969 and had immediately become active in the church. I had baptized their children and would eventually officiate at the marriages of their daughters. Then, when they began to have marital problems, they had come to me for counsel.

In time, however, they divorced, and I lost contact with them. By then working at the prison and conducting my services at the Shiro church, I had struggled through my own personal difficulties and was slowly growing comfortable with my life as a single father.

It was a year later when I stepped to the pulpit one Sunday morning and was pleasantly surprised to see Jane and two of her daughters among my small congregation. It was good to see an old friend and flattering when Jane explained that she had decided to visit because she missed my sermons.

Though still active in the Huntsville church, she began to attend Shiro services on a fairly regular basis. Then, as I was making preparations to attend an annual meeting of church officials in nearby Bryan, I learned that she would also be attending as the First Presbyterian representative. I suggested that we make the day trip together.

Something remarkable happened that afternoon as we sat together, listening to a moving sermon delivered by Joan Salmon Campbell. As I listened and later sang along with the closing hymn, "Have Thine Own Way Lord," I came to a realization that my firm determination to remain a bachelor for the rest of my life was pure folly.

Later, as we sat in the car, its heater warding off the twenty-six-degree temperature outside, Joan was quiet for some time, then asked, "Did you feel something during the sermon?"

"What I heard," I replied, "was that you and I should talk about making a life together."

She smiled the most beautiful smile I'd ever seen and nodded. "That's what I heard, too."

Six months later, we met with our children—her three and my four—and asked how they felt about our getting married. The vote to move ahead with our plans was quick and unanimous.

Jane was a remarkable woman—a devout Christian, loving mother, and tireless worker in International Rope Skipping Organization, a worldwide activity designed to encourage physical fitness and competition for youngsters looking for something other than Little League baseball or summer basketball camps. A fine athlete herself, she quickly became my mixed doubles partner on the tennis court.

She was, of course, aware of what I did at the prison, yet quick to admit that she had no real understanding of the death penalty. We had been married only a short time when she got her baptism into my world. My daughter Charlotte had answered the phone one evening to hear a raging voice lashing out against capital punishment in general and me in particular. "If your father was a real Christian," the unidentified woman said, "he would do something to stop these murders. He would jump onto the gurney and pull the needles from the arms of the man they are killing." Before Charlotte could respond the woman had called me a murderer and slammed the phone down.

Later, Jane and I sat and talked late into one night. I confided some of the problems I'd begun to have with my role in the process, the struggle I was having. "I know it must be terribly hard for you," she had said, "but what you're doing for these men is important. I want to help you, but I can't unless you tell me how."

She could help me by being a sounding board, I said; someone to talk with when the pressures mounted would be a godsend. "I'm a good listener," she acknowledged. As a bonus she fell into a routine of having freshly cooked banana pudding waiting on the kitchen table when I arrived home in the wee hours following an execution. The gentle sounds of Bill Gaither gospel music would be flowing through the house.

It was like being rescued from an Arctic cold to the warmth and comfort of a blazing hearth.

In time she even began to occasionally accompany me to the prison when a visiting minister arrived to preach, sitting beside me in the chapel, coming to an understanding of what could only be learned firsthand. The Chapel of Hope, I had tried to explain, was the only sanctuary of freedom in prison, the only remnant of the real world left for those who came to it. Meeting inmates, she also soon realized that they weren't all the beasts and ogres depicted in lurid detective magazines. She made friends and soon realized that despite past mistakes many of those behind bars were people not so different from us. And in that realization she embraced the philosophy of my prison ministry.

And, over time, she came to understand the source of my frustration. The seemingly endless succession of executions was taking me farther from what I had vowed to accomplish at The Walls. Those being transported to the Death House, I knew, needed me. But so did those who looked to the chapel and my office for whatever comfort I could provide. I began to worry that the dilemma of serving two responsibilities had begun to leech away my effectiveness at both.

Perhaps, I confided to Jane, it was time to begin thinking of stepping down.

SEVENTEEN

Dread, I have long believed, is one of the darkest, most oppressive of all emotions. Whether so simple as the apprehension attached to a visit to the doctor or to the annual homage paid the Internal Revenue Service, it can, if allowed, become suffocating, accompanying one's every waking hour, distracting thought of all else. While the early days of May of 1991 served for many as a welcome harbinger of the summer to come, I found myself more anxious about an upcoming execution than any I'd ever prepared for.

For the first time, I would be asked to minister to a man who had dramatically affected my own life, leaving a scar that still remained after seventeen years.

Ignacio Cuevas, at fifty-nine the oldest inmate residing on Death Row, was finally scheduled to die for his role in that long-ago prison siege that had first drawn me to The Walls.

And as his execution date drew near, I found myself reliving those horrifying eleven days and nights in 1974 when innocent prison employees had been held hostage by Fred Carrasco, Rudolfo Dominguez, and Cuevas. The distant faces of worried family members returned to play in my mind's eye, and the brave voices of Judy Standley and Yvonne Beseda began to whisper to me in my restless sleep. I could not escape the idea that by ministering to Cuevas I would somehow be betraying them and their memories.

It all came rushing back: talking to Judy on the phone while she was being held hostage, just hours before her death, discussing plans for her funeral and promising to move ahead with the preparations for her daughter's wedding. Then gathering with her family to tell them that their loving mother and wife was dead. All of the agony and rage, desperate prayers, and unresolved questions associated with that senseless time in history had been burned into my memory. Ignoring them was impossible.

I worried that all Cuevas would want to talk about was the siege, and I wasn't at all sure that I could deal with it.

Despite all efforts to focus on my daily routine of chapel services, choir practices, and visits to hospitalized inmates, the weight of what lay ahead pressed on me. Since that day in 1982 when Warden Pursley had announced that the death penalty had been reinstated, I had privately hoped that the date now officially scheduled would never come. After so long on Death Row, so many stays of execution ordered by the courts, I had begun to doubt that Cuevas's sentence would ever be carried out and secretly welcomed the thought of endless stays. Twice, legal technicalities had resulted in the verdict against Cuevas being overturned. The state of Texas had spent over a million dollars to support the physical existence and maintain the civil rights of a man who had been tried and convicted of an unspeakably inhumane act, not once but three times. Now it appeared that the appeal process would endlessly drag on until, one day, Ignacio Cuevas would quietly die in prison, an old man never required to face punishment for his crimes.

It was, quite honestly, a scenario that had long provided me a degree of selfish relief.

Now, however, a new reality had emerged, and with it questions that I struggled with mightily. How was I to properly minister to a man who had caused me and many close to me such great and lingering pain? And what might the inmate's reaction be if he learned that on that dark August night when the siege had ended so tragically, I had not been a prison chaplain but, rather, the minister of the First Presbyterian Church, which his victims attended? How, I wondered, does one counsel families of the living and the dead—as I knew I would be required to do—on the day of execution? Should any man who has served as pastor to a murder victim be called on to serve as chaplain to the man convicted of that murder? Would it be possible to summon the proper degree of strength and honest conviction to do so?

I prayed for answers. And, for the first time since assuming the role of Death House chaplain, I began to consider asking to be relieved of the task that awaited me. Finally, a greater power told me that I had to embrace the responsibility. Like those who had traveled to the Death House before him, Ignacio Cuevas deserved my time, my help, my emotional support—and perhaps even my sympathy.

Thus, on the morning of May 22, I was nervously standing in the hallway of the Death House when guards escorted him to the small cell in which he would spend his final hours.

For all the ugly pictures that had long played in my mind, the images I'd conjured of the desperate and evil men who had boarded them-selves into the prison library, Cuevas was not at all what I expected. The bigger-than-life persona I'd mentally created immediately disap-peared when I saw a five-foot-two, 140-pound man quietly walk to a nearby chair to be released from the shackles he'd worn on the trip from the Ellis Unit. The coal black hair I'd seen in newspaper pho-tographs was now specked with gray, and his brown eyes were not mirrors of spite and hate but instead dull and hidden behind horn-rimmed glasses.

Lifting his head, he silently turned to me and nodded.

Through the years, I had been warned, Cuevas had become an expert at the I-don't-understand-English ploy. On the advice of the lengthy parade of court-appointed lawyers who had represented him and civil rights leaders who chose to champion his cause, he had hidden behind a feigned ignorance of the language despite the testi-mony of numerous hostages who clearly recalled him yelling out angry threats and commands to them in English throughout the siege. Now, to portray himself as an illiterate victim of a bloodthirsty legal system determined to put him to death had become his life's role. True to form, his first response to the warden was, "No hablo inglés."

In anticipation of the problem, I had requested that Sgt. Gilbert Cervantes, fluent in Spanish, be assigned to serve as an interpreter. Though convinced that Cuevas understood everything I was saying, I began the routine of going through the necessary paperwork by speaking first to Sergeant Cervantes, who would then translate.

While the documents the inmate had filled out earlier in the week indicated that he wished to have no witnesses to his execution, he now insisted that he had requested that his children be on hand. He particularly wanted his son, Ricardo, to be there "to make sure he was dead."

An angry tone rose in his voice as he explained. For years, he said, he had heard rumors that Death Row inmates did not actually die by lethal injection but, instead, were simply buried alive in the prison cemetery.

He even refused to acknowledge that the signature on various forms was actually his. Someone had forged it. The amount in his inmate trust fund, he insisted, was seventeen dollars shy of the total he'd carefully tabulated. His defiant message was clear: the system continued to treat him unfairly—lying to him, stealing from him, wishing him dead.

Each argument he made was delivered in perfectly good English. Sergeant Cervantes shook his head in disgust and announced that he had better things to do. "You don't need me here," he said to Cuevas, then left. The inmate laughed in response.

While he did not want to write a will, the prisoner indicated that his possessions as well as his body should be turned over to his son if and when the execution was completed.

The formalities finally completed, I began to describe what he could expect of the remainder of the day. His attorney from the Texas Resource Center was, I assured him, at the prison, monitoring the appeal process, which would likely continue throughout the day. He would be notified, I promised, as soon as any decision was made.

On the visiting list he had prepared were the names of ten children, a wife, an ex-wife, a Catholic nun, and a friend. He seemed surprisingly confident that all of them would be waiting their turn to see him despite the fact that prison records indicated he had not received a single visitor in over a year.

The only two who came were his son Ricardo and Ricardo's wife, Juana. They had driven from the little Texas Panhandle community of Abernathy.

For much of the afternoon, they sat outside his cell, quietly speaking in Spanish. My job, for the time being, was reduced to bringing the occasional cups of black coffee that Cuevas always politely asked for. Relieved that he had apparently made no connection between me and the victims of his crime, my thoughts had turned to other concerns. Once the visiting period ended and we were left alone to count away the final hours, I would have to set all personal feelings aside and focus on my purpose for being there. *God,* I silently prayed, *give me the strength to provide comfort to this man.*

It was shortly after four when I was called upstairs to the prison director's office to meet with Cuevas's attorney, a pleasant and cooperative young woman named Elizabeth Cohen. She had just received word that she and Cuevas's son would not be allowed to witness the execution because the deadline for such requests had long passed, and she wanted to personally tell her client of this fact. Though I expressed concern that her news might only serve to upset him, she was adamant. And she made it clear that she held no great faith in the role I was playing. "I'm afraid," she said, "that no one is telling him that he has anyone on his side."

She followed me into the Death House, where she and Cuevas spoke briefly. His appeal, she explained, was still with the district court. And even if the judge's ruling should not be in his favor, there remained the Fifth Circuit Court of Appeals and the Supreme Court

to be heard from. I heard her assure him that there was good reason
to believe that another stay of execution was possible, and I felt a new
wave of emotions boil in my stomach. Was it possible that her argument that Cuevas was, in fact, mentally retarded—a condition of
which I'd seen no evidence—and that he should not have been held
to the same degree of blame as the others involved in the standoff
and murders—something I could not find it in my heart to agree
with—going to again postpone the long-overdue justice that the victims' families had waited a lifetime for? Or was Cuevas's attorney only
offering up a false and empty hope that, in its own way, was as cruel
as the fate now assigned him?

Such were the questions I pondered as I escorted her out and allowed Cuevas's son to return for his final good-bye. When the time
came for the visit to end, Ricardo asked for three more minutes as he
stood and placed his hands against the mesh wire of the holding cell.
And with that, his son, a young man with no ordination, no official
call by his church, began to give his father, a man who had referred
to himself as a nondenominational Christian on the forms he had
filled out, the last rites of the Catholic Church.

It was shortly before 6:00 P.M. when word came that the district
court had denied his request for a stay. It was time, I explained, that
we discuss what would transpire over the next few hours. Calmly, the
former migrant worker agreed. And for the remainder of the night, we
conversed in the language he'd claimed not to know.

During the day, a Baptist minister had appeared at the administration building, claiming that he had been the one who had led Cuevas
to the Lord during a prison ministry fifteen years earlier. Though he
was not on the visitors list, I was prepared to allow him in until
Ignacio said that he did not wish to see him. Nor, he said, did he wish
to speak with a San Antonio minister who had arrived early in the
afternoon, asking to pray with the condemned prisoner. I asked if there
was a chaplain from the Ellis Unit he might like to see. He laughed.
"None of them did me any good," he said.

It appeared matters of the spirit were of little concern to him.

He seemed more eager to spend his final hours making long-distance phone calls to family members who had not seen fit to bid him farewell in person and to his son, who had returned to his room at a local Motel 6.

And he bragged to me of his ability to kill and the notoriety that it had earned him in the free world.

I sensed no remorse, no attempt at a cleansing confession, as he spoke in great detail of the crime that had resulted in his being sentenced to forty years in prison. In fact, there was a faint sparkle in his eyes as he told of stabbing a man to death during a drunken barroom fight in 1970. Thereafter, he noted, his reputation had been such that on one occasion fearful authorities in Mexico arrested him, then simply escorted him across the border, chaining him to a tree on the U.S. side of the Rio Grande. That done, they placed a call to American officials to alert them to his location. "He's yours," they supposedly said. "We don't want him." For some time he talked boastfully of a wasted life of crime and pain inflicted on others, yet not once did he ever mention the prison siege. He spoke neither of Judy nor Yvonne nor of the other hostages forced to endure the nightmare he had caused.

Nor did I attempt to draw him into such a discussion, still fearful that my own fragile emotions might surface.

By early in the evening the Fifth Circuit had also denied the request for a stay, and the realization that he was soon to die began to set in. While I described the procedure as carefully and thoroughly as I could, his only interest seemed to be in how long it would take and whether he would feel anything once the needles were inserted into his arms. He wasn't afraid to die, he said; he just didn't want it to be painful.

As he talked, I struggled to avoid thinking back on those days when he'd threatened the hostages, handcuffed them to that grotesque makeshift tank, and then used them as human shields during the attempted escape. Why had he felt no concern for their fears and pain?

In those final hours he never gave up on the idea that he could manipulate the system that he so obviously despised. Following an evening call to his son, he asked me if it was true that under the rules a spiritual advisor was allowed to witness his execution. I acknowledged that was the case, and immediately he began to insist that he had filled out paperwork, making such a request, before being transferred from the Ellis Unit. And, unlike all the others he'd disavowed, the signature on that particular document was his own, he said. I immediately telephoned an Ellis chaplain, asking that he locate the request and bring it to the administration building as quickly as possible. On the form, filled out well after the deadline for listing witnesses had passed, Cuevas had written that Ricardo Martinez—his son—was the spiritual adviser he wished to be allowed into the witness area. Upon learning that, I couldn't help but wonder if the last rites scene I'd watched earlier in the day had been more for my benefit than Cuevas's, if perhaps it was part of a carefully planned last-minute scheme to admit his son into the witness room.

Of course, it was something that I could not be sure of. On the other hand, one thing was becoming increasingly clear: for a man supposedly too mentally handicapped to understand the consequences of his actions, Ignacio Cuevas seemed quite calculating.

The warden quickly ruled against his request.

It was not until late in the evening, after his final appeal had been denied, and after he had showered and begun to eat his final meal, that we finally began to discuss matters of the heart. No longer the bragging criminal, he was, he told me, soon going to be in a better place. He'd put his life in the hands of the Lord years earlier, he said, and had been reading the Bible daily for almost eighteen years. He was at peace.

His only real regret was that he'd failed his children, some of whom were dealing with many of the same problems he'd experienced as a young man. And he lamented the fact that he'd never been able to hold any of his grandchildren.

As I sat listening, my fears that I would be unable to deal with the unique situation returned. Among the files I had read earlier in the week had been a letter sent to the warden by the children of Judy Standley. In it, they movingly described how their family had been affected by the murder of their mother, pointing out that she had not lived to enjoy the pleasure of seeing her grandchildren. As I listened to Cuevas talk of his own family, I could not help but make the comparison between the two lovely women who had died and this man who had a hand in their deaths.

Finally, shortly after 11:00 P.M., he asked to make a final call to one of his daughters. Moving away from the cell, I walked down the hall to the shower room and sat on the brick entryway. And immediately a wave of uncontrolled nausea swept over me. The pain and resentment, so long stored away, overwhelmed me as everything that had happened during that long-ago August rushed back. At that moment I would rather have drowned myself in the shower than endure what was to take place in the next hour. As I sat, perspiring and shaking, trying to calm myself before returning to the man whom I had promised to comfort, I questioned the whole idea of fairness and justice. And came to the decision that the system in which I worked provided neither.

He was hanging up the phone as I approached and looked up at me with an almost childlike expression. "What do we do now?" he asked. "How do I get ready to die?"

"We'll do whatever you want to do," I replied. "We can pray, we can read Scriptures, you might want to confess your sins. . . ."

It was at that moment that he said the words that haunt me to this day: "I've been confessing what I've done every day for the last eighteen years."

The sincerity in his voice, suddenly soft, even gentle, took me by surprise. In every article that I'd read about him, he had never assumed any moral responsibility for his participation in the siege, had shown no remorse for the lives he'd helped destroy. To the world he had always proclaimed himself an innocent victim. "I have never killed anybody," he had told the court shortly before his sentencing. And now, only ten feet and twenty minutes away from the death chamber, he was admitting that he had been seeking God's forgiveness for years.

And suddenly I felt a new confidence in my purpose. "Is there some Scripture I can read for you?" I asked.

"The Twenty-third Psalm," he replied, "has always given me comfort."

When I finished, he nodded. "You know, it is important that all people be pastors to those in need. You've done a good job of representing Jesus here today. Like He said, I was a stranger, and you came to me. The Lord said to bring water to those who are thirsty, and you've been bringing me coffee all day. You've been kind. You've been everything a good pastor should be."

I asked if he wished to pray, and he shook his head. "My prayers are finished," he said.

Minutes later the warden was at the door of the cell, asking that Cuevas step into the hall to begin the short walk to the death chamber. Before he was taken away, he turned and silently stared at me for several seconds. "I've had a good day," he said, "and I'm ready to die."

I reached out and shook his hand, then followed him to the waiting gurney.

The death of Ignacio Cuevas came quickly. Seconds after the drugs began to flow into his veins, he uttered a faint sigh and closed his eyes. He was pronounced dead at 12:18 A.M. But not before one final surprise.

Though already aware that he had planned no final statement, Warden Pursley was obligated to ask if the inmate had any last words. Cuevas turned his head toward the window that separated him from the nearby witnesses and smiled. "Beautiful faces," he said. Then, in a last whisper, two words that I could not believe I was hearing: "I'm innocent."

Only minutes earlier he had spoken of the remorse he'd lived with for eighteen years, had confessed and talked of God's forgiveness. Yet in public, the pride and misguided ego, the years of programming by the lawyers and the judicial system, had made it necessary for him to die a liar.

. . .

Later that night I walked into the still and steamy night where Judy's daughters waited outside the prison and told them it was over. They asked if he had said anything about their mother, if he had admitted his wrongdoing, and if he had felt any pain as he died. I answered their questions as best I could. As they turned to go to their cars, which were parked across the street in my driveway, it was Dru who stopped and looked at me. "It isn't what I expected," she said. "All these years I've thought this would bring the closure I've heard so much about. But it doesn't. My mother is still dead." And with that she turned and disappeared into the darkness.

I then drove to the motel to meet with Cuevas's son, to assure him that his father had died a painless death and to deliver his belongings and a check for the $115.92 that had remained in his trust fund. I also gave him the watch and small cross and chain that Cuevas had handed to me before showering.

Ricardo Martinez admitted that he had been relieved that the request to allow him to witness the execution had been denied. It had not been a memory with which he wanted to live. He told me that he had known in his heart that this time there would be no stay to prevent his father's dying. In anticipation, he had hand built a casket in which he planned to bury his father. Rather than wait until daylight, he wished to begin the nine-hour trip home as quickly as possible.

I contacted the funeral home to make them aware of his wishes, and they quickly set about preparing the body to be transported.

Thus Ignacio Cuevas, whose evil legacy had haunted the community of Huntsville for almost two decades, left town in a makeshift box fashioned from pieces of cardboard in the bed of a pickup. Soon he would be placed in a homemade casket, lowered into a grave, covered by earth, and forgotten. And very few people would care.

In the days to come I would find myself thinking back on that long and trying day, again seeking an answer to the question I'd asked so many times before. Was there really justice? Clouding the answer on this occasion had been the memory of not one but two people whom I'd spoken with in the last hours of their lives: the victim and the person charged with the crime.

Judy Standley had told me, "It isn't how you die, but, rather, how you live. I'm prepared to die. I know where I'm going, and God will take care of me."

The deeds of Cuevas's life had been vile and despicable, yet he too seemed confident that a new life awaited him. "I'm going to a better place," he had said.

Despite a lifetime of studying the Scriptures and listening to the theological interpretations of men far wiser than me, I'm still not sure what to make of it all. Judy died for others, her passing mourned, her memory honored by tributes and scholarships and professions of great admiration. Cuevas had died a cold-blooded murderer, proclaiming a blatant, unforgivable lie to the end, and was hauled away in a pickup truck and destined for a lonely grave.

Perhaps it was justice, at least as our society and judicial system choose to define it. There had even been a time when I would have agreed. But all that had changed. Where was the fairness? In the days following Cuevas's execution, a reporter for the Huntsville *Item* wrote that . . . "seventeen years of 'fairness' was quite enough."

Still, I wondered what good had been done. And I could find no answer.

EIGHTEEN

As the summer of 1995 neared, I began to seriously consider retirement. Too many distractions had begun to blur the goals I had long ago set for my ministry at The Walls. Changes in philosophy were coming rapidly, many of them the by-products of the ongoing battle by the state with federal judge Justice to regain control of the Texas prison system. The function of the chapel, I felt, was fast sliding down a growing list of bureaucratic priorities. Throughout the system, in fact, there were rumors that other chaplains were preparing their resignations.

Never a quitter, I found myself considering the options that lay ahead: I could call it a career, try to assure myself that I had fought a good and noble fight, all the while feeling guilt at having left behind unfinished business and a concern that I was turning my back on the needs of others. Or I could step aside and allow someone with fresh, new ideas and greater energy to assume my position.

Such a decision is particularly difficult when one's emotional bank balance is depleted. And I was tired, particularly of the executions. As I pondered what to do, the thirteenth execution of the year was scheduled to be carried out. Since that night in 1982 when Texas resumed capital punishment with the execution of Charles Brooks, ninety-seven people had been executed.

Over the years my belief had grown that Texas's espousal of the virtues of the death penalty was badly misguided. My participation in the process had begun to gnaw at me; keeping my silence had become increasingly difficult.

"Perhaps," Jane suggested, "it is time for you to consider the possibility of speaking out."

Despite her remarkable perceptiveness, I doubt that even she knew how badly I wanted to do just that—to finally hear myself talk from the heart about the moral and spiritual shortcomings of a legal system that condoned state-sponsored murder. Perhaps that was the new call I was beginning to hear.

It is, I suppose, human nature to view ourselves as being so vital to our work that we've become irreplaceable. While I did not look on myself quite so grandiosely, I did find myself concerned at the small number of clergymen who might embrace the unique kind of ministry I'd conducted. There were few, I feared, who aspired to become the Death House chaplain. On numerous occasions, in fact, fellow prison chaplains had clearly stated they could and would not do what I had been doing for years. I'd seen preachers of virtually every faith visit condemned men waiting out their final hours and watched as they shook and broke into a sweat the moment I escorted them to the Death House. Few had ever stayed more than a few minutes, and none made more than one trip. Despite their strong commitment to spreading the gospel, most had made it clear to me that they would never return.

I found myself reflecting on those times a great deal.

Stephen Morin had come to prison as a rapist and murderer in 1982. His life story was as sad and sordid as any I'd ever heard. He had shot and killed a young woman outside a San Antonio restaurant, abducted another woman, and fled in her car. It was while the frightened hostage drove him deep into the Texas Hill Country, he would later tell me, that his life changed.

A sermon from a Texas evangelist was playing on the tape deck. The words he heard, the promise of redemption and the glories of a good life, so moved Morin that he suddenly decided that he would end his life of crime and turn himself in to the authorities. But not before making a trip to Fort Worth for a personal visit with the charismatic minister. Reaching Kerrville, the woman drove him to a bus station and provided him money for a ticket.

Then she had driven to the police station to report the nightmare that she'd just experienced. Morin was arrested when his bus made a stop in Austin.

During the years he spent on Death Row, he was a model prisoner, strong in his faith. He wrote regularly to the evangelist, praising his work and thanking him for directing him to a Christian way of life.

It was when he came to the Death House that I learned of the almost childlike admiration Morin felt for the evangelist. He had, in fact, even included him on his visitors list. The evangelist, he insisted, had assured him that he would be with him as he prepared to die.

And so I spent much of the day attempting to contact the evangelist to remind him of his promise. It was not until late in the afternoon that he returned my call. Explaining who I was and that the inmate was expecting him to visit, I asked when he might arrive. My question was quickly greeted by a lengthy tirade about pressing matters that would make such a visit impossible. I felt my patience slip away. "You've corresponded with this man since he came to prison, right?" I said.

For several seconds there was silence on the other end of the line. "Yes . . . yes, I have," he finally replied.

"From what I understand, you have had a great impact on his life. You are the person who led him to Christ, encouraged him to seek salvation. I doubt that there is anyone among your following who holds you in higher regard."

More silence.

"And apparently you made a promise. Am I right?"

"Okay," he responded, "I'll try to get there." I sensed a tone in his voice that bordered on anger.

It was almost ten in the evening, long past the established time for visits, when I was informed that the evangelist's private jet had landed at the Huntsville airport and that he would soon be en route to the prison. When I passed the information on to Morin, an almost angelic smile spread across his face. "He's really here? He's coming?"

"I'm going to go upstairs and escort him down," I said.

In the lobby I met a man clearly anxious about his mission. There was no trace of warmth in his voice as he said, "You know that I don't want to be here."

"Sir," I acknowledged, "none of us wants to be here."

"How long do I have to stay?" he asked. Despite the late hour, I explained, the warden had agreed that I could assure him a lengthy visit.

In the years that I spent time in the Death House, I never saw a man's spirits soar as Stephen Morin's did upon seeing the evangelist's approach. The look on his face was like that of a wonderstruck child seeing Santa Claus for the first time.

The evangelist stayed less than five minutes. "Son," I heard him say, "I wish I could stay longer, but they limited my time."

No sooner had we stepped beyond the Death House door than the evangelist took a deep breath and said, "I'll never come to this place again." As I escorted him back to the waiting room, he was silent until we reached to doorway that led to the street. Then, pointing a finger toward my face, he said, "Don't you ever call me again." He was gone before I could tell him that he need not worry.

These were some of the thoughts that raced through my mind as I wrestled with the decision I'd committed myself to make. I weighed pluses and minuses, and reflected on successes and failures, the good times and the bad. Jane and I would sit up late into the night, talking. The faces of men I had come to know, some asleep in their nearby cells, some back in the free world, many now dead, began to flip through my mind like the pages of a photo album. My appetite disappeared, and I began sleeping only in fitful interludes.

The time, I decided, had come. And so I made the director and the warden aware of my intent to retire.

· · ·

Inmate Vernon Sattiewhite would be the last man I would meet in the Death House. Ironically, he illustrated perfectly many of the reservations that had prompted my decision. A high school dropout, he was poorly educated. A black man, he'd spent much of his adult life in jails and prison. Experts who had tested him had agreed that he suffered mental problems resulting from brain damage due to childhood abuse. A career criminal and drug abuser, he was someone I would not have trusted to roam in the free world. Yet, in prison, he had quietly served his time, harming no one.

A cell and supervision had clearly served the needs of Sattiewhite and society quite nicely. Yet the law insisted that he die.

In 1986, unable to accept the rebuff of a longtime girlfriend, he had stalked her relentlessly, angrily urging her to return to the relationship. For over a month Sandra Sorrell, a nursing student and the mother of two, had complained about Sattiewhite's harassment to San Antonio authorities, but to no avail.

Then, one morning as she walked to school in the company of her new boyfriend, Willington Mingo, Sattiewhite approached the couple on the street. Wrapping one arm tightly around Sorrell's neck, he pulled out a twenty-two-caliber pistol, held it to her head, and began dragging her down the sidewalk. Mingo hurried into a nearby office and asked that someone phone the police, then caught up with Sattiewhite and the woman, pleading that she be released.

For a moment Sattiewhite glared at the frightened young man, then cursed and said, "If I can't have her, ain't nobody else going to." And then he fired two point-blank shots into the woman's head. As her body fell to the pavement, he put the gun to his own head. Mingo would later tell authorities that Sattiewhite must have pulled the trigger at least a dozen times, but the gun failed to fire.

Later that day, dazed and bewildered, his shirt still stained with the blood of his dead former girlfriend, he surrendered to the police.

Crimes of such violence, committed in an insane display of frustrated love, were among the most difficult for me to understand. Yet I had encountered tales of them at virtually every turn inside The Walls. With the exception of Blue, every clerk who ever worked for me had come to prison convicted of murdering his wife. So had many who were among my most faithful chapel attendees. My barber had shot and killed his wife. A trustee who was allowed to come to my home and do yard work was adored by my children—who did not know that years earlier he had shot and killed his wife.

And, clearly, such crimes of passion were not the sole property of any single segment of the inmate population. The only lawyer ever sentenced to death in Texas was George Lott, a docile, soft-spoken man who had walked into a crowded Fort Worth courtroom one morning, pulled a nine-millimeter handgun from his briefcase, and begun randomly firing. Clyde Marshall, an assistant district attorney, was killed, and the presiding judge, John Hill, was badly wounded. When Steve Condor, an attorney who had only been watching the proceedings from the gallery, ran from the courtroom, Lott calmly followed him into the hallway and killed him.

Lott then fled the scene, only to turn up a few hours later at a Dallas television station, where he sat with a reporter, admitting his crimes to a stunned noonday news-viewing audience before police could arrive.

He explained that the rampage had been triggered by divorce hearings during which his wife, whom he insisted he still loved dearly, was seeking to prevent him from seeing his two-year-old son.

Representing himself at trial, Lott was quickly convicted. During less than two years on Death Row—the shortest time any inmate had been there since the death penalty had been reinstated—he made no attempt to appeal his case. On the night he was scheduled to die, he told me that his only wish was that he could have been executed sooner.

Sattiewhite's inexcusable act, one that left two children without a mother and a family devastated, was more than a crime of misguided passion. It was the culmination of a life of self-destructive behavior spent striking out against others. In 1977 he had been sentenced to five years in prison for murder, but he was paroled two years later and granted clemency. In 1984 he returned to prison, convicted of robbery, and stayed only six months before again being paroled.

Then, after his girlfriend had broken off their relationship, he began suffering blackouts, heard voices, and on several occasions attempted suicide. Finally he had murdered Sandra Sorrell.

Among the new changes that were being discussed by prison officials was the routine of bringing the condemned men to Huntsville early in the morning, providing a full day in which to see visitors, make phone calls, and tend to the last bits of business before their postmidnight execution. It had already been decided that Sattiewhite would be the last man put to death in the first minutes of his court-ordered execution date. Instead, the new plan would have executions carried out at 6:00 P.M. Additionally, inmates would not be transferred to the Death House until midafternoon on the day they were to die.

It was but another step toward an assembly-line approach, an approach for which the state was already being roundly criticized. The criticism I could tolerate. What I could not accept was the idea that one could offer any real counsel and support, that the delicate process of helping someone mentally and spiritually prepare for death could be accomplished in the abbreviated time frame being proposed. I strongly believed that the role of the chaplain was being greatly diminished.

I did not greet Vernon Sattiewhite until five in the afternoon. And almost immediately I realized that the judgment of psychologists who had spent time with him was valid.

Shortly after he was settled into the holding cell, I had received a call from the warden's office explaining that Bettie Sattiewhite, the inmate's sister, had phoned to say that she wished to speak with him. I relayed the message and received only a blank look. "I don't know any Bettie Sattiewhite," Vernon said.

I was nonplussed. In the folder that had been given me by the

guards who accompanied him from the Ellis Unit was the paperwork
he had filled out. On the form addressing how he wished his property
disposed of, he had clearly written that it was to go to Bettie Sattiewhite, even including her address in San Antonio. Yet now he was
insisting that he did not even know such a person. Feeling the pressure
of the time constraints forced by his late arrival, I opted not to press
the issue and simply moved quickly forward through the routine of
legal work.

I assured him that his attorney, Nancy Barohn, had arrived and
would immediately contact him if there was any news regarding the
last-minute appeal process that was underway. I double-checked his
intent to will his body to the University of Texas Medical Branch at
Galveston, and made sure that he expected no visitors other than his
lawyer. When I outlined the schedule we would follow over the course
of the remaining hours, he would only occasionally nod until I reached
the point where I explained that at some point it would be necessary
for us to discuss what would take place once he was escorted into the
death chamber.

"That part," he said, finally smiling faintly, his voice only a soft
whisper, "can wait until we've heard whatever the appellate courts
have to say."

It was not until he'd showered and was finishing his meal that he
showed interest in conversation. "You and me," he said, "we need to
talk about something."

I pulled my chair near the bars.

"All the guys out on the Row, they understand you're quitting," he
said.

Aware that few secrets are kept in the system, I was not surprised
that word of my plans had reached the Ellis Unit. "I've been doing
this for a long time. . . ."

"They don't like it," he interrupted. "Why you want to quit? Everybody on the Row says you're the only person really cares about us.
They say you treat us like human beings. My friends, they say you
probably don't even think killing people like this is right. Everybody

I know—including me—wishes you would stay on, keep doing what you're doing."

He looked squarely at me, his sad, piercing brown eyes appearing larger as he leaned toward the bars. "Why you quitting, Chaplain?"

I couldn't explain that it was because men like him were being put to death. I couldn't rant against a system that would keep him locked up and waiting to die for over ten years, yet now wanted to hurry him through his final hours. I couldn't tell him that I'd spent too much time in this cramped, ugly place, listening to frightened men whose lives began to slip away even before they made the walk to the gurney. I couldn't tell him that I was tired of it, saddened and angered by it; that I was bone weary of going through what he and I would be dealing with in only a matter of hours.

Sattiewhite continued talking. "Too bad you won't be here," he said. "Look what happened when you wasn't. Poor Chaplain Taylor—a good man—winds up losing his job. You ask me, I think that was a tragedy. Lot of guys out on the Row liked him. They miss seeing him."

During my career as chaplain at The Walls, I had attended all but two of the executions that took place there. In one case, it was assumed by everyone that the inmate's appeal would be granted and that his execution would not take place. The warden had urged me to join Jane on a brief business trip to the West Coast. Another of the chaplains, he assured me, would be standing by.

However, the execution did go off as scheduled. Shortly after my return, the chaplain who had replaced me was in my office. Still shaken by the experience, he said that he would resign if ever called on to go through the experience again.

On the other occasion when I was away, Ellis Unit chaplain Alex Taylor had been called on to minister to an inmate named Raymond Kinnamon as he awaited the carrying out of his sentence. A friend for years, Taylor had given me invaluable help as I prepared to meet the men who arrived from Death Row. If he thought a particular prisoner might present any sort of problem, he would alert me to it

and suggest ways that trouble might be avoided. At times he would
pass along small but important bits of information about the condemned men I would soon meet—one might have a particular fond-
ness for chocolate or peppermint candy, and thus I could be sure to
have it on hand; another might be open to discussion of anything but
a particular family member against whom he held a grudge, and thus
I knew not to bring up that person's name.

I had gone through the Death House routine with Taylor with a
mixture of confidence and wariness. Alex, I knew, was a good and
caring man who would keep the needs of the inmate foremost in mind.
On the other hand, I could not help but think of the warning Warden
Pursley had made years earlier. It was not a good idea, he said, for me
to get to know those on Death Row. It was his firm belief that I would
be able to carry out my responsibilities most effectively if I did not
have any kind of relationship with the inmate until his arrival in
Huntsville. In time I had come to realize the validity of his argument.
Chaplain Taylor, on the other hand, would be ministering to a man
he'd known for years at the Ellis Unit.

There were, however, no problems until Kinnamon was escorted
into the death chamber and strapped to the gurney. When asked if he
had any final words, he launched into a filibuster that he clearly hoped
would last until the sunrise deadline for his execution passed. The
more he talked—lashing out at the judge and jury involved in his
conviction, decrying the death penalty—the more agitated he became.
Finally, he began writhing on the gurney, trying to free himself from
the leather straps. Several times he managed to raise himself into a
half-sitting position. As the warden reached out to restrain the prisoner, Taylor, acting on instinct, attempted to help. Placing his hands
on the inmate's shoulders, the chaplain pushed him down onto the
gurney as stunned members of the media watched from the witness
gallery.

The following day, the headline in the Huntsville paper read,
"Chaplain Restrains Inmate During Execution." Soon thereafter, Taylor was removed from the Death Row position he had held for years.

Angered by what they had read, prisoners refused to attend his chapel services or welcome his visits to their cell blocks. He was transferred to a desk job in the administration office. The death chamber incident and the subsequent publicity had cost him a job he dearly loved and had done effectively. Eventually he left the prison system.

One night in the Death House, one innocent but ill-advised gesture inside the death chamber, had been responsible for the ruin of a career.

"There's other guys out there," Sattiewhite pointed out, "whose dates have done been set. They were counting on you being here." A sudden wave of guilt swept over me, and I was relieved when he changed the subject before I could reply.

"I'd like to call my sister now," he said.

"Your sister?"

"Yeah, her name's Bettie."

"Vernon, just a couple of hours ago I told you she had called and you said you didn't know her."

"I don't remember that," he said.

I looked at him as he sat on his bunk, wondering where the fine line between the real and unreal existed in his mind. How could he be so lucid one moment, discussing his feelings about my retirement, and at another not remember something that had occurred only an hour or so earlier?

He and his sister talked for several minutes, then he asked that I try to reach his son, whom he hadn't seen since coming to prison. I sensed a nervous hesitation on the part of Eric Sattiewhite when I reached him, but he agreed to speak with his father. For most of their conversation, he only listened.

As the brief conversation ended, I overheard Vernon say to his child, "There's lots of things I did in my life that I don't remember, and maybe that's just as well. But I want you to be sure you remember something. I don't want you to ever forget it. Don't get in trouble with the law. You be a good boy."

Over the next few hours, the ritual began. I'd watched it so many times that I could almost anticipate everything that would take place. Sattiewhite wrote a few letters, and I gave him envelopes and stamps, promising to see that the letters were mailed. The calls came to say that the appellate courts had ruled against a stay of the execution. He showered, changed into the civilian clothing that he would wear into the death chamber, then had his final meal. And then we began to talk of things that would take place in the final minutes of his life.

It was well after nine when he asked if it was possible to see the Catholic chaplain who was assigned to Death Row. "I'm Catholic, you know. I think I'd like it if Father Lopez could give me last rites."

Since he'd given no previous indication that he wished to have Fr. Richard Lopez there, I had to make several calls before locating him and asking that he come to The Walls as soon as possible. I was pleased to hear him say that he would come right away.

It was after he and Sattiewhite had talked for quite some time that I walked with the priest to the exit. Thanking him for coming, I watched as he left, then felt the hand of Director Wayne Scott on my shoulder. "You've done a good job," he said. "I can't let you quit." I didn't reply as we walked toward the warden's office. "Sattiewhite would like to see his attorney one more time," was all I said.

As soon as we entered the room, however, Scott returned to the subject. "Is there any chance that I could persuade you to stay on and just help with executions?" he asked. Not waiting for an answer, he turned to Jerry Peterson, the deputy director for operations. "Write up a contract," Scott said. "We can't do executions without him. Have it ready for him to sign tomorrow."

I cannot say the blame rests with ego, triggered by sudden flattery, or whether it was the fragile presence of second thoughts that prompted me not to immediately reject the idea.

All I said was that I needed to get back to Vernon Sattiewhite.

It was eleven-thirty when his lawyer told him that all avenues of appeal had closed. I began to describe the procedure that would take place in the nearby death chamber. His chin cradled in his hands, Sattiewhite sat on his bunk, saying nothing.

It was several minutes before he spoke. "Chaplain," he said, "I've been a good inmate. Maybe that counts for something."

"I believe it does."

"And me giving my body to science—I got no idea what they're going to do with it—maybe that'll be like the giving you been doing here. I wish I was going to be missed like I know you will be."

Soon the moment was at hand. Vernon Sattiewhite said nothing as he was being strapped in, did not flinch as attendants had difficulties getting the needles inserted into his arms. His eyes never left me.

At 12:25 A.M., he was dead.

Later that night, as I slowly made my way home, I knew I would have no appetite for the banana pudding that Jane had prepared. I also knew that I would not sign the contract that I had been told would be on my desk later in the day.

I had kept vigil in the Death House for the last time.

In my last week at The Walls, I focused my attention on the chapel and saying my good-byes. During the final Wednesday-night service I conducted, the choir took over the evening, singing a medley of my favorite hymns. Several inmates stood to wish me well. A steady stream of requests to visit my office came in from cell blocks throughout the unit. I had more volunteers—inmates and guards alike—to help me pack my things than I could possibly use.

The new chaplain came by to introduce himself, and we talked for several hours. He asked my advice, and I gave it, knowing full well that most of the things he would eventually need to know he would have to learn himself. My phone rang often as families of inmates called to ask if the news that I was leaving was true. When I assured them that it was, there was warm and genuine well-wishing mixed with concerns for their loved ones whom I would be leaving behind. The warden from Colorado's state prison phoned to ask if I would be interested in coming to work there.

Still, it was not until the first Sunday of my retirement that I felt the full impact of my decision. As had been my practice for years, I woke early, only to realize that I would not be having breakfast with old friends in the prison dining hall. There would be no choir practice, no chapel sermon to deliver.

I dressed, paced the house, and read the paper, yet the morning was still young. Finally, as Jane slept, I got into the car and drove toward the prison. And as I neared the familiar redbrick walls, I parked, rolling down my window in an effort to see if I could hear music, hoping for reassurance that something I had been part of for such a long time would continue.

Real or imagined, I heard a faint chorus of voices. They were singing "What a Friend We Have in Jesus."

I sat there for some time, years of memories flooding my thoughts, and then felt a warm and welcome peace begin to embrace me.

POSTSCRIPT

Occasionally, when I least expect it, my mind wanders back to the days about which you've just read. It might be only a sudden sweet smell of raspberry Pixy Stix that seems to come from nowhere, to remind me of that long-ago night spent in the company of Ronald O'Bryan, the Candy Man. Or a visit to my grandchildren during which I encounter the waxy aroma of crayons and find myself thinking of the childlike manner of condemned murderer John Paul Penry, coloring and reading comic books as he sat in a tiny cell with no idea what was about to take place. I smell the smoke of an old friend's cigar and am instantly lost in memory of the last request of an inmate named David Holland. For reasons I shall never understand, he wished to have a cigar in his shirt pocket when executed. Although it seemed to be a frivolous request, I felt obligated to fulfill it. Hurrying to a nearby drugstore, I purchased a cigar that he would never be allowed to smoke and slipped it into his pocket that night as he lay on the gurney.

On late nights, when all is still and the Texas air is ripe with the gentle whispers of darkness, I can sometimes hear the muted cries from the death chamber gallery and am reminded of the burdens still borne by the living. New-mown grass or the rich smell of the soil takes me back to those early mornings in the prison graveyard when I conducted funeral services for twenty of the ninety-five men I saw executed. The arrival of a letter from a former inmate or an encounter with some other retired prison employee on the steps of the post office is certain to open the floodgates that hold my memories.

The mental visits are not always discomforting. To this day I cannot hear a choir without comparing it to those who sang in the Chapel of Hope—strong, beautiful voices rising in melodious splendor that briefly drowned out the cries of anguish and despair inside The Walls. And for every man who spat in my face or cursed my message, there were many more whom I liked, even admired. In the cruelest world I can imagine, I saw deeds of love and compassion, even heroism, and I make no apologies for calling those who performed them my friends. I think often of those whose paths I crossed, their presence affecting my life in good ways and bad.

My favorite clerk, Blue, is dead now. So, too, are many other inmates who served their sentences and paid their social debts, rebuilt their lives, and returned to the outside world. That they died free men, no bars still casting long shadows on them, gives me comfort.

On nights when sleep eludes me and I wander the house alone, I am still visited by the faces of those in whose innocence I believed. And I see those who went to their deaths still filled with hate and anger, proclaiming innocence that was a lie, bound by whatever demons that possessed them to never admit the cruel deeds they had done. Yet even those distressful images are mitigated by reminders of those who displayed genuine remorse for their acts—men who did wrong in their youth yet managed to grow into something better in adulthood.

Today, I am free to express my feelings about the death penalty and do so often, sometimes to audiences receptive to my concerns, at other times to those determined to hold fast to what they view as a righteous eye-for-an-eye form of justice. As the old pastoral proverb suggests, one's message is never effective if delivered only to the choir. And so I often speak out to those not likely to receive me warmly. Not long ago, as I stood before a large gathering of Rotarians, suggesting that vengeance is not the property of the state, providing statistics that demonstrated that the death penalty is not a deterrent to crime, and warning them of the very real possibility that judges and juries have convicted innocent men, I saw my audience thin as time passed. First to leave midspeech was the chief of police, soon followed by a representative of the local district attorney's office. Others followed until the once-packed room was less than half filled.

It is an uphill battle. A number of Texas legislators, in their most recent gathering, argued eloquently for a two-year moratorium on the death penalty, during which its application could be closely reexamined. Even strong advocates of executions spoke out. Sam Millsap, Jr., a former Bexar County district attorney who had successfully prosecuted several death-penalty cases during his career, rose to say, "The system in Texas is broken, and until it is fixed and we are satisfied that only the guilty can be put to death, there should be no more executions." Yet the proposal died in committee, and the killing continued. Even a bill that would have banned the execution of those judged to be mentally retarded was vetoed by the governor. And the image of the Texas legal system, labeled callous and bloodthirsty by critics worldwide, grows darker even as the questions, moral and legal, become louder and more profound.

It took a ruling by the Supreme Court to save John Paul Penry from yet another visit to the Death House. Joining the six-to-three majority that voted to overturn Penry's death sentence was Justice Sandra Day O'Connor. Later, to the surprise of many, she would voice her newfound concern that innocent people were, in fact, being put to death. And as I learned of her comments, I was reminded of the times when it had been her vote that cleared the way for executions that I witnessed. And I found myself wondering how such a learned body as the Supreme Court can be so changeable in its opinions.

Logic is continually tested and defied. In the dozen states that have chosen not to enact the death penalty, homicide rates have steadily decreased over the past twenty years. In those where executions continue, the murder rates have grown steadily higher. I can state the case no better than does Steven Messner, a criminologist at the State University of New York at Albany. "Whatever the factors are that affect change in homicide rates, they don't seem to operate differently based on the presence or absence of the death penalty," he says.

What level of arrogance, I wonder, allowed the legal minds of our country to openly defy the World Court and proceed with executions that were in clear violation of international law? In 1999 brothers Karl and Walter LaGrand, citizens of Germany, were put to death for the murder of a Tucson, Arizona, bank manager. The German judiciary, arguing that the men were denied representation by a German consulate that might have helped save their lives, took the United States to court. In proceeding with the executions, the World Court ultimately ruled, the United States violated the 1963 Vienna Convention on Consular Relations. And what was our response? The government admitted that no consular notification had ever been made and issued a hollow apology to the German government. When a similar situation occurred in Texas—a Canadian was convicted of capital murder—then-governor George Bush, now our president, took the podium and proclaimed that his state had the right to execute anyone who comes to it and kills.

What of the inalienable rights granted by the United Nations and the Council on Human Rights? Have we reached a point where we worship polls and political clout more than we treasure the sanctity of human life? Has the commandment that we shall not kill simply fallen on deaf ears, giving way to the angry voices of those I too often saw demonstrating in the streets outside The Walls, urging another death?

I am not a doomsayer. Nor am I an idealistic Bible-thumper. I am simply a man who saw the system at work, not from the distant vantage point of political office or the halls of academia, but close enough to smell fear's sweat and foul breath. And, despite the wrongs I saw and still see, there is reason for some optimism. The death penalty, no longer hidden in the shadows, seems to have emerged as a social issue that is causing soul-searching and has given our nation pause. In that I see hope.

When a Texas inmate named Christopher Ochoa, who had spent twelve years on Death Row, was released after DNA tests proved that he could not have committed the murder for which he'd been convicted, new governor Rick Perry lent his support to a bill that would offer DNA testing to those sentenced to die. Even as I write this, a Waxahachie man named Victor Thomas has been freed after fifteen years of insisting that he was not the rapist who attacked a convenience-store clerk in 1985. In Waco the family of Calvin Washington welcomed him home from prison after testing proved him innocent of the rape and murder of a Waco woman fifteen years ago.

In Illinois, Gov. George Ryan, long a death-penalty advocate, recently declared a moratorium after being presented with evidence that no fewer than thirteen residents of that state's Death Row had been wrongfully convicted. In Texas, editorials urging that Ryan's lead be followed now appear with greater frequency.

The steps are small, but in the right direction.

Even as the controversy grows more heated, I find it difficult to understand why it is so hard to come to grips with basic truths. Killing to prove that killing is wrong turns logic on its head. With each execution that is conducted, a new set of victims is created. Even those justifiably angered by the senseless loss of a loved one at the hands of a criminal have to admit that another death does not balance the scales or result in closure.

Are we a nation so driven by revenge—to a barbaric degree, in the minds of many Europeans—that we can't even consider alternate punishment for those who have committed evils against us? And to whom do we answer when we put an innocent man to death?

In fifteen years I saw the painful loss suffered by the families and friends of victims. I wept at their grief and marveled at their courage. I also saw bad men die deaths less horrible than those they had inflicted. And I saw people killed who I was convinced were not guilty of the crimes of which they were accused. I met those who lacked the basic intelligence to even comprehend the system that had doomed them. And I saw men die who had changed from angry and irresponsible youths into good and thoughtful adults, put to death only for revenge and political gain. And I wondered each time: what good was being accomplished?

I know that I shall never be free of the questions any more than I can erase the memories. They are as much a part of me as my own heartbeat. And I know that I am not alone.

When Jim Estelle, the man who persuaded me to accept the position of prison chaplain, retired and moved to California, he asked one promise of me. And I have kept it dutifully. Each year on the anniversary of the deaths of prison librarians Yvonne Beseda and Julie Standley, shot down in the evil climax of that long-ago standoff that first introduced me to the prison, I place a single red rose on each of their graves.

As I visit the cemetery, the sun warming my back, soft breezes blowing, a quarter of a century ago miraculously turns to yesterday. Standing there with only my thoughts for company, I remember. Because I must.

ACKNOWLEDGMENTS

God, I know, sends people into our lives at different times and for different reasons. For that I am thankful—to Him and to so many people who helped me through my career as a prison chaplain.

No man had more influence on the days you've just read about than W. J. Estelle, who remains at the top of the list of those for whom I feel great respect. He not only provided me a challenge and a tremendous responsibility, but offered advice that I continue to abide by to this day. Think how much better the world would be if his simple words—"always deliver what you promise, and never promise what you can't deliver"—were followed by everyone.

To Warden Jack Pursley, I'm thankful for the support and freedom afforded me. Too many times we visited the Death House together, each time learning a little bit more both about life and death and about ourselves.

And to Warden Morris Jones, who also lent trust and support for which I am deeply grateful. I saw your suffering and your caring and know the toll that doing a difficult job well took on your body and spirit.

No one functions alone in a prison system, and the management I witnessed at The Walls serves as a prime example. I shall forever remember how coworkers became friends; how they stood together, lending each other strength during times of pain and disappointment and during dark moments of soul-searching. My heartfelt thanks to Maj. A. J. Murdock, Maj. Al Losack, and a lengthy list of security personnel who spent long hours with me in the Death House. Many of you eventually opted to remove yourself from the death-penalty process for reasons that I embraced and understood. Know that you and your efforts were appreciated. Just as were those of Dorothy Coleman, a good friend and a good listener, who always stood by with a cool glass of orange juice at just the right time.

To the staff of the Office of the Presbytery of New Covenant, to whom I am responsible, I owe sincere appreciation. It helped greatly to always have the vocal support of our executive presbyter Jack Boelens, despite the fact our church opposed the death penalty. That my role was understood made things so much easier. Knowing that staff devotionals led by Sharon Darden, herself a victim of the Texas justice system, were held on the days executions were scheduled was a prayer loudly answered.

And to the prophet, Prof. Henry Quinius of Austin Presbyterian Seminary, who had no idea how important his words would one day be to me and my ministry, my sincere thanks. For his insight and for providing that awakening, he is both loved and appreciated.

My thanks to agent Janet Wilkens Manus for finding this project a home and to Charles Spicer and Anderson Bailey for making it welcome. And a deep bow to Paul Montazzoli for smoothing rough edges.

Finally, this undertaking would not have been possible without the help of Carlton Stowers. His spirit of kindness and understanding, knowledge and patience, brightly pointed the way.